Growing Up in Christ

52 New Testament Lessons for Ages 8-12

STANDARD PUBLISHING™

Growing Up in Christ

Standard Publishing, Cincinnati, Ohio
A division of Standex International Corporation

Printed in the United States of America

Credits
Cover design: Liz Howe
Interior design: Dale Meyers
Illustrations: Ron Wheeler
Editors: Kristi Walter, Theresa Hayes, Bruce E. Stoker
Writing team: Karen Jesse Becker, Sandra Collier, Sandra Friesen, Dianna Golata, Robin Griffin, Joyce Hardin, Kathy Johnson, Shawn Lewis, Sarah Lyons, Diane Mansfield, JoDee McConnaughhay, Kristi Walter
Syllabus development: Ruth Frederick, Carol A. Jackson

07 06 05 04 03 02 01 00 7 6 5 4 3 2 1

ISBN 0-7847-1182-8

Contents

	UNIT TITLE	SCRIPTURE	APPLICATION	MEMORY VERSE
September	Growing in Faith (Lessons about faith in Jesus based on his miraculous signs)	John 2:1-11 (1st miracle, wine) John 4:46-54 (2nd miracle, healing) John 9:1-38 (healed blind) John 11:1-45 (Lazarus to life)	Believe that Jesus is from God	John 20:30, 31
October	Growing in Obedience (Lessons about obeying based on Jesus' life of obedience)	Luke 2:39-52 (obeyed parents) Matthew 3:13-17 (obeyed God, bap.) Matthew 4:1-11 (obeyed Scripture) Matthew 26:36-46 (Gethsemane)	Obey like Jesus (using Scripture and prayer to help)	1 John 5:1-5
November	Growing in Attitude (Lessons about godly attitudes based on Jesus' life and teaching)	Matthew 5:1-12 (Beatitudes) Philippians 2:1-8 (Jesus' attitude) Luke 18:9-14 (Pharisee, tax collector) Matthew 18:21-35 (unmerciful serv.) Matthew 19:16-26 (rich young man)	Grow in Jesus' attitudes: servanthood, humility, forgiving & merciful	Mark 10:43-45
December	Growing in Worship (Lessons about worship based on events surrounding Jesus' birth)	Luke 1:57-75 (Zechariah) Matthew 1:18-21 (Joseph & Mary) Luke 2:8-18 (shepherds) Luke 2:21-38 (Simeon) Matthew 2:21-38 (wise men)	Worship the Savior in response to knowing why Jesus is the only one who can save us	Matthew 1:20, 21
January	Growing in Discipleship (Lessons about being and making disciples from the book of Matthew)	Matthew 4:18-22; 9:9-13 (followers) Matthew 5:13-16 (salt and light) Matthew 5:38-48 (love enemies) Matthew 20:20-28 (servant)	Choose to be a disciple and disciple others	Matthew 28:16-20
February	Growing in Prayer (Lessons about prayer based on Jesus' teaching and example)	Luke 3:21; 5:16; 6:12; 22:41 (Jesus' prayer times) Luke 11:1-4 (model prayer) Luke 11:5-13 (ask, seek, knock) John 17:1-26 (Jesus' prayer)	Follow Jesus' example of praying regularly (how & who)	Matthew 6:9-13

	UNIT TITLE	SCRIPTURE	APPLICATION	MEMORY VERSE
March	Growing in Goodness (Lessons about being and doing good from the Letters)	Romans 12:9-21 (examples) Colossians 3:12-17 (wear it) Galatians 5:19-25 (fruit of Spirit) Ephesians 5:8-20 (children of light)	Know what is good, put goodness on every day, live in the Spirit	Philippians 4:8, 9
April	Growing in Love for Christ (Lessons about loving Jesus based on Peter's view of Jesus' last week)	John 13:1-17, 31-38 (last supper) John 18:15-18, 25-27 (denial) John 20:1-9, 19, 20 (resurrection) John 21:3-17 (catch of fish)	Love Jesus by believing, following, serving (like Peter)	John 14:23, 24
May	Growing in Devotion to the Church (Lessons about what the church does from the book of Acts)	Acts 2:42-47 (four ways) Acts 2 (Pentecost) Acts 3, 4 (Peter and John speak out) Acts 4, 6 (believers share) Acts 4, 5 (Peter & John jailed)	Be devoted to the church by following the example of the believers in the early church	Acts 2:42, 46, 47
June	Growing in Grace (Lessons about showing God's grace from the book of Acts)	Acts 8:26-40 (Philip, Ethiopian) Acts 9:1-19 (Ananias, Saul) Acts 10 (Peter, Cornelius) Acts 11:19-26 (Barnabas in Antioch)	Accept people, show God's grace, in order to help them know and love Jesus	1 Peter 4:10, 11
July	Growing in Confidence (Lessons about telling the good news from the life of Paul)	Acts 17:16-32 (Athens) Acts 21:27–22:29 (Jerusalem) Acts 24, 25, 26 (Felix, Agrippa) Acts 28:17-31 (Rome, guards)	Build confidence to tell Jesus' good news—like Paul (personal testimony)	1 Peter 3:15, 16
August	Growing in Hope (Lessons about Jesus' return from his teaching and the book of Revelation)	Revelation 21, 22 (new Jerusalem) Matthew 24, 25 (end times, parable) Matthew 25 (talents) 2 Timothy 3, 4 (godlessness) Revelation 1, 3 (Sardis)	Be ready, use gifts to help others get ready, live a godly life, obey what you know	Matthew 24:36, 42, 44

Materials Needed

Typical Classroom Supplies

atlas or maps
Bible
Bible concordances
cassette player
cellophane tape
chalk board and chalk or white board and markers
colored chalk
construction paper
cotton balls
craft sticks (large and small)
crayons
dictionaries (Bible and English)
glue (white and glue stick)
index cards
markers (permanent and washable)
masking tape
paper clips
paper punch
pencils
pens
rulers
scissors
stapler and staples
string
sturdy paper or poster board
tempera paint
thesaurus
white paper

Clothing Supplies

adult-size hat
backpacks
belts
Bible-times costumes
boy's suit coat
child-size hat
coats
crown
fake jewelry
girl's vest
gloves
hat
man's suit coat
paint shirts or smocks
rings (for fingers)
sash
scarf
shoes
socks
sunglasses
wedding ring
wide shoestrings
women's vest

Household Supplies

bag ties
blanket
bleach
bowls
candles
clear drinking glass
cups
dental floss
drinking straws
facial tissues
flat bed sheet
hand towels
jars with lids
knives
matches
measuring cups
mixing bowls
napkins
paper bags
paper lunch bags
paper plates
pitcher
plastic grocery bags
plastic knives
sauce pan
self-sealing bags
serving tray
small plastic bags
spray bottle of ammonia
spray bottle of cologne or air freshener
table cloth
tablespoons
thread
toothpicks
two-liter bottles
wooden spoons

Special Supplies

adding machine tape
American flag
award certificates
award ribbons
badge
balloons
basket
beanbag
blindfold

book of baby names
bricks
butcher paper (white, black, brown)
church bulletins
clean garbage can
corrugated cardboard
cross
dead potted plant
dowel rods
envelopes
eyedropper
fertilizer
fishing net
flashlights and batteries
gavel
highlighting pens
hook-and-loop fastener strips
Jenga or Uno Stacko games
large box
large coffee cans
logs (for a campfire)
magazines
magnetic tape
magnets
manila clasp envelopes
name tags
newspapers
one-liter bottles
packing tape
pennies
plants
Plasti-Tak
play money
postcards
ribbon
rocks
shoe boxes with lids
silk plants
small ball
small box
small gift-wrapped box
small nails
small prizes
small toys
sports equipment
stickers
trophies
variety of plastic fruit
watering can
wrapping paper
wrapping paper tubes
yarn

Food Supplies

brownies
candy coins in foil
cheese
communion bread and juice
cookies
eggs
flour
food coloring
juice
lemonade
mayonnaise
peanut butter
pecan pieces
potato
raisins
rice
salt
snack crackers
sugar
sugar cubes
tubes of frosting
variety of fruit
various candies
various snack foods

Technology Supplies

blank cassette tape
buzzer boards
cassette of praise music
microphone (real or toy)
Polaroid camera and film
timer or stopwatch
TV
VCR
video camera

Introduction

Welcome to an exciting and challenging growth experience for the eight- to twelve-year-olds in your church. It's exciting because your students will be called to depend on God and will see God at work in their lives. It's challenging because your students will be taken out of the ordinary to put their faith in action. They will grow up in Christ!

Ask any child what he wants to be when he is grown, and he'll have an answer or two. Children look forward to being adults. They know that their purpose as children is to grow up. After all, everyone grows up.

What is sadly lacking in the forward thinking of children is that spiritual growth is as necessary as physical growth. No newborn baby remains a baby; he grows into a beautiful child who grows into a useful adult. The moment of salvation is not the beginning and ending of a spiritual life, it is only the beginning. God intends for his babies to grow into beautiful people. Certainly, he admonishes us to "grow in the grace and knowledge of our Lord and Savior Jesus Christ" (2 Peter 3:19).

Physical growth is helped along by proper nutrition, rest, and exercise. Visit any home with children, and you'll most likely find a cherished place where the physical growth of the children is logged. The marks on the wall are benchmarks of the physical side of life.

Spiritual growth is no less demanding, needing regular feeding in God's Word, rest in prayer, and the exercising of faith. What are the benchmarks of spiritual growth? While they may not be as easy to measure, they should be more cherished and remembered than their physical counterparts. Growing Up in Christ was written to provide those cherished and remembered benchmarks of spiritual growth. This series contains a wealth of activities that will teach children that growing up spiritually is indeed more exciting than growing up physically.

Growing Up in Christ Benchmarks

- **Action grows faith.** Growing up in Christ means doing what Jesus calls children to do now. Children do not need to wait until they are adults to serve God. Children need to know that they are important enough to God that he has work for them to do now. Action builds faith because it gives children a chance to see God at work in their lives. There's no better spiritual benchmark for children than to have a history with God. The Growing Up in Christ lessons use action to build faith. When the students leave class, they will know without a doubt what they can do to live out what they just learned.
- **Accountability grows faith.** Growing up in Christ happens when a young

Christian is accountable to an older Christian. As parents, we teach our children to check in with us on a regular basis. If they don't, we check on them. We expect our children to be accountable to us. Each Growing Up in Christ lesson sets aside time for accountability. Students report on how they handle growing up assignments. Teachers give feedback. Students learn from each other. Growth happens. Faith builds. Students are more likely to complete their assignments when they know that they will have to check in with the class.

- **God's Word grows faith.** Growing up in Christ can't happen without knowing and remembering God's Word. Researchers have learned that understanding and repetition are critical parts of remembering. Because Growing Up in Christ units are centered around a memory passage and each lesson supports the passage, students gain a lasting understanding of the passage. Scripture hidden in the heart is ready for children to recall and use when they need to put faith behind their actions.

About the Growing Up in Christ Lessons

Each Growing Up in Christ unit is a month of study—most units have four lessons, while others have five. Over the course of a unit, you will focus on one area of growth such as faith, attitude, goodness, testimony. This will happen by teaching four or five Scripture passages and one Bible memory passage.

Growing Up in the Word

This section contains the memory passage that emphasizes the area of growth for the unit. Think of the memory passage as the meat of the lesson, and think of the lesson passages as the support material for the memory passage. Make the memorization of the memory passage a goal for each unit.

Growing Up in the Word offers two activities that are geared to help students memorize and understand the memory passage. Teachers may choose one of the two activities for the lesson or offer them both. These activities give students ample time to review, study, repeat, and ponder the passage. Since the memory passage is the focal point of the unit, it is always discussed in each lesson. Conversation is important during the memory passage activities because it will guide students to mentally interact with the passage.

Consider the following when working with the memory passage:

- **Use long term vs. short-term memory.** Our short-term memory contains five to nine items. Our long-term memory contains an infinite number of items. Because the short-term memory is so limited, new information crowds out the old. We want students to move Scripture passages from the short-term to the long-term memory. We don't want God's Word crowded out when new information comes along!
- **Use time.** Time is the most important element needed to store information in the long-term memory. Time is needed to test what the memory knows and to smooth out difficult sections. One or two study sessions on a memory passage is not enough time to store a passage in long term memory. Research has shown that time spent on memory work must be spaced out

rather than done in one sitting. It takes less total time to memorize a passage if the work on it happens in several sessions over a period of time. Use every opportunity in each lesson to encourage students to say the memory passage. Encourage students to practice it during the week as well.

- **Use mental activity.** Memory is tied to understanding and association. A student will not remember what he doesn't understand or cannot associate with other material he has stored in his memory. Passages to be memorized must be processed and evaluated by the mind. The mind must act and interact with the material. It must be thought about, categorized, and related to what is already known. A student's mind must be actively involved in thinking about the verse. Questions are provided in each lesson to help students understand and ponder the meaning of the passage. Object lessons are also provided to help students make connections between what they already know and what they need to know—the memory passage. Growing Up in Christ lessons involve the senses in learning the memory passages. While many activities break the memory verses into smaller pieces to aid in memorization, they also present the entire passage as one unit. This helps the mind associate the entire group of words as one unit, and therefore, makes memorization and application easier.
- **Use review.** Once a passage is stored in long-term memory, it needs only to be reviewed occasionally. This book provides a review activity with each unit that will serve this need—an activity that can be prepared and used in future units to review the passage. Prepare a permanent memory passage review center. It can be as simple as a box that contains envelopes with the prepared activities from the unit pages. Since students will be able to do each activity on their own, allow them to take the materials home and review the passages. Always have the activities available in class for students who arrive early or for those who finish another activity early.

Why Grow Up?

This section of each lesson answers the question every kid asks: Why do I need to know this? An object lesson or demonstration will help to communicate the need for every child to grow up in Christ. When students are faced with the why-grow-up question, they should respond by saying, "Yes, I want to grow up in Christ."

How to Grow Up

This section focuses on key New Testament passages that highlight and illustrate how to grow up in Christ. During this presentation of the Scripture passage, students will discover for themselves what God says about growing up.

Ready to Grow Up

Students use information gained in How to Grow Up to accept an assignment that will help them grow up. This section includes meaningful and memorable activities for students to apply what they have learned. Students will practice the focus of the lesson or prepare to practice the focus during the week. Each unit has its own theme that will inspire students to "stick" with the challenge to grow and will "spur" them to action. Because these activities spill over into the week, students will have take-home assignments that will challenge them to grow up in Christ. These are not pencil-and-paper assignments; they are action assignments that will engage them mentally, spiritually, and physically. Then at the next week's session, students will report on how the assignment went. These weekly assignments will put faith into action and grow faith from action, and students will remember the lessons long after the unit is over.

If students are not used to having homework from church, it may take a few weeks to get them acclimated. Stick with it. Keep making assignments. Keep asking students to report. Send a postcard reminder. Don't give up.

Growing Up Every Day

This final section of the lesson is a time to wrap up the lesson. It briefly summarizes the theme of the lesson along with the challenge to grow for the unit. It's a time to encourage students in their assignment. Sometimes it will be a quiet or reflective time. In other sessions, it will be a loud, cheering time. Your students will leave knowing that yes, they can grow up in Christ.

Reproducible pages are included to complement and enhance the *Growing Up in Christ* units.

Let the Holy Spirit guide you as you adapt these lessons for your growing children. May the Lord bless you and your work as you help children "grow up in every way to be like Christ" (Ephesians 4:15). You may even find that you've grown an inch or two!

Growing in Faith

Unit Aims

Know:	Describe four miraculous signs Jesus did and people's responses to them.
Feel:	Feel awed by the power Jesus displayed.
Do:	Believe that Jesus is the Christ, the Son of God.
Memorize:	John 20:30, 31

Why Grow in Faith?

This first unit is the cornerstone of the coming year. In these first lessons you'll introduce your students to the basic precept of our Christian faith: Jesus is the Son of God. The memory passage for this month, John 20:30, 31, tells us that we can believe Jesus is God's Son because of the miracles he preformed. This unit explores four of the miraculous signs that Jesus performed. Each one demonstrates an important aspect of his love for us: his interest and intervention in our daily concerns; his power and willingness to heal us; his power of life over death; and the gift of eternal life we receive through him.

A primary goal of this unit is to teach eight- to twelve-year-olds how to recognize the presence of Jesus in their lives. They will begin to see this by looking for examples of God's love and care, and recording them to share in class. Growing in faith requires work; we must teach ourselves to see what God has done for us; we must actively look for his hand on our lives; and we must remember what he has done for us. This unit's lessons will provide your students the opportunity to identify and remember what Jesus has done for them and for others.

Summary

Grow in the grace and knowledge of Jesus Christ by believing that Jesus is from God.

- Jesus' power to change things and improve circumstances proves that he is from God.
- Jesus' power to heal proves that he is from God.
- Jesus' power to raise the dead proves that he is from God.
- Jesus is the Christ, the Son of God.

Lesson Aims

Scripture focus	Bible focus	Life focus
Lesson 1 John 2:1-11	When Jesus turned water into wine, his followers believed in him.	Believe that Jesus can change things and improve circumstances.
Lesson 2 John 4:46-54	When Jesus healed an official's son, the official and all the people of his house believed in Jesus.	Believe that Jesus can heal.
Lesson 3 John 9:1-38	When Jesus healed a man born blind, the man responded with belief.	Believe what Jesus can do even when no one else believes.
Lesson 4 John 11:1-45	When Jesus raised Lazarus from death, many people believed in Jesus. Martha believed that Jesus was from God.	Believe that Jesus is the Christ, the Son of God.

Memory Passage: John 20:30, 31

"Jesus did many other miraculous signs in the presence of his disciples, which are not recorded in this book. But these are written that you may believe that Jesus is the Christ, the Son of God, and that by believing you may have life in his name."

Classroom Supplies
- index cards
- marker

Curriculum Supplies
none

Memory Passage Review Activity

Make several sets of cards for the students to play Concentration. For each set, write the following verse segments on separate cards so that you have two for each phrase: John 20:30-31/ "Jesus did many other miraculous signs/ in the presence of his disciples,/ which are not recorded in this book./ But these are written that you may believe/ that Jesus is the Christ, the Son of God/ and that by believing you may have life in his name."

One complete set is fourteen cards, including the reference. Make enough of these sets so that several students can be playing at the same time. Mix up the sets, and then place the cards face down on a tabletop. Tell students that as they uncover matches, to place the matches in biblical order. The first student to complete the Bible passage wins.

Lesson 1

Growing in Faith

Believing Jesus Can Change Things

John 2:1-11

Bible Focus

When Jesus turned water into wine, his followers believed in him.

Life Focus

Believe that Jesus can change things and improve circumstances.

Growing Up in the Word: John 20:30, 31

Set up one or both of the following activities for students to do as they arrive. Greet students by name and direct them to the activity.

Classroom Supplies
- Bibles
- paper
- pencils

Curriculum Supplies
none

Memory Activity 1

Distribute paper and pencils. Tell the class you're going to read John 20:30, 31 aloud, and they are to write it down on their papers as you read. Begin reading the verses aloud as fast as you can. The students will protest that you're going too fast. Read the verses aloud again, slowing down a little bit, but still go too fast for the class to keep up. The students will protest again. Tell them to turn to John 20:30, 31 in their Bibles and copy down the verses and that they may have all the time they need.

Say: **Which was easier—remembering the verses when I recited them or when you read from the Bible?** Let students respond. **Because God's Word is written, anytime we need help remembering what God says, we can read it again. We're blessed to have our Bibles to read whenever we want. Almost 2,000 years ago, Christians started writing down the stories and teachings of Jesus so that we will always have them. These writers have given us proof that Jesus is God's Son.** Lead the students in reciting John 20:30, 31 in unison.

Memory Activity 2

Before class, write the following phrases of the memory passage on separate sheets of paper: "Jesus did many other miraculous signs/ in the presence of his disciples,/ which are not recorded in this book./ But these are written that you

Classroom Supplies
- paper
- marker

Curriculum Supplies
none

may believe/ that Jesus is the Christ, the Son of God,/ and that by believing you may have life in his name" (John 20:30, 31).

Play a modified game of Red Light, Green Light. Have students stand on one of the side of the room across from you. Tell them that you'll show them a sign that you'll read aloud, and they will repeat after you. Then when you say green light, they may move forward until you say red light. Continue until all the phrases have been shown and read. Then mix the phrases and begin the game again. This time just the students will read the signs aloud.

Say: **Red and green traffic lights are types of signs that help drivers know when to go and when to stop. We used them in our game today as part of the rules. They helped us know what to do. In an ordinary day, what other types of signs do you see?** Let students respond. **Signs give us directions, and they also give us important information.** Lead the students in saying John 20:30, 31 aloud. **The Bible gives us signs as well. These signs also give us directions and important information. This month we're going to study the signs that tell us that Jesus is the Son of God.**

Why Grow Up?

Classroom Supplies
two-liter bottle with label of same kind of soft drink used in the "Growing Up Every Day" activity but filled with water

Curriculum Supplies
none

Hide the bottle with the soft drink for use during "Growing Up Every Day." Show the class the bottle of water. Say: **Here is a bottle of water. What would it take to convince you that I can change this water into a soft drink? What if I poured this water into these cups and told you that as I pour the water it will change? None of you would believe me. Why? I'm only human. I can't perform miracles.**

Let's pretend that I did change this water into a soft drink. What would you think of my claims then? Yes, you would believe that I could do what I said I could do. You would have faith in my ability to change water to a soft drink.

Our goal this month is to grow in faith. The word "faith" is used to describe our belief that Jesus is the Son of God. What is faith? Let students respond. **Faith is a little word for a very big idea; it's the idea that we can know or believe that something is real without having to actually see or touch it. Not being able to see or touch Jesus sometimes makes it hard to believe that he is always with us. But thankfully, the Bible gives us signs that point us in the right direction—these signs point us to faith in Jesus.**

Signs in the Bible give us the information we need to have faith that Jesus is the Son of God. One sign we have in the Bible is the story about Jesus changing water to wine. It is a story that builds our faith in Jesus.

How to Grow Up

Before class, write the following questions on separate sheets of paper and attach them to the walls around your classroom: What was the first miracle Jesus performed? Why did the master of the banquet say, "Everyone brings out the choice wine first and then the cheaper wine, but you have saved the best till now"? Who changed the situation at the wedding? How did Jesus' miracle affect the master of the banquet? Who believed in Jesus? Why did Jesus' disciples put their faith in him? Why do we need to know about this miracle?

Distribute the Scripture Sleuth handouts. Divide students into pairs. Say: **We're going to be Scripture sleuths today. These sheets contain our Scripture passage along with clues to help us find the answers to the questions posted around the room. Work with your partner to complete your sleuth sheets. Then we'll use those clues to answer the questions on the walls.** When all the students have finished, discuss the handout answers. Then discuss each question posted on the wall.

Classroom Supplies
- paper
- marker

Curriculum Supplies
reproducible page 34
(Scripture Sleuth)

What was the first miracle Jesus performed? (He changed water to wine at a wedding in Cana.) **Why did the master of the banquet say, "Everyone brings out the choice wine first and then the cheaper wine, but you have saved the best till now"?** (The wine Jesus made was better than the wine that had already been drank.) **Who changed the situation at the wedding?** (Jesus did.) **How did Jesus' miracle affect the master of the banquet?** (It brought him joy.) **Who believed in Jesus?** (His mother believed before the miracle, and his disciples believed after the miracle.) **Why did Jesus' disciples put their faith in him?** (They saw his glory through his changing of water to wine.) **For Jesus' disciples this miracle was the first sign that showed Jesus is the Son of God, and their faith in him grew because of this. Why do we need to know about this miracle?** (So we can put our faith in Jesus and believe that he is the Christ, the son of God.)

Read John 20:30, 31 aloud in short phrases and have the students repeat each phrase after you. **How is this story a miraculous sign?** (It reveals Jesus' glory and his power to change things.) **Does this story help us believe that Jesus is the Son of God? Who else could change water to wine?** Let students respond. **Why is it important to believe that Jesus is the Christ the Son of God?**

The story of Jesus turning the water into wine is a sign that's been written down so that we may believe that Jesus is the Christ, the Son of God and by believing have life in his name. This story builds our faith in Jesus.

Ready to Grow Up

Faith is believing that Jesus can change things and can improve circumstances in our lives. How did Jesus improve the circumstances at the wedding. How did he change things? Discuss.

We build faith by reading about the miracles Jesus performed when he was a man. We also build faith by seeing Jesus work in our lives and in the lives of those around us. We have to learn to look for Jesus. He is with us, and he blesses us everyday. We build faith in Jesus by looking at the signs of his love and care in our own lives.

Classroom Supplies
none

Curriculum Supplies
reproducible page 35
(Jesus Search)

If Jesus has the power to change water to wine in an instant, what does Jesus have the power to do in your life? Jesus can change things in each of our lives. Jesus can change little things, and he can change big things. In fact, he blesses us every day.

Distribute handouts. **We're going to use these sheets to write down how Jesus blesses us—how he cares for us and shows his love for us. Each day this**

week, look for evidence of Jesus in your life. It may be something good that happens to you, or maybe it's some kind of good behavior that you wouldn't normally do. It may be an answered prayer, an act of kindness someone shows to you, or an encouraging letter or phone call from a friend. If you find yourself being more patient or less angry than you normally would feel in a bad situation, that's evidence of Jesus in your life. If you feel calmer about something that's been worrying you or find a way to get along with someone, or find it easier to obey your mom or dad or listen to the teacher, each could be evidence of Jesus working in your life.

At the end of the week, we'll have a written record of Jesus working in our lives. It will help our faith in him grow. Evidence that Jesus works in our lives assures us that he is the Son of God.

Classroom Supplies
- two-liter bottle filled with a soft drink
- cups

Curriculum Supplies
none

Growing Up Every Day

Say: **Remember how Jesus changed the water into wine and how I couldn't change the water into a soft drink? That shows us that only God can make miraculous changes. Are there things about you that you want to change?** Allow students to respond; try to direct the students toward spiritual changes rather than physical ones. **Are these things easy to change?** (No.) **There are plenty of things about each of us that don't always make God happy, and all of them are related to sin. Is it easy for us to avoid sin all the time?** (No.) **God wants all of us to be changed so that we no longer sin and do things that are related to sin. And even though it is not always easy for us to make those changes, God promises us that he can change us if we have faith in him. Just as Jesus was able to change the water into wine, he is able to change us into people who try to please God. We have faith that he is able to change us because we read the Bible to see Jesus' miracles, evidence that he is has the power to do what he promises. That's exactly why Jesus did his miracles, to show that he is God's Son.**

Let's pretend that you have all known me for years and years and have always thought I was the most selfish person you have ever known. I never share my possessions with other people. I always try to get more things for myself, even if other people need the things more than I do. If you were dying of thirst right in front of me, you know I wouldn't help you even if I could. Would you like me? Do you think someone like that could ever change? What if I did change? Bring out the soft drink and cups and start pouring. **Even though I can't turn water into a soft drink, if I started to share with you after years of being super selfish, wouldn't that be just as much of a miracle? That's the kind of miraculous changes God can do with people. People who are worriers learn to trust their futures to God. People who are afraid learn to rely on God for courage. People who are hateful learn how to love others.**

Say: **At the end of each day this week, I want you to use this handout to write down how Jesus shows you that he is with you. Look for small things as well as big things. Once you begin looking for Jesus, you'll find that Jesus is everywhere around you, helping you know that he is the Christ, the Son of God. As you begin to see God at work in your lives, don't forget to thank him.**

Lesson 2

Growing in Faith

Believing Jesus Can Heal

John 4:46-54

Bible Focus

When Jesus healed an official's son, the official and all the people of his house believed in Jesus.

Life Focus

Believe that Jesus can heal.

Growing Up in the Word: John 20:30, 31

Set up one or both of the following activities for students to do as they arrive. Greet students by name and direct them to the activity.

Memory Activity 1

Before class, make one copy of the reproducible for each student. Cut each sheet into about 15 pieces. Keep the pieces for each sheet together in separate envelopes.

In class, distribute the envelopes and have students put the pictures together. If there is time, let the students turn their assembled puzzles over, tape them together, and color them.

Say: **In order to assemble these pictures, you used your memories and your abilities to recognize a pattern. Did it get easier the longer you worked at it?** Let students respond. **It did, didn't it, because after you put a couple of pieces together, you could begin to see the picture that was forming and begin to recognize the pattern of the words.**

Did you know that the Bible has a pattern too? Let students respond. **The Bible has a pattern that helps us see the larger picture it makes. Piece by piece, we can put together the stories of Jesus' miracles to tell the big picture story that he is the Son of God. Today's Bible story is another piece that will help us believe that Jesus is the Christ, the Son of God.**

Classroom Supplies
- envelopes
- crayons or markers
- cellophane tape

Curriculum Supplies
reproducible page 36 (stained-glass picture)

Memory Activity 2

Give each student two pieces of paper. Have them fold the paper in half, then layer the folded sheets one inside of the other. Have them punch at least three holes in the folded edge of their booklet and string yarn through each hole to

Classroom Supplies
- Bibles
- paper
- paper punch
- yarn
- scissors
- markers
- crayons

Curriculum Supplies
none

make a book. Have the students turn to John 20:30, 31 or post the verses on the wall. Instruct students to write the following six phrases of the memory passage on pages two through seven. Read the passage aloud in these six parts, pausing after each one to give the students time to write: "Jesus did many other miraculous signs/ in the presence of his disciples,/ which are not recorded in this book./ But these are written that you may believe/ that Jesus is the Christ, the Son of God/ and that by believing you may have life in his name" (John 20:30, 31).

Say: **On each page, draw an illustration, make a design, or rewrite that section of Scripture in your own words. For the first phrase you might draw an illustration showing Jesus performing a miracle. Or for miracles that weren't written down in the Bible, you might draw a picture showing a miracle Jesus performed in your own life. When you are finished with the six phrases, think of a title for your book that would tell anyone seeing it what your book is about.**

Why Grow Up?

Classroom Supplies
- a scarf
- newspapers

Curriculum Supplies
none

Blindfold one student. Lead the student to the center of an open space. Have the rest of the students crumple up sheets of newspaper and then place them around the open space. Tell the blindfolded person that he will listen for directions for how to walk through the maze of papers. Here's the catch: all the students in the class will be giving him or her directions to avoid the papers, but only one of them will be telling the truth. The blindfolded student will have three chances to determine which person is telling him the correct directions before he is out. Silently choose one person to give the correct directions. Signal the class to begin giving directions.

If a person makes it through the papers, ask: **How did you know who to listen to? What made you trust that person?** If a person does not make it through the papers, have him remove the blindfold and begin again. He still must follow directions from the class. When the student navigates the paper field, ask: **How much easier was it to trust the directions this time?**

It's hard to know who to believe when you can't see the way you should go yourself. You can get easily confused or led in the wrong direction. But when you know that the person giving you the instructions is telling you the truth, it's much easier to trust him. Today's story is about a man who needed Jesus' help. The man had faith in Jesus and trusted that what he said was the truth. The Bible says that the man took Jesus at his word.

How to Grow Up

Before class, copy the following information and tape each road sign to a separate index card. Prepare a handout for each student with space to write their answers to the road sign questions, including Road Sign Six.

Road Sign One

Jesus' power to do miracles and heal people was becoming well-known. But there were still some people who didn't understand that Jesus had the power to heal because he is the Son of God.

- What town was Jesus in (John 4:46)?
- What had Jesus done there before?

Go to Road Sign Two.

Road Sign Two

A royal official, a man who worked for the king, had a son who was so sick that the man was afraid his son would die.

- What did the royal official do (John 4:47)?
- How did Jesus reply (John 4:48)?
- Why do you think Jesus said this?
- Do you think Jesus understood the royal official's problem?

Go to Road Sign Three.

Classroom Supplies
- index cards
- marker
- tape

Curriculum Supplies
road sign information listed with this section

Road Sign Three

The royal official persisted and asked Jesus to come home with him so that Jesus could heal his son.

- What did Jesus say to this man (John 4:50)?
- Why do you think Jesus didn't go home with the royal official?

Go to Road Sign Four.

Road Sign Four

Jesus told the man, "You may go. Your son will live."

- What did the royal official do (John 4:50)?
- Why do you think the royal official did this?
- What did the royal official find out (John 4:51, 52)?

Go to Road Sign Five.

Road Sign Five

Then the father realized that this was the exact time at which Jesus had said to him, "Your son will live." So he and all his household believed.

- Do you think the royal official's belief in Jesus was stronger before or after Jesus healed his son?
- What did the official do while he waited to see the truth of Jesus' words?

Go to Road Sign Six.

Road Sign Six

Jesus is the Son of God.

Keep sign six out of the students' view. Arrange the five cards randomly around the room in out-of-the-way locations. If you have a large class, make two or three sets of these signs.

Say: **Today we're going on a trip. What do you do if you're on a trip, and you're not sure of the right way to go?** Let students respond. **You could ask directions or use a map or follow road signs. Today, you and a traveling partner are going to rely on the road signs posted around the room. I'll get you started on your journey.** Group the students in pairs. **Use your Bibles and work with your traveling buddy to get the information you need to complete your journey. Answer all the questions on each road sign, then move on to the next one.**

Let students work, and as pairs begin to ask where sign six is, have them sit down in a circle and wait for the rest of the class to finish with signs one through five. Expect students to wriggle and fidget as they wait. Remind them often that you'll show them sign six when everyone is done; they need to be patient.

When the last pair is done and has joined the rest of the students in the circle, pass around Road Sign Six so that all students have a chance to read it.

Say: **This is the last road sign you need to finish your journey: Jesus is the Son of God. This was also the end of the royal official's journey too. He came to believe that Jesus is the Son of God. Did he believe that when he first came to Jesus for his help?** Let students respond. **He had just heard stories about the miracles Jesus could perform. While he believed that Jesus could heal his son, he probably didn't believe yet that Jesus is the Son of God.**

When Jesus said, "You may go. Your son will live," what proof did the official have that Jesus was speaking the truth? Let students respond. **The royal official took Jesus at his word. In other words, he believed Jesus could heal, and he was willing to trust Jesus to do as he said he would. It was when the official discovered that his son was healed at the very moment Jesus spoke that he believed that Jesus was the Son of God.**

This story helps us build our faith in Jesus. Faith is believing that Jesus is God's Son and is able to change our lives, even when we are sick, when we are well, whenever.

Classroom Supplies
none

Curriculum Supplies
none

Ready to Grow Up

Lead students in saying John 20:30, 31 aloud. Say: **During this past week you were to look for evidence of Jesus' care and love in your lives. How did Jesus show you his love and care? What did you write in your diary?** Allow students to share. Be sure to share some of your experiences too. Ask: **Which of these experiences helped your faith in Jesus to grow?** Discuss. **Did you remember to say thank you for what Jesus did?**

Today's Bible story was written so that we may believe that Jesus is the Christ, the Son of God. Jesus' power to heal was a sign that he truly is the Son of God. While it was a great thing for Jesus to heal the official's son, Jesus healed the boy not simply to make him well but to show that Jesus is God's Son. We can believe, just as the official did, that Jesus is the Son of God.

The official trusted Jesus' word, and we ought to trust Jesus, even when we are sick. Sometimes we are healed or made well, and we can thank Jesus for that, but even when people are not made well or even die, we can know that Jesus is God's Son because of the evidence we find in the Bible.

Classroom Supplies
none

Curriculum Supplies
reproducible page 35
(Jesus Search)

Growing Up Every Day

Distribute handout. Say: **We will continue this week to keep track of how Jesus works in our lives. Keep looking for ways that Jesus shows his love and care. Don't forget to say thank you for what Jesus does.**

Lead students in singing the following song to the tune of "Frère Jacques":

He is God's Son. He is God's Son.
Jesus Christ! Jesus Christ!
Jesus has the power, each and every hour,
In our lives, in our lives.

If time permits, have students write their own words to the tune.

Lesson 3

Growing in Faith

Believing Jesus When No One Else Believes

John 9:1-38

Bible Focus
When Jesus healed a man born blind, the man responded with belief.

Life Focus
Believe what Jesus can do even when no one else believes.

Growing Up in the Word: John 20:30, 31
Set up one or both of the following activities for students to do as they arrive. Greet students by name and direct them to the activity.

Memory Activity 1
Play this modified version of "Wheel of Fortune." Before class, break John 20:30, 31 into manageable segments. For each segment, make a large sheet of paper with a blank line for each letter. Include the punctuation. At the top of each sheet write John 20:30, 31 so that students have a clue about what they are trying to solve. Mix your segments up so that they are not in order. Don't make this too easy for students who may have already memorized this month's passage. Either let the individual students attempt to solve the puzzle or split the class into teams. Cut the construction paper into small squares. Make three green squares to one red square. Conceal the squares in a container.

Classroom Supplies
- large sheets of paper
- marker
- red and green construction paper
- individually wrapped candy

Curriculum Supplies
none

To play, individuals or teams take turns drawing a paper from the container. A green paper allows them to guess a consonant; a red paper allows them to guess a vowel. If the letter is a part of the phrase, write it in the correct blanks. Students may guess the phrase only when it is their turn. After a student or team correctly solves a segment, let them each choose a small candy as a prize. Continue playing until all the segments have been solved correctly.

When finished solving all the phrases, have students put them in order and say the memory passage in its entirety. If you notice that some students are still struggling or are unsure, encourage them individually with how well they're doing so far, and if there is time, help them phrase-by-phrase until they have said the memory passage correctly at least once. Hand out a small piece of candy to each person in class.

Say: **It is much easier to read our memory passage when it is written out. We don't have to guess what the words are. That is why the miracles and signs of Jesus have been written down in the Bible. We don't have to guess about who Jesus is. We know that he is the Christ, the Son of God, because we have written proof.**

Memory Activity 2

Classroom Supplies
Bibles

Curriculum Supplies
none

Have students stand in a circle. Tell them that you're going to whisper the first part of the memory passage in one student's ear. That student will then pass it on by whispering in the next person's ear and so on until it is whispered into your ear. Then say the phrase that was whispered back to you aloud. Expect some changes! Then say the phrase correctly. Continue by whispering the next phrase. Keep the portions of the memory passage as short as possible so that students can easily pass them on. Keep playing until the entire memory verse has been passed around the circle. Then have students recite the memory passage without your help—do not lead them and do not prompt them.

Say: **Words can get changed when they are spoken from person to person. That's why, almost 2,000 years ago, Christians began to write down the events of Jesus' life so that we would always have them to help us remember that Jesus is the Son of God. We're blessed to have the Bible to help us remember not only the miracles of Jesus but also the words of God.**

Open your Bible to John 20:30, 31. Pass the opened Bible to a student standing on one side of you. Have that student read a few words of the memory passage aloud, then pass it to the person next to him in the circle. Continue until all the students have had a chance to read a portion of the passage aloud. When the Bible comes back to you, lead the students in reciting the passage in unison.

Why Grow Up?

Classroom Supplies
- paper
- scissors
- marker or pen

Curriculum Supplies
none

Before class, cut pieces of paper into slips, one for each person in class. On each slip write one of the following: soccer player, actor, doctor, baseball player, crossing guard, photographer, pastor, fireman, construction worker, singer.

Have the students sit in a circle. Tell the students not to show what is written on the slips of paper you will give them. Then hand out a slip of paper to each student. Say: **On each slip of paper is an occupation. Your job is to silently act out clues that will help the rest of the class guess your occupation. When it's your turn to act, you will not be allowed to speak. Be thinking of actions that will help the rest of the class guess what occupation is written on your slip of paper.** Allow the students a few minutes to think about how they're going to portray the people. Then have the students stand up one by one and do their actions. The person doing the actions is not to speak. If the class is having a hard time guessing from a person's actions what occupation they're portraying, you may help out. Continue until all the students have had a turn acting out their roles.

Say: **How hard was it to guess what someone was acting out?** Let students respond. **It would have been easier if the person doing the actions could have**

given you some clues using words, wouldn't it? Let students respond. **But the actions still gave us a lot of information.**

When you don't know someone, how can you tell if they're someone you'd like to know? Let students respond. **A person's actions give us lots of information about them. Someone who thinks of fun games on the playground is usually someone we want to play with. Their actions tell us that they're creative and fun. Or sometimes, if you notice that someone picks on other kids, that person's actions tell you that you don't want to play with them. Have you ever decided whether or not you wanted to get to know someone better based only on his actions?** Let students respond. **Even though we aren't always aware of it, we all make decisions about other people based on their actions.**

In today's Bible story, a blind man was healed by a man he didn't even know. But the healed man made some decisions about the person who had healed him based upon the unknown man's actions. Let's look at how the healed man came to know the man who had healed him.

Classroom Supplies
- Bibles
- pencils or pens

Curriculum Supplies
reproducible pages 37, 38 (Breaking Good News)

How to Grow Up

Say: **Today, we're going to create television news reports about a miracle that Jesus performed and also tell people's reaction to the miracle.** Divide the class into two groups, one for each news segment. Distribute handouts to the groups and assign them their segment. **Open your Bibles to John 9:1-38. Use your Bibles and work together to fill in the facts for your groups' part of the story.**

Once students have finished their assigned segments, have each group select either one reader or suggest that they take turns reading their group's "Breaking Good News" segment aloud. Make sure they read in chronological order.

Say: **Jesus is the Son of God. How do we know this?** Let students respond. **Jesus showed that he is the Son of God by the many signs or miracles he performed. In other words, his actions showed that he is the Son of God.** Lead students in reciting John 20:30, 31.

Classroom Supplies
none

Curriculum Supplies
none

Ready to Grow Up

Say: **During this past week you continued to look for evidence of Jesus working in your life. What happened this week? How did Jesus show his love and care for you?** Discuss. **Were any of you sick? Did you remember that Jesus was with you when you were sick? Now that you feel better, do you remember that Jesus heals? Did you tell Jesus thanks?**

Seeing Jesus at work builds our faith in him. In today's Bible story, we had an example of a man making a decision about who Jesus was based only on what Jesus' actions told him. The blind man believed that Jesus is the Christ, the Son of God because of what Jesus did for him. We believe too when we see what Jesus does in our own lives.

We are going to meet people all of our lives who don't believe that Jesus is God's Son. Some of these people may try to steal your faith; they will try to convince you that Jesus is not God's Son. The Pharisees tried to convince the

man born blind that Jesus was a sinner and not God's Son. But because the man had a personal experience with Jesus, the Pharisees could not steal his faith.

When we remember what Jesus has done for us, no one will be able to steal our faith. That is why we are working each week on our "Jesus Search" sheets. The things listed on our search sheets are evidence of who Jesus is.

The man born blind didn't even know who Jesus was when Jesus healed him, but Jesus' actions told the man that Jesus was someone very special. Jesus' actions in your life will tell you that he is someone very special too.

Classroom Supplies
none

Curriculum Supplies
reproducible page 35 (Jesus Search)

Growing Up Every Day

Distribute search sheets. **This week I'd like you to think about the actions of Jesus and what they tell you about him. Jesus' actions tell us a lot about who he is. We can all get to know Jesus better just from looking at what his actions tell us about him. Keep looking for Jesus in your life and record it on your Jesus Search sheets. Your faith in him will grow.** Close with prayer.

Lesson 4

Growing in Faith

Believing Jesus Is the Son of God

John 11:1-45

Bible Focus

When Jesus raised Lazarus from death, many people believed in Jesus. Martha believed that Jesus was from God.

Life Focus

Believe that Jesus is the Christ, the Son of God.

Growing Up in the Word: John 20:30, 31

Set up one or both of the following activities for students to do as they arrive. Greet students by name and direct them to the activity.

Memory Activity 1

Classroom Supplies
paper

Curriculum Supplies
none

Before class, divide John 20:31, 32 into six phrases and write them on separate sheets of paper. Make a seventh paper with the reference and an eighth that reads "Jesus is the Son of God." On five other pieces of paper write these words: "Go," "One Way," "Yield," "No Left Turn," "Slow."

Place the signs with verses on the floor in an orderly pattern. Once you've arranged the verse signs, write directions beneath each phrase such as take two steps to the left so that students will move in sequential order through the entire passage. You can also add instructions such as jump up and down three times, take three steps sideways and one step forward, take two giant steps, take six baby steps, and so on to make this an enjoyable activity for the students. Spread the memory passage papers out so that students take more than one or two steps at a time. Put the "Go" sign at the beginning of the path, the "Jesus is the Son of God" sign at the end of the path, and intersperse the other directional signs among the memory passage.

Tell the students to start at "Go" and follow the directions on each sign. Tell students to read aloud the memory passage on each sign before moving on. If they have time, students can follow the signs while walking backward, hopping on one foot, and so on.

Lead the students in saying John 20: 30, 31 aloud. Say: **Today you followed signs that told you where to go, what to do, and how to get to the next step. In an ordinary day, what types of signs do you see?** Let students respond. **Signs are everywhere in our lives. There are signs that tell us how to get where we want to go. There are also signs that give us information. There are also signs in the Bible that tell us that Jesus is the Son of God.**

Classroom Supplies
- masking tape
- paper
- marker
- four wads of paper in two different colors

Curriculum Supplies
none

Memory Activity 2

Use the masking tape to make a large tic-tac-toe grid on the floor. Divide the memory passage into three phrases. Number each phrase in order. Make two copies of phrase one, four copies of phrase two, two copies of phrase three, and one copy of the reference. Place the papers in the tic-tac-toe grid in the following order. Row 1: phrases 1, 2, 3. Row 2: phrase 2, reference, phrase 2. Row 3: phrases 3, 2, 1. For a large class, make several grids.

Players choose one color of paper and take turns tossing the wads onto the grid, trying to get one each of the three phrases, preferably in a row. As each wad lands in a square, that player reads that portion of the verse aloud.

Say: **Listen carefully to this part of our memory passage: "Jesus is the Christ, the Son of God, and that by believing you may have life in his name." What do you think this means?** Discuss their answers. **Jesus said that we will have eternal life. Our bodies will die, but our souls, the part of us that makes us unique and special, will live forever with him and God in Heaven.**

Classroom Supplies
12-inch lengths of yarn—three red, three blue, three green for each student

Curriculum Supplies
none

Why Grow Up?

Lead students in reciting John 20:30, 31. **Jesus loves and cares about us because he is the Son of God. And we love him too! What color do you think of when you think of the word love?** Discuss. **Red is the color that usually stands for love. The red yarn will remind us that Jesus loves us and we love Jesus.**

Jesus is the Son of God. The blue yarn we'll use today will remind us that Jesus is God's Son.

Because Jesus is the Son of God, we have hope. What does the word "hope" mean? Let students respond. **Hope is believing that things will work out for the best. The green yarn will remind us that we have hope because Jesus is God's Son, and someday we'll live forever with him in Heaven. These three things, love, belief, and hope, are important by themselves, but when we weave them together they become faith.**

Show the students how to braid their lengths of yarn together. Have the students twist or braid three strands—of any color—together to make one thicker strand. When they have created three of these thick strands, have them braid those to form one bracelet. Then have students help tie the yarn around each other's wrists to make bracelets. **We've made faith bracelets today. Wear these bracelets to remind you that Jesus is the Son of God. Jesus loves you and cares about every part of your life, not only the big issues, but also those small daily needs you have. When you feel uncertain, look at your bracelets to remind yourself that you have hope because you can always trust Jesus to do**

what's best for you.

In today's Bible story, we're going to find out about Mary and Martha. These two women loved Jesus and believed that he is the Son of God. But they didn't fully understand the hope Jesus gives until their brother Lazarus died.

How to Grow Up

Lead the students in the following action skit. Make a name tag from the index cards, using the yarn to hang the name tag around the neck. Make one for each of the following characters: Narrator, Mary, Martha, Lazarus, Jesus, Thomas, Messenger. Make several of the following so that each student gets a part: Disciples and Mourners. (If you are short of players, one person can play a dual role as the Messenger/Mourner. Just have the person flip his name tag over at the appropriate time.) Please feel free to have students of either gender play any character. Remember, the important thing is to get your students involved in telling the story and to have fun. Italicized text is stage directions that the players should follow as they act out the story.

Classroom Supplies
- yarn
- index cards
- marker

Curriculum Supplies
one copy of the script printed in this section for each student

Have Mary, Martha, Lazarus, and Messenger stand in the center of the room. Have Jesus, Thomas, and the Disciples stand on one side of the room. Keep the Mourners next to you.

Narrator: In a small town called Bethany lived two sisters, Mary and Martha, and their brother, Lazarus. Mary, Martha, and Lazarus were all good friends of Jesus. One day, Lazarus became very sick.

Lazarus lies down.

Narrator: Mary and Martha sent a messenger to Jesus to come help Lazarus.

Mary and Martha (*to the Messenger*): Go Tell Jesus that the one he loves is sick. We need him.

Narrator: The messenger had to travel for a whole day before he reached Jesus.

The messenger walks around the room once then walks to where Jesus and the disciples are gathered.

Messenger: Lord, the one you love is sick.

Narrator: But when Jesus heard this, he didn't leave for Bethany right away. Jesus and his disciples stayed where they were for another two days. And then Lazarus died.

Mary and Martha: Lazarus is dead! If only Jesus had been here, he would have healed Lazarus.

Mourners join Mary and Martha.

Narrator: Then two days after Mary and Martha had sent for him, Jesus told his disciples they were going to Bethany. But the disciples were afraid.

Disciples: But Jesus, the town of Bethany is very close to Jerusalem. Those who hate you are in Jerusalem. They just tried to kill you. If you go back there, they'll try again.

Narrator: Jesus told them that he was doing God's work, and until Jesus' work was done here on earth, no one could hurt him.

Jesus: Our friend Lazarus has fallen asleep, but I am going there to wake him up.

Disciples: Lord, if he sleeps, he will get better.

Narrator: The disciples didn't understand what Jesus had said, so Jesus explained.

Jesus: Lazarus is dead, and for your sake I am glad I was not there, so that you may believe. Let us go to him.

Jesus walks a few steps away from the disciples.

Thomas: Let us also go, that we may die with him.

Thomas and the disciples join Jesus, and they all walk around the room once.

Narrator: So Jesus and the disciples traveled for a whole day to get to Bethany.

Jesus and the disciples stop walking and come stand a few feet from Mary, Martha, Mourners, and Lazarus.

Narrator: When Jesus got to Bethany, Lazarus had been dead for four days. Martha heard that Jesus was coming and went out to meet him.

Martha moves to stand in front of Jesus.

Martha: Lord, if you had been here, my brother would not have died. But I know that even now God will give you whatever you ask.

Narrator: Martha believed that Jesus had wonderful powers from God. But Martha felt that Jesus was too late to do anything for Lazarus.

Jesus: Your brother will rise again.

Narrator: But Martha still didn't understand that Jesus is the Son of God.

Martha: I know he will rise again in the resurrection at the last day.

Narrator: Jesus had to make it plain to Martha who he really is, so he told her.

Jesus: I am the resurrection and the life. He who believes in me will live, even though his body dies; and whoever lives and believes in me will never die. Do you believe this?

Narrator: Now Martha finally understood who Jesus is; he was not just a wise teacher, but he is the Son of God.

Martha: Yes, Lord. I believe that you are the Christ, the Son of God.

Martha goes and stands by Lazarus. Mary and the mourners come and stand before Jesus. Have them make crying sounds and say things such as "Lazarus is gone forever" and "Jesus is too late to help."

Mary: Lord, if you had been here, my brother would not have died.

Narrator: When Jesus saw how sad Mary was and saw all the people grieving for Lazarus, he felt sad for them. Jesus was so troubled by their sadness that he wept.

Jesus bows his head.

Mourners: Jesus loved Lazarus, too. Jesus healed the blind man. Couldn't he have healed Lazarus?

Then Mary leads Jesus, the disciples, and the mourners back to Martha and Lazarus.

Narrator: Mary led Jesus to the tomb of Lazarus, which was a cave with a stone rolled in front of it to seal it.

Jesus: Take away the stone.

Martha: But, Lord, by this time there is a bad odor; he has been dead for four days.

Jesus: Didn't I tell you that if you believed, you would see the glory of God?

Narrator: So they rolled away the stone from in front of Lazarus' tomb. Jesus looked up and prayed.

Jesus: Father, I thank you that you have heard me. I knew that you always hear me, but I say this for the benefit of the people standing here that they may believe that you sent me. (*In a loud voice.*) Lazarus, come out!

Lazarus stands up.

After the skit, lead the students in reciting John 20:30, 31. Say: **Mary, Martha, and those at Lazarus's tomb saw Lazarus raised from the dead, and they believed that Jesus is the Son of God. Faith is believing that Jesus is the Christ, the Son of God.**

Ready to Grow Up

Classroom Supplies
none

Curriculum Supplies
none

Say: **Our goal this month has been to grow in faith. We have looked at four miracles Jesus did so that we would have faith in him. We have also searched our own lives for the work of Jesus. We have recorded events that happened each day that show us that Jesus loves and cares for us. How did Jesus work in your lives this week?** Discuss. **I hope you remembered to say thank you for all these good things.**

We also see evidence of Jesus in our lives when he answers our prayers. What prayers of yours has Jesus answered? Give students an opportunity to share.

Say: **We may feel let down or disappointed or even sad when Jesus doesn't seem to hear our prayers. Like Martha from our story today, we also might sometimes feel that Jesus came too late to help. But was Jesus late?** Let students respond. **No, Jesus wasn't late. He came to help Mary and Martha at just the right time. Because Lazarus had died, Jesus was able to give Martha, Mary, Lazarus and the people there that day hope—the hope of life over death. Not only does Jesus have the power from God to change our circumstances and to heal us, but also he has the power of life over death. This power gives us the hope of everlasting life. Our memory passage says that by believing that Jesus is God's Son, we may have everlasting life in his name.**

Growing Up Every Day

Classroom Supplies
none

Curriculum Supplies
reproducible page 35 (Jesus Search)

Say: **The miracles that Jesus performed weren't just to show the people of long ago that he is the Son of God. These miracles were written for us so that we too will always have the proof we need to know and believe that Jesus is the Son of God.**

We believe that Jesus is the Christ, the Son of God because of the signs recorded in the Bible. We believe because we see signs of Jesus' presence in our lives. Distribute handout. **Look again this week for what Jesus is doing in your life and write it down.**

Do you believe that Jesus is the Son of God? Let students respond. Lead students in reciting the memory verse.

SCRIPTURE SLEUTHS

Follow these instruction to mark the Scripture passage.

- Circle the name of the fourth Gospel.
- Underline the chapter and verses that contain the story of Jesus changing water to wine.
- Draw a box around what happened to all the wine at the wedding.
- Mark an exclamation point next to the idea that Jesus' mother had for more wine.
- Draw a jar beside each instruction that Jesus gave to the servants.
- Put quote marks around the words that tell how the wine tasted.
- Place dots under the words that tell that Jesus' disciples believed in him.
- Draw a cloud around the words that tell why this miracle was important.
- Draw a wavy line under the name of the place where Jesus performed this miracle.

John 2:1-11
Jesus Changes Water to Wine

2 On the third day a wed-
ding took place at Cana in
Galilee. Jesus' mother was
there, 2and Jesus and his disci-
ples had also been invited to the
wedding. 3When the wine was
gone, Jesus' mother said to him,
"They have no more wine."
4Dear woman, why do you
involve me?" Jesus replied,
"My time has not yet come."
5His mother said to the ser-
vants, "Do whatever he tells
you."
6Nearby stood six stone water
jars, the kind used by the Jews
for ceremonial washing, each
holding from twenty to thirty
gallons.
7Jesus said to the servants,
"Fill the jars with water"; so
they filled them to the brim.
8Then he told them, "Now
draw some out and take it to
the master of the banquet."
They did so, 9and the master of
the banquet tasted the water
that had been turned into wine.
He did not realize where it had
come from, though the servants
who had drawn the water
knew. Then he called the bride-
groom aside 10and said, "Every-
one brings out the choice wine
first and then the cheaper wine
after the guests have had too
much to drink; but you have
saved the best till now."
11This, the first of his miracu-
lous signs, Jesus performed in
Cana of Galilee. He thus
revealed his glory, and his disci-
ples put their faith in him.

"Jesus did many other miraculous signs in the presence of his disciples, which are not recorded in this book. But these are written that you may believe that Jesus is the Christ, the Son of God, and that by believing you may have life in his name" (John 20:30, 31).

Jesus Search

1. ______________________________

2. ______________________________

3. ______________________________

4. ______________________________

5. ______________________________

6. ______________________________

7. ______________________________

He thus revealed his glory, and his disciples put their faith in him (John 2:11).

Then the father realized that this was the exact time at which Jesus had said to him, "Your son will live." So he and all his household believed (John 4:53).

"I believe that you are the Christ, the Son of God" (John 11:27).

"If this man were not from God, he could do nothing" (John 9:33).

Jesus did many other miraculous signs in the presence of his disciples, which are not recorded in this book. But these are written that you may believe that Jesus is the Christ, the Son of God, and that by believing you may have life in his name (John 20:30, 31).

BREAKING GOOD NEWS

News has reached this reporter that a _______________ [John 9:1] was healed this week. _________________ [John 9:8] are expressing amazement and disbelief at the man's miraculous healing. "Isn't this the man that used to sit and _______ [John 9:8]," they asked. When questioned by his neighbors about who had done this miracle, the blind man could only say, "The man they call ____________________ [John 9:11]."

As Jesus and his disciples passed by the blind man, the disciples asked Jesus to explain why the beggar was blind. "Who ______________________ [John 9:2]?" they asked. The man heard Jesus reply, "Neither this man or his parents sinned, but this happened so that the _____________ [John 9:3] might be displayed in his life." Then Jesus made some __________ [John 9:6] and placed the ____________ [John 9:6] on the blind man's eyes. Jesus told the blind man to wash his eyes in the ___________ [John 9:7]. When the blind man washed the mud from his eyes, he could see! He had been completely healed!

Unfortunately, this miracle has caused a great deal of confusion for all those who know the healed man. At this point, concerned neighbors have brought the blind man to the ______________ [John 9:13] to find out more about how this miracle has happened.

Jesus' action has drawn the criticism of religious leaders, the _______________ [John 9:13]. In his testimony before the Pharisees the formerly blind man has revealed that this miracle took place on the __________________ [John 9:14], a day when no work may be done.

This fact has the Pharisees arguing among themselves. Some Pharisees argue that Jesus is not _________________ [John 9:16] because Jesus broke God's law about resting on the Sabbath. Other Pharisees maintain that working a miracle, even on the Sabbath, doesn't make Jesus a sinner, since the power to heal can only come from God. Unable to come to an agreement about Jesus' action, the Pharisees continue to seek answers from the healed man about Jesus. Under further questioning, the healed man now says of Jesus, "____________________ [John 9:17]," or one sent from God.

We'll be continuing to cover this story in future broadcasts.

BREAKING GOOD NEWS UPDATE

Here's an update on the miraculous healing that Jesus performed in our city recently. Suspecting that the blind man is secretly a disciple of Jesus only pretending to have been healed, the Pharisees have now called in the man's ____________________ [John 9:18] to testify. The man's parents confirmed that the man __________________________ [John 9:20]. But they have told the Pharisees to ______________________ [John 9:21]. The Pharisees have finally reached a decision about Jesus' action. In his second meeting with the Pharisees, the man was told to "____________________ [John 9:24]. We know Jesus is a sinner. He broke one of God's laws by working on the Sabbath." The healed man didn't agree with their decision, and stated again, "___________________ [John 9:25]"

The Pharisees then again asked the man, "What did he do to you? ____________________ [John 9:26]?" The man was tired of being asked to explain Jesus' action, for the Pharisees refused to believe. So the man said, "I have told you already and you did not listen. Why do you want to hear it again? ____________________ [John 9:27]" This proved to the Pharisees that the healed man is a disciple of Jesus. The Pharisees told the man, "________________ John 9:29], but as for this fellow, we don't even know where he comes from." To which the man replied, "___________________ [John 9:33]. This has so angered the Pharisees that the healed man was kicked out of the meeting.

Jesus, the man whose actions have caused all the uproar in our city lately, was later seen talking to the man he had healed. Jesus was heard to ask the healed man, "_______________________ [John 9:35]?" The healed man asked, "___________________ [John 9:36]?" And Jesus said, "You have now seen him; in fact, he is the one speaking with you." The healed man then said, "___________________ [John 9:38]," and began to worship him.

Growing in Obedience

Unit Aims

Know:	List examples of Jesus' obedience to God's will.
Feel:	Feel a desire to please God.
Do:	Use Scripture verses and prayer to help you obey God in all areas of life.
Memorize:	1 John 5:1-5

Why Grow in Obedience?

This unit takes an in-depth look at the importance and necessity of having an obedient heart. Why obey? The reasons are many. This unit focuses on willing and immediate obedience out of love for God. First John 5:3 says, "This is love for God: to obey his commands." Obedience is fundamental to the Christian faith. In fact, it is evidence of faith—the faith that overcomes the world. Obedience shows the world that we believe Jesus is the Son of God.

Life in the twenty-first century promotes disobedience, and our children can't always escape the influence of someone who makes disobedience seem appealing. It is crucial that children learn to discern what is God's way and what is not. Eight- to twelve-year olds must see that living in obedience to God is the most rewarding and exciting life they can experience. And of course, the rewards are eternal.

Summary

Grow up in every way to be like Christ by using Scripture verses and prayer to help you obey as Jesus obeyed.

- Jesus obeyed his earthly parents.
- Jesus obeyed his heavenly Father.
- Jesus obeyed Scripture.
- Jesus obeyed even if it meant suffering.

Lesson Aims

Scripture focus	Bible focus	Life focus
Lesson 1 Luke 2:39-52	Jesus was obedient to God by obeying his parents.	Use Scripture verses and prayer to help you obey your parents.
Lesson 2 Matthew 3:13-17	Jesus' baptism pleased God and marked the beginning of his ministry.	Use Scripture verses and prayer to help you obey God, to please him.
Lesson 3 Matthew 4:1-11 Mark 1:12, 13 Luke 4:1-13	Jesus used Scripture verses to help him obey God when Satan tempted him.	Use Scripture verses and prayer to help you obey when tempted.
Lesson 4 Matthew 26:36-46 Mark 14:32-42	Jesus prayed to do God's will.	Use Scripture verses and prayer to help you when it is difficult to obey.

Memory Passage: 1 John 5:1-5

"Everyone who believes that Jesus is the Christ is born of God, and everyone who loves the father loves his child as well. This is how we know that we love the children of God: by loving God and carrying out his commands. This is love for God: to obey his commands. And his commands are not burdensome, for everyone born of God overcomes the world. This is the victory that has overcome the world, even our faith. Who is it that overcomes the world? Only he who believes that Jesus is the Son of God."

Classroom Supplies
- branch (real or constructed from paper)
- markers
- ribbon
- scissors
- hole punch

Curriculum Supplies
reproducible page 57 (leaf pattern)

Memory Passage Review Activity

Make twelve copies of the leaf pattern and cut them out. Divide the memory passage into twelve phrases and write one phrase on each leaf. Punch a hole at the base of the stem of each leaf and thread ribbon through it. Scramble the leaves and have students tie the leaves on the branches in the order of the memory passage.

Lesson 1

Growing in Obedience

Obey Willingly

Luke 2:39-52

Bible Focus
Jesus was obedient to God by obeying his parents.

Life Focus
Use Scripture verses and prayer to help you obey your parents.

Growing Up in the Word: 1 John 5:1-5
Set up the materials for one or both of the following activities. As the students arrive, greet them by name and direct them to an activity or briefly explain the chosen activity for this lesson.

Memory Activity 1
Before class, copy the reproducible page and cut it into separate strips. Make two copies of the code.

Divide the class into two teams. Name one team "Love" and the other "Obedience." Write these names on the board and keep score during the game. Teams will race to see who can decode phrases of the memory passage faster. Distribute a copy of the code to each team. Give each team one of the phrases from set one. Award the team that finishes first one point. Then give the phrases for round two. Continue until all the phrases have been decoded.

After the teams have decoded the first few messages, it should become evident that the phrases they decoded simultaneously belong together; that is, one completes the other. For example, "Everyone who believes that Jesus is the Christ is born of God" matches "and everyone who loves the father loves his child as well."

Once the game is completed, have the students place the decoded messages on the table. Have several students find 1 John 5:1-5 and read it aloud. As they read it aloud, have other students place the messages in order on the table.

Say: **Once you started playing the game, you realized that the phrases you were decoding belonged together. You were two teams working against each other to win, but you were working together to complete the memory passage. Who remembers what names I gave to your teams? That's right, "Love" and**

Classroom Supplies
- Bibles
- paper
- pencils
- scissors

Curriculum Supplies
reproducible page 58 (Bible Code Breaker)

"Obedience." These two things never work against each other; they belong together and complete one another. We show our love for God through our obedience. When we obey, we show our love; when we love, then we obey. Which part of the memory passage tells us that obedience shows our love for God?** (1 John 5:3.)

Classroom Supplies
Bibles

Curriculum Supplies
none

Memory Activity 2

Instruct students to find 1 John 5:1-5. Students will read the passages in various styles. Give them the command, and then give them this signal to begin: "Do what you are told." Commands follow:

Command: Chant verse 1. Do what you are told.
Command: Sing verse 2. Do what you are told.
Command: Laugh while saying verse 3. Do what you are told.
Command: Read verse 4 slowly. Do what you are told.
Command: Jump while reading verse 5. Do what you are told.

As time permits, allow students to give some commands.

Say: **You did a great job doing what you were told! While we were memorizing this passage, we learned the definition of obedience. What is obedience?** (Doing what you are told.) **Our memory passage is about obeying God's commands. God doesn't usually tell us to jump, but he is serious about our obedience. How serious is our obedience to God? Look in verses three and four. Obedience shows that we have faith or belief in God.**

Classroom Supplies
• slips of paper
• marker

Curriculum Supplies
none

Why Grow Up?

Before class, write the following attitudes on separate slips of paper: guilty, tired, surprised, sad, angry, happy, frustrated, confused, frightened, suspicious, willing.

Distribute pieces of paper with attitudes written on them. Have students pantomime the attitude they have been given and let the other students guess what attitude it is. Write their guesses on the board to create a list of attitudes we can display on our face. They may think of some that aren't on the list, and that's OK.

Say: **We have different attitudes depending on what is going on in our lives.** Discuss each attitude listed, and ask students if they have this attitude when life goes well or when life doesn't go well.

Say: **Most of us think that situations cause our attitudes and determine how we feel. If life goes bad, then we are angry. If life goes well, then we are happy. Let me see you make a "life is going well with you" face. God's Word tells us one sure way for life to go well for us—and that is to display an attitude first! Let's find out what attitude that is.**

How to Grow Up

Have students locate Luke 2:39-52 and read it silently.

Ask: **Where did Jesus live?** (Nazareth in Galilee.) **Why did Jesus go to Jerusalem?** (For the feast of the Passover.) **What happened when it was time for Jesus to return home?** (Jesus stayed behind in Jerusalem.) **Why do you think it took a day for Mary and Joseph to miss Jesus?** (They trusted that he was with them and thought he was traveling with others in the group.) **Why were Mary and Joseph upset with Jesus?** (They did not know where he was.) **How did they feel when they were searching for Jesus?** (Anxious.) **What was Jesus doing when his parents found him?** (He was talking with the teachers.) **How did Jesus' parents feel when they saw him?** (Astonished.) **Was Jesus being disobedient by staying in the temple?** Allow the students time to answer and discuss the answers, particularly the fact that he was obeying God first. **What happened when Jesus returned to Nazareth?** (He was obedient to his parents.)

Choose three readers to read the conversation between Jesus and Mary in Luke 2:48-50. One will read the words of Mary, one the words of Jesus, and one the narration. Instruct students to read Mary's words with an astonished voice. Read Jesus' words with a soft, gentle, obedient voice. Help students understand that Jesus was not arguing with his parents. He was respectfully answering their questions. The narrator should read with a compassionate voice. Give several trios an opportunity to read the conversation.

Say: **Jesus willingly obeyed his earthly parents. He was busy with the work of God, yet he still obeyed his earthly parents.**

Classroom Supplies
- Bibles
- paper
- pens or pencils
- white board
- marker

Curriculum Supplies
none

Ready to Grow Up

Say: **Jesus has given us an example of willing obedience. He obeyed his parents without arguing or complaining. Instead, he respectfully answered their questions about where he was and what he had been doing.**

Like Mary and Joseph, our parents sometimes ask us where we have been and what we've been doing. How do you answer them? Discuss. **The way we talk to our parents shows them how we feel about them. It shows God whether or not we love him. It is not so much the words we use as it is the way we say the words.**

Our attitude can make the same sentence have a different meaning. Let's use this sentence as an example: "I've been at the ballgame." Direct students to repeat the sentence with a respectful voice and then with a disrespectful voice. **What difference do you notice in the meaning of the words?** (Same words, different attitude. One shows love, one doesn't.)

What is your attitude when you talk to your parents? Is your attitude cheerful and willing? Do you love your parents? Do you act like you love them when you talk to them? Do you act like you love them by willingly doing what they ask you to do? Discuss.

A willing attitude is an important part of obedience. Without a willing attitude, we may do what we are asked, but we are not obeying. If we are not obeying, then we are not loving. God commands us to obey, and not only that, we have to realize that "just doing it" is not good enough.

We need God's help to obey with a willing attitude. Sometimes we would rather do things our way and not God's way. So we need some help. We're going to make a reminder to help us obey our parents willingly. Ask students to make their "life is going well with you" face again so that you may take an individual snapshot of each student displaying that face. Distribute the reproducible page. Direct students to frame their picture. A new prayer will be added to the frame border each week. Hold pictures to use later.

Classroom Supplies
- Polaroid camera and film (use a regular camera and film if a Polaroid is unavailable)
- marker
- clear tape
- sturdy paper for frame backing
- glue

Curriculum Supplies
reproducible page 59 (picture frame)

Classroom Supplies
- Bibles
- photographs and frames from previous activity
- tree branch or substitute
- ribbon
- colored paper
- scissors

Curriculum Supplies
reproducible page 57 (leaf pattern)

Growing Up Every Day

Before class, set up a tree branch in the classroom on which to tie leaves from the reproducible page. If a tree branch is not available, make one by twisting long sheets of brown butcher paper. Staple together the twisted paper to form branches and attach them to the wall. For class today, prepare four leaves. Use different colors of paper. Write the following information:

What? Doing what you are told
Who? Parents
How? Willingly
Result? Life will go well with you.

Punch a hole at the base of the stem and thread ribbon through it. Gather students around the tree branch. Say: **We're going to keep track of what we learn this month. As we grow in obedience, our tree will grow as well.** Show the four leaves. Review what is written on each, and ask students to tie them to a branch of the tree.

Ask students to find and read Ephesians 6:1-3. Say: **God promises us that if we obey our parents, life will go well with us. Look at your picture. This is what you will feel like when you obey your parents willingly and life goes well with you. Your assignment this week is to use Scripture and prayer to help you willingly obey your parents. Place your picture beside your bed. Each night, pray this prayer. Read the verse. Then smile along with your picture because you know that when you willingly obey your parents, life will go well with you. Let's pray the prayer together now:**

"Dear Father, I love my parents. Help me to show my love for them by obeying them willingly. Thank you for your promise that 'it will go well with me' when I obey my parents. In Jesus' name, amen."

Lesson 2

Growing in Obedience

Obey Immediately

Matthew 3:13-17

Bible Focus

Jesus' baptism pleased God and marked the beginning of his ministry.

Life Focus

Use Scripture verses and prayer to help you obey God, to please him.

Growing Up in the Word: 1 John 5:1-5

Set up one or both of the following activities for students to do as they arrive. As you greet each student by name, direct them to an activity or explain the one chosen for this lesson.

Memory Activity 1

Classroom Supplies
- index cards
- marker
- masking tape

Curriculum Supplies
none

Write the memory passage in short phrases on separate index cards. Make enough so that each student will have a card containing part of the memory passage. On the opposite side of each card, write the name of an animal. The card containing the beginning phrase of the Scripture should have the name of a very small animal such as a fly or mouse. As you progress to the end of the passage, the animals should increase in size so that the last phrase card contains the largest animal such as an elephant. Use the tape to create a straight line on the floor long enough for all the students to stand on it side-by-side.

Mix the memory passage phrases so they are not in order. Distribute the cards to the students, and ask them not show anyone what is on the card. Ask the students to line up side-by-side on the tape line. Explain that the object of the game is to get the memory passage into correct order. Students are not allowed to say their phrase or to look at each other's cards. Instead, students are to act like and make the sound of the animal listed on the back of their card. From this students will determine their place in line. The smallest animal has the beginning of the passage and so on. Students work until the animal sounds are in order ranging from the smallest to the largest. At that point, direct students to read their cards to see if they have achieved their goal.

Say: **Our memory passage tells us that we must be obedient to show our faith in and love for God. It is easy to say I love you. It is harder to back up**

our words with action. In this game, you were not allowed to use words to find your place in line, and yet your actions showed others what animal you were. When we obey God, our actions show others that we love God.

Memory Activity 2

Classroom Supplies
none

Curriculum Supplies
memory passage script printed here

Before class, make one copy of the script below for each student. In class, have students read through this choral reading several times. Consider presenting it for a worship service.

All: Everyone
Solo boy: who believes that Jesus is the Christ is born of God,
All: and everyone
Solo girl: who loves the father, loves his child as well.
Duet boys: This is how we know that we love the children of God:
Duet girls: by loving God and carrying out his commands.
All: This is love for God: to obey his commands.
Solo girl: And his commands are not burdensome,
All: for everyone born of God has overcome the world.
Solo boy: This is the victory that has overcome the world,
All: even our faith.
Solo girl: Who is it that overcomes the world?
Solo boy: Only he who believes that Jesus is the Son of God.

Say : **How many times does this passage use the word everyone?** (Three.) **Who is everyone?** (All people.) **This passage narrows everyone down from all people to a everyone in a certain group of people. What group of people is that?** (Everyone who believes that Jesus is the Son of God.) **What is important about this group of people?** (They are born of God.) **What does everyone who is born of God do?** (They obey God.) **What does their obedience show?** (It shows that they love God and are born of God.) **Do people around you know that you are born of God by the way you obey God? Do they know that you believe Jesus is the Son of God?**

Why Grow Up?

Classroom Supplies
- Bibles
- timer or stopwatch
- paper
- pencils

Curriculum Supplies
none

Say: **Think of a fast-food restaurant. What kind of service do you expect at a fast-food restaurant? What would you do if it took over an hour to get a hamburger or French fries? Would that be acceptable? We usually receive our food immediately at a fast-food restaurant. We're going to think like a fast-food restaurant to play this game. We will have to act immediately. In order to complete the task before the time expires, you will have to start as soon as I give the instruction.**

Give students a task to complete, and give them a certain amount of time to complete it. Start with simple activities and an adequate amount of time so that students are able to complete the task given to them. As the game continues, the activities will grow longer and the time shorter. Decrease the time so that students are unable to finish the given task in time. Task suggestions follow:

1. Switch chairs with the person across from you.
2. Take your Bible and find the book of Numbers.

3. Stand up, turn around three times, and sit down.
4. Look in your Bible for John 3:16.
5. Stand up. Walk around the table counterclockwise until you reach your chair.
6. Find Ephesians 4:2 and write down the last word in that sentence.
7. Take off both shoes, untie or unbuckle them completely, and then put them back on.
8. Walk to the four corners of the room, touch each corner three times, and return to the seat that was on your right.
9. Draw a picture of your house.
10. Recite the alphabet.

Continue as time allows, making up your own activities.

Ask: **As the activities took more time to complete, what happened to the time? Did you find it hard to finish the activities in the time allowed? What happened when you didn't start on your task immediately after it was assigned? It was likely that you ran out of time!**

How did it feel to finish the task before the buzzer went off? (Good, happy, joyful.) **How did it feel not to finish the task before the buzzer went off?** (Sad, disappointed.)

In order for you to experience the feeling of doing a good job, you had to act immediately. In order for us to experience the joy God has for us, we must obey immediately. Have students read 1 John 5:1-5. **Acting immediately was important to play this game. Obeying immediately is important for pleasing God.**

How to Grow Up

Have students read Matthew 3:13-17.

Ask: **Why did John the Baptist try to discourage Jesus from being baptized?** (John thought he needed to be baptized by Jesus.) **How did Jesus answer John?** (Jesus said that he needed to be baptized in order to obey God.) **How soon did Jesus want to be baptized?** (Immediately.) **So how and when did Jesus obey God in this passage?** (Jesus obeyed God by being baptized right away.)

Let's talk about John the Baptist. Did John know that Jesus is the Son of God? (Yes.) **How did John feel about baptizing Jesus?** (He didn't think he was worthy.) **What if John had refused to baptize Jesus or had asked for a couple of days to think about it?** (John would have been disobedient to God.) **So how and when was John the Baptist obedient to God in the passage?** (John obeyed God by baptizing Jesus, and he did it when Jesus told him to do it—now.)

Was God pleased with Jesus and with John? (Yes.) **How do we know that God was pleased with them?** (God said so from Heaven, and he sent a dove to rest on Jesus.) **Nothing is said about God being pleased with John, but John obeyed, and God is pleased with obedience.**

God calls us to obey him and to obey him immediately. He doesn't tell us that it OK for us to think about obeying him. We are to do it now—immediately. Both John and Jesus showed their love for God when they obeyed him immediately. When we obey God, we please him. In fact, we show that we love God when we obey him.

Classroom Supplies
Bibles

Curriculum Supplies
none

Classroom Supplies

- Bible
- ribbon
- scissors
- colored paper
- hole punch

Curriculum Supplies

reproducible page57 (leaf pattern)

Ready to Grow Up

Before class, prepare three leaves. Use different colors of paper. Write the following information:

Who? God

How? Immediately

Result? Please God.

Punch a hole at the base of the stem and thread ribbon through it. Gather students around the obedience tree. Say: **Last week we learned that obedience is willingly doing what we are told to do. Let's review the leaves that were placed on the tree last week: What?** (Doing what you are told.) **Who?** (Parents.) **How?** (Willingly.) **Results?** (It will go well with you.) **Your assignment was to obey your parents willingly. You had a Scripture verse and a prayer to help you. How did the week go? How did your prayer and Scripture help you obey at home?** Let students report.

Not only does God want us to obey willingly, he wants us to obey immediately, not to be ones who say, "Yeah, well, I might get back to you on that in a couple of days!" Obedience does not give us a choice when to obey. Obedience is immediate. When our parents ask us to do a chore, do they mean next week or next month or the second time that we are asked? No, it means now.

We've added to our definition of obedience this week. Show students the three leaves. **Obedience is willingly and immediately doing what you are told. So far we have a list of two people we need to obey. Who are they?** (Our parents and God.) **Let's add these new leaves to our tree.** Have students do so.

Classroom Supplies

Bibles

Curriculum Supplies

reproducible page 59 (Pleasing God Prayer)

Growing Up Every Day

Ask students to find and read John 14:15. Say: **We often don't think about what our actions show about how we feel about God. This week your assignment is to willing and immediately obey God. Our obedience pleases God.** Distribute the Pleasing God Prayer. **At home paste this prayer to one edge of your picture frame. Each night before you go to bed, pray this prayer and read the Scripture. When it is time to obey God, remember this prayer and Scripture. Let's pray the prayer together now:**

"Dear Father, I love you. I want to show my love for you by obeying you. Help me to remember this. Help me show you I love you by obeying you. In Jesus' name, amen."

Lesson 3

Growing in Obedience

God's Word Helps Us Obey

Matthew 4:1-11; Mark 1:12, 13; Luke 4:1-13

Bible Focus

Jesus used Scripture verses to help him obey God when Satan tempted him.

Life Focus

Use Scripture verses and prayer to help you obey when tempted.

Growing Up in the Word: 1 John 5:1-5

At the beginning of class, set up the materials for one or both of the memorization activities. As the students arrive, greet them by name and direct them to an activity or briefly explain the chosen activity for that day.

Memory Activity 1

Classroom Supplies
- bricks
- paper
- marker
- gloves

Curriculum Supplies
none

Before class, cut one piece of paper for each brick. The paper should be the size of the side of one of your bricks. The more bricks used for this activity, the more students will have to move around, and the better the point will be made. Divide the memory passage into the same number of phrases as you have bricks. Write each phrase on a separate piece of paper. Attach each one to the side of a brick. Provide gloves if bricks are rough.

In class, put the bricks in a pile. The order of the passage should be shuffled. Instruct students to stack the bricks in order with verse one at the bottom and verse five at the top. When finished, students should read the passage aloud. Next ask them to move the pile of bricks across the room and again stack the bricks in memory passage order, but this time they should make the stack look different from the first stack. When finished, students should read the passage aloud. Continue in the same manner for one more round. At the start of the fourth round, students should begin to complain about moving the bricks. This time tell them to take the papers off the bricks and to move only them across the room. They can then lay the papers in order on the floor and recite the passage.

Say: **Carrying bricks is a lot of work. It was fun the first time, but it got old quick! This is what disobedience is like. We think it looks fun, and it may be the first few times. Then it becomes a burden. Our memory passage tells us that God's commands are not a burden. They won't weigh us down. They**

aren't hard to carry. In fact, even when God's commands seem hard to obey, they don't burden us; they bless us. God blesses us when we obey his commands.

Classroom Supplies
- poster board
- masking tape

Curriculum Supplies
none

Memory Activity 2

Before class, make a large heart from the poster board. Write the memory passage on the heart clearly marking the verses. Place it where it can be seen easily. Use the masking tape to make seven lines an equal distance from each other on the floor. They should look similar to the five-yard lines on a football field. Label lines in the following order: "Start," "Verse 1," "Verse 2," "Verse 3," "Verse 4," "Verse 5," "Finish."

Explain that the heart represents God's love that is available to us, love that he wants to shower on us, if we obey him. Then play this version of Simon Says in which the words "To obey" are substituted for "Simon Says." The goal is for students to reach the "Finish" line. At each line, students are to stop and recite the indicated verse from 1 John 5.

Most of the commands should move the students forward, however not all of them have to. Try using some of these commands: "To obey, hop on one foot forward"; "To obey, waltz to the next line"; "Touch your nose"; "Turn around"; "To move forward, sing loudly"; "To obey, crawl six steps." If students obey a command that hasn't been preceded with the words "to obey," they must return to the starting line. Instruct the first student to reach the finish line to grab the heart with the memory passage and take a victory lap, holding the heart high.

Say: **Were the instructions in this game hard to follow? For some of us, the only problems were with our hearing! Who won the victory in this game?** Name the student. **We all like to win. Our memory passage tells us how we can win a victory. What does it tell us in verses 4 and 5?** (Our faith is the victory.) **What is faith?** (Faith is believing that Jesus is the Son of God.) **How do we show that we believe Jesus is the Son of God?** (We obey.)

Classroom Supplies
- three eggs—two hard-boiled and one raw
- napkins
- bowl

Curriculum Supplies
none

Why Grow Up?

Call students' attention to the bowl of three eggs. Say: **Two of these eggs are the same; one is different.** Pass the bowl of eggs around the table, and have each student take a turn investigating the eggs in order to detect a difference. They are to look but not to touch. After everyone has had a turn, crack open the eggs to reveal the inside and how they are different.

Say: **These eggs appeared to be the same, but in fact they were not the same. Many things in life can appear innocent when they are really dangerous. When this happens, we are deceived. Satan fools us with deception.**

The difference in something that looks innocent but is dangerous can actually be enormous, and once we realize this, it may be too late. For instance, what if I had asked one of you to hit your head with an egg? What difference would it have made if you had picked the raw one instead of the hard-boiled one? It's the same with other choices, like choosing friends or going to

the movies. We can choose to be friends with anyone, but we have to be careful about not choosing friends who will help get us into trouble. Going to the movies isn't necessarily bad, but we have to be sure we don't choose bad movies to watch. We have to be on our guard, not relying on our own power, but relying on God's power and his Word to catch Satan's deceptions.

Jesus was a master at catching Satan's deceptions. Jesus knew just what Satan was up to and just how to handle him. Let's find our how Jesus handled Satan.

How to Grow Up

Distribute the reproducible page. Direct students to read the Scripture silently and follow the instructions given on the page.

When the page is complete, say: **Satan worked hard to get Jesus to sin—to disobey God. He tried to deceive Jesus. What method did he use?** (He wanted Jesus to think that he needed to prove he was God's Son. He misused Scripture.) **These are both examples of how Satan uses deception. He makes us think that we have something to prove. He makes something seem right when it is wrong.**

It is important for us to understand how Jesus dealt with Satan. What was Jesus' answer to each of Satan's temptations? (Jesus quoted Scripture.) **How many times did Jesus have to answer Satan with Scripture?** (Three.) **We can follow Jesus' example when Satan tries to deceive us.**

Classroom Supplies
Bibles

Curriculum Supplies
reproducible page 60
(The Temptation of Jesus)

Ready to Grow Up

Before class, prepare two leaves. Use different colors of paper. Write the following information:

How? Use Scripture

Result? Defeat Satan.

Punch a hole at the base of the stem and thread ribbon through it. Show reproducible page. Say: **We've tried to trick you into thinking these two pictures are the same. Are they? Look closer.** Distribute pages and give students time to find the differences. When students are finished, say: **This was a fun activity, but Satan's tricks of deception are serious.**

Satan uses temptation deceptively in our lives to trick us into doing wrong or making bad choices. We know that Satan tried to trick Jesus by quoting Scripture and by trying to make Jesus think he had to prove he was God's Son. We know that Satan will try to trick us into disobeying God by making something wrong look right or innocent. We have to realize that sin or temptation will not always appear in the way we expect it.

When Jesus was tempted, he trusted in God, relied on the Scripture, and was obedient to his father. We must rely on God and use his Word to help us obey. With God's help, we can become a master at catching Satan's deceptions.

Gather students around the obedience tree. Say: **So far this month, we have learned that obedience is willingly and immediately doing what we are told to do. Let's review.** Review the leaves on the tree: **What?** (Doing what you are told.) **Who?** (Parents and God.) **How?** (Willingly and immediately.) **Results?** (It will go well with you and you'll please God.) **Last week your assignment was**

Classroom Supplies
- colored paper
- scissors
- ribbon
- hole punch
- marker
- pencils

Curriculum Supplies
reproducible pages 57 and 61 (leaf pattern and What's the Difference?)

to please God with your obedience. You had a Scripture and a prayer to help you. How did the week go? How did your prayer and Scripture help you obey? Let students report.

Say: **Today, we will add two more leaves to our tree.** Select students to read the leaves and add them to the tree. **Jesus used Scripture to help him obey God. In doing so, his obedience defeated Satan.**

Growing Up Every Day

Classroom Supplies
Bibles

Curriculum Supplies
reproducible page 59
(Temptation Prayer)

Before class, copy and cut out one Temptation Prayer for each student.

Ask students to find and read 1 Peter 5:8, 9. Say: **Satan is like a lion, and he wants to deceive you into doing wrong. Your assignment this week is to use Scripture and prayer to obey when you are tempted.** Distribute the Temptation Prayer. **At home paste this prayer to one edge of your picture frame. Each night before you go to bed, pray this prayer and read the Scripture. Then when you face temptation, remember this prayer and Scripture. Let's pray together now:**

"Dear Father, Help me stand strong against my enemy Satan. Help me be alert to the tricks he will use to get me to do wrong. Help me remember these words. In Jesus' name, amen."

Lesson 4

Growing in Obedience

Prayer Helps Us Obey

Matthew 26:36-46; Mark 14:32-42

Bible Focus
Jesus prayed to do God's will.

Life Focus
Use Scripture verses and prayer to help you when it is difficult to obey.

Growing Up in the Word: 1 John 5:1-5
Set up the materials for one or both of the memorization activities. As the students arrive, greet them by name and direct them to an activity center or briefly explain the activity chosen for this lesson.

Memory Activity 1
Have the students sit in a circle. Give a student the heart and ask him to read the first verse, then pass the heart to the next student, who in turn reads the next verse, and so on. Once the heart has made it around to all students, begin again. This time, turn the heart so the words are facing the group and away from the person holding the heart. The first student recites the first verse from memory and passes the heart to his neighbor for him to recite the next verse. The group can provide clues or hints to the person reciting. Continue this until the heart has made it all the way around a couple of times.

Say: **What does it mean to overcome the world? The apostle John uses the word "world" in this passage to refer to sin and evil. So to overcome the world means to overcome evil, sin, and temptation. What does obedience have to do with overcoming temptation? When we obey, we overcome or defeat evil. We obey because we love God and believe that Jesus is God's Son. Overcoming evil is choosing obedience over disobedience.**

Classroom Supplies
memory passage heart from lesson 3

Curriculum Supplies
none

Memory Activity 2
Before class, write key words from the memory passages on small pieces paper that will fit on a student's forehead. Prepare one for each student.

In class, use tape to attach one slip of paper to the forehead of each student. This will enable them to easily see other people's papers but not their own.

Classroom Supplies
- paper
- pens
- tape
- basket

Curriculum Supplies
none

Gather together in a circle or around the table. Each student is allowed to ask yes or no questions to try and guess what word is written on their forehead. For a small class, choose one student to begin asking the group questions. Allow several questions and then have another student take a turn. For a large class, have students find a partner. Each partner asks one question of the other and then the entire class switches partners. Continue the game until everyone has discovered his word.

Say: **Was it easy to guess the words? Did anyone guess the correct answer on the first try? Most of us had to keep asking and guessing. It took time, patience, and perseverance. Commitment also takes time, patience, and perseverance. It requires dedication, and we can apply this to our study on obedience. Obedience isn't a one-time thing; it requires a commitment to obey again and again.**

Why Grow Up

Invite a talented musician, artist, or one who fluently speaks a foreign language to come and share what was involved in mastering his talent. Once the guest has shared with the class, encourage the students to ask questions concerning how this person discovered their gift, how long have they had it, how long have they been dedicated to it, how often do they practice, and so on.

Classroom Supplies
- a guest speaker who has mastered a skill (if someone is not available, bring a musical instrument)
- index cards
- pens or pencils

Curriculum Supplies
none

If you cannot find someone to visit your class, or if time does not allow this, bring a musical instrument to class. Pass the instrument around the room and invite the students to try to play it. Some may have the ability and others won't.

After the guest has shared their talent or after the class has tried to play the instrument, ask: **How does a person achieve a goal or develop a talent? What does it require?** (Dedication and commitment.) **Most people can't expect to sit down at a piano the first time and play beautifully; it requires practice, dedication to lessons, and a commitment to learn. Commitment applies to many areas of life, but none are as important as our commitment to God.**

How to Grow Up

Have students find and silently read Matthew 26:36-46. When finished, assign the following roles to students: Jesus, Peter, James and John (the two sons of Zebedee), and disciples. All students other than Jesus, Peter, James, and John can be disciples. Distribute the costume materials to the students and help them assemble a Bible-times outfit. Lead students to pantomime the scene from the Garden of Gethsemane. If weather permits, move outside to create a more realistic feel. As you read the passage aloud, students will perform the actions and mouth the words.

Before you begin, determine where the disciples will wait while Jesus prays. Determine the places where Jesus will pray. Instruct students to show the way they think Jesus and the disciples felt that night.

Say: **The disciples were sleepy. How does someone who is sleepy act? Show me. Jesus was sorrowful. How does someone who is sorrowful look? Show**

me. Discuss how the disciples probably looked and acted. Discuss Jesus' attitude toward the disciples. Determine his body language during that time and when he was praying to God.

When all the instructions have been given, practice the pantomime, and when students are somewhat comfortable with their roles, perform it. If possible, videotape the performance and watch it together in the classroom.

Ask: **How many times did Jesus pray and then return to his disciples?** (Three.) **Why was Jesus sorrowful?** (The time had come for him to be crucified.) **Why did Jesus continue to pray? This was a hard time for Jesus. Jesus had a burden to carry for us; he knew that suffering was in store for him the next few days. He continued to pray to seek comfort and to speak with his father. He had made a commitment to obey, and he followed through.**

What is the main idea of this passage of Scripture? (Prayer.) **What caused Jesus to pray?** (The difficult time ahead of him.) **Jesus shows us here how important it is for us to pray when we need help obeying God.**

Classroom Supplies

- costumes (sheets, pieces of material, robes)
- pieces of poster board cut in half to write the script on
- video camera and TV/VCR (optional)

Curriculum Supplies

none

Ready to Grow Up

Before class, prepare two leaves. Use different colors of paper. Write the following information:

How? Pray

Result? Able to do what is difficult.

Punch a hole at the base of the stem and thread ribbon through it. Make one copy of the Difficult Time Prayer for each student.

Gather students around the obedience tree. Say: **We've been working hard this month to grow in obedience. We've learned that obedience is willingly and immediately doing what we are told to do. Let's review what we've learned.** Review the leaves that are on the tree: **What?** (Doing what you are told.) **Who?** (Parents and God.) **How?** (Willingly; immediately; using Scripture.) **Results?** (It will go well with you; you will please God; you will resist Satan.)

Last week your assignment was to use Scripture and prayer to resist temptation. How did the week go? How did your prayer and Scripture help you obey? Let students report.

Say: **In today's Scripture, we saw that Jesus had a difficult time ahead of him. We may never face anything as difficult as dying on a cross, but we will have difficult times. Let's name some difficult times that we might have or that we have had.** Discuss. **These could include a loved one's death, divorce of parents, sickness, missing family member, addiction problems, and so on. Why might it be difficult to obey during these times?** (We feel sad; we don't want to; we are angry.)

Difficult times are important times to pray. When we have a difficult thing to do or a difficult situation to face, we must still do what God has asked us to do, and we must do it with prayer.

Let's add the last two leaves to our tree. Select students to read the leaves and

Classroom Supplies

- ribbon
- scissors
- marker
- colored paper

Curriculum Supplies

reproducible pages 57 and 59 (leaf pattern and Difficult Time Prayer) add them to the tree. **Prayer helps us to obey God. Jesus showed us how important prayer is. He prayed until he knew he was ready to do the difficult thing that he needed to do.**

Ask students to find and read Philippians 4:6. Say: **We often feel anxious when we are having a difficult time. This week your assignment is to use Scripture and prayer to help you obey during a time that is difficult or a task that is difficult.** Distribute Difficult Time Prayer. **At home, paste this prayer to the last edge of your picture frame. Each night before you go to bed, pray this prayer and read this Scripture. When you have a difficult time, remember this prayer and Scripture. Let's pray together now:**

"Dear Father, I feel anxious. Your Word tells me to pray when I feel anxious. I ask for your help through this difficult time. Thank you for your help. In Jesus' name, amen."

Growing Up Every Day

Classroom Supplies
none

Curriculum Supplies
reproducible page 59 (four prayers)

Before class, make one copy of the four prayers for each student. Say: **At the beginning of class, we talked to a person who is accomplished in** (name area of accomplishment). **We talked about what it takes to be exceptional at something. It takes hard work and commitment. Both hard work and commitment are needed in our relationship with God. We must work hard to obey, we must be committed to know Scripture, and and we must pray in every situation. These actions are necessary ingredients for obedience.**

We've used four Scriptures and four prayers this month. We're going to read each Scripture and pray each prayer as we close out our unit on obedience.

Ask a student to find and read Ephesians 6:1-3, then lead the class in the Parents' Prayer.

Ask a student to find and read John 14:15, then lead the class in the Pleasing God Prayer.

Ask a student to find and read 1 Peter 5:8, then lead the class in the Temptation Prayer.

Ask a student to find and read Philippians 4:6, then lead the class in the Difficult Time Prayer.

Ask the class to find and read 1 John 5:1-5 together.

BIBLE CODE BREAKER

Code:	A	B	C	D	E	F	G	H	I	J	K	L	M	N	O	P	Q	R	S	T	U	V	W	X	Y	Z
	1	2	3	4	5	6	7	8	9	10	11	12	13	14	15	16	17	18	19	20	21	22	23	24	25	26

5.22.5.18.25.15.14.5 who 2.5.12.9.5.22.5.19

20.8.1.20 10.5.19.21.19 9.19 20.8.5

3.8.18.9.19.20 9.19 2.15.18.14 15.6 7.15.4,

1

1.14.4 5.22.5.18.25.15.14.5 23.8.15 12.15.22.5.19

20.8.5 6.1.20.8.5.18 12.15.22.5.19 8.9.19

3.8.9.12.4 1.19 23.5.12.12.

A 10.15.8.14 E:A

1

20.8.9.19 is how 23.5 11.14.15.23 20.8.1.20

23.5 12.15.22.5 20.8.5 3.8.9.12.4.18.5.14

15.6 7.15.4,

2

2.25 12.15.22.9.14.7 7.15.4 1.14.4

3.1.18.18.25.9.14.7 15.21.20 8.9.19

3.15.13.13.1.14.4.19. A 10.15.8.14 E:B

2

20.8.9.19 is 12.15.22.5 6.15.18 7.15.4:

20.15 15.2.5.25 8.9.19 3.15.13.13.1.14.4.19.

3

1.14.4 8.9.19 3.15.13.13.1.14.4.19 1.18.5

14.15.20 2.21.18.4.5.14.19.15.13.5.

A 10.15.8.14 E:C

3

6.15.18 5.22.5.18.25.15.14.5 2.15.18.14 15.6

7.15.4 8.1.19 15.22.5.18.3.15.13.5 20.8.5

23.15.18.12.4.

4

20.8.9.19 is the 22.9.3.20.15.18.25 20.8.1.20 has

15.22.5.18.3.15.13.5 20.8.5 23.15.18.12.4, even

15.21.18 6.1.9.20.8. A 10.15.8.14 E:D

4

23.8.15 9.19 9.20 20.8.1.20

15.22.5.18.3.15.13.5 20.8.5 23.15.18.12.4?

5

15.14.12.25 he who 2.5.12.9.22.5.19 20.8.1.20

10.5.19.21.19 is the 19.15.14 15.6 7.15.4.

A 10.15.8.14 E:E

5

Read
Ephesians 6:1-3

Dear Father, I love my parents. Help me to show my love for them by willingly obeying them. Thank you for your promise that "it will go well with me" when I obey my parents. In Jesus' name. Amen.

Lesson 2

Lesson 3

Lesson 4

Read
John 14:15

Dear Father, I love you. I want to show my love for you by obeying you. Help me to remember this. Help me show you I love you by obeying you. In Jesus' name. Amen.

Read
1 Peter 5:8

Dear Father, Help me stand strong against my enemy Satan. Help me be alert to the tricks he will use to get me to do wrong. Help me remember these words. In Jesus' name. Amen.

Read
Philippians 4:6

Dear Father, I feel anxious. Your Word tells me to pray when I feel anxious. I ask for your help through this difficult time. Thank you for your help. In Jesus' name. Amen.

Photo Frame

Instructions

- Cut out the picture frame along the outside lines.
- Cut out the dotted square photo area.
- Center your photo behind the frame in the photo area.
- Secure with tape.
- Glue the picture frame to a piece of sturdy paper the same size.
- Each week add a Scripture reference and a prayer to one side of the frame.

The Temptation of Jesus

- Draw a book shape over each time Jesus or Satan quotes Scripture. Hint: Look for the words "it is written."
- Write a big number 40 over the number of days and nights Jesus went without food.
- Make a check mark over the times that Satan asked Jesus to prove that he is God's Son.
- Draw an arrow over the words Jesus used to send Satan away.

Matthew 4:1-11

Then Jesus was led by the Spirit into the desert to be tempted by the devil. After fasting forty days and forty nights, he was hungry. The tempter came to him and said, " If you are the Son of God, tell these stones to become bread."

Jesus answered, "It is written: 'Man does not live on bread alone, but on every word that comes from the mouth of God.'"

Then the devil took him to the holy city and had him stand on the highest point of the temple. If you are the Son of God," he said, "throw yourself down. For it is written:

"'He will command his angels concerning you,
and they will lift you up in their hands,
so that you will not strike your foot against a stone.'"

Jesus answered him, "It is also written: 'Do not put the Lord your God to the test.'"

Again, the devil took him to a very high mountain and showed him all the kingdoms of the world and their splendor. "All this I will give you," he said, "if you will bow down and worship me."

Jesus said to him, "Away from me, Satan! For it is written: 'Worship the Lord your God, and serve him only.'"

Then the devil left him, and angels came and attended him.

WHAT'S THE DIFFERENCE?

UNIT 3

Growing in Attitude

Unit Aims

Know: Identify attitudes Jesus had and taught us to have.
Feel: Feel a desire for the blessings of Jesus attitudes.
Do: Grow in Jesus' attitudes.
Memorize: Mark 10:43-45

Why Grow in Attitude?

The words that begin this month's memory passage—"Not so with you"—introduce us to the fact that Christians are set apart. They are different from the world. The truth of this is overwhelmingly apparent in the area of attitude. Students see a world around them that puts self first. Many of today's role models are arrogant and selfish people. Unfortunately, the world praises these people and sees humility as a sign of weakness. But Jesus said, "Not so with you." We are not to have this world's attitude.

This unit encourages students to examine their attitudes. The lessons and activities focus on changing me-first attitudes into God-first attitudes. Students will be encouraged to do this through serving others. They will put others first, look out for the interests of others, consider others more important than themselves, and show mercy and forgiveness to others. These servant actions toward others certainly are "not so" with the world. But they are the actions that stem from a God-first attitude.

Summary

Grow up in every way to be like Christ by developing the attitudes he had.

- Jesus taught us that right attitudes bring blessings.
- Jesus showed us an attitude of servanthood.
- Jesus taught us to be humble.
- Jesus taught us to be forgiving and merciful.
- Jesus taught us to replace me-first attitudes with God-first attitudes.

Lesson Aims

Scripture focus	Bible focus	Life focus
Lesson 1 Matthew 5:1-12	Jesus taught that right attitudes bring blessings.	Realize the need for right attitudes in your life.
Lesson 2 Philippians 2:1-8	Jesus was a humble servant.	Identify Jesus' attitude.
Lesson 3 Luke 18:9-14	Jesus taught us to be humble and meek.	Choose a way to grow in humility.
Lesson 4 Matthew 18:21-35	Jesus taught us to be merciful.	Choose a way to grow in showing mercy and forgiveness.
Lesson 5 Matthew 19:16-26	The rich young man did not choose to have a God-first attitude.	Give up a me-first attitude and replace it with a God-first attitude.

Memory Passage: Mark 10:43-45

"Not so with you. Instead, whoever wants to become great among you must be your servant, and whoever want to be first must be slave of all. For even the Son of Man did not come to be served, but to serve, and to give his life as a ransom for many."

Classroom Supplies
- tag board or poster board
- marker
- magnet strip (found in craft aisles for a few dollars)
- metal cabinet or some other metal surface where students can place a magnet

Curriculum Supplies
none

Memory Passage Review Activity

Glue a length of magnetic strip to sturdy paper. Write the words of the memory passage on the magnet strip. Leave space between words so they can easily be cut apart. Place the words in scrambled order on the side of a metal cabinet. Student can put the words in order and scramble them for the next person.

Lesson 1

Growing in Attitude

Let Others Go First

Matthew 5:1-12

Bible Focus

Jesus taught that right attitudes bring blessings.

Life Focus

Realize the need for right attitudes in your life.

Growing Up in the Word: Mark 10:43-45

Set up one or both of the following activities. Greet the students by name and direct them to the activity chosen for this lesson.

Memory Activity 1

Before class, write the memory passage on the poster board. Plan a service project for your class in which they adopt a younger class in your church that meets the same time as yours. Each week of this unit during Memory Activity 1, students will serve their adopted class.

Have the students search Mark 10:43-45 for Jesus' attitudes. To get them started, point out the first section: "whoever wants to become great among you must be your servant." Have students share the attitudes they found in the passage.

Ask: **Who wants to be great in God's kingdom? Can you become great and be arrogant according to Jesus? What must you do to be great?** (Serve.) **Who wants to be first? Can you be first and be selfish according to Jesus? What must you do to be first?** (Be a slave.)

Introduce the service project, then ask: **How can we be servants to these people over the next month?** Discuss. Each week suggestions will be given in the lesson outline, but use some of your students' ideas as well.

Have each students create a card of encouragement for someone who teaches in the class you have chosen. Instruct students to pick up an idea from the memory passage and use it in the message. For example, "Thank you for the way you serve the kids of this church. You are great because you are a servant." Team students up with a partner, and they can make a card together. Collect the cards, read over them, and take them to the teachers. Be sure to have a contact person in the class so you can plan ahead and not interrupt their schedule.

Classroom Supplies

- pens
- pencils
- constructions paper
- stickers
- markers
- scissors
- glue
- poster board

Curriculum Supplies

none

Classroom Supplies
- the game Jenga or Uno Stacko
- poster board
- marker

Curriculum Supplies
none

Memory Activity 2

Before class, write the memory passage on the poster board. Use a blank line in place of the following words: whoever, great, whoever, first, slave, all, Son of Man, served, serve, life, ransom, many, 43-45. Write these words on slips of paper and attach them to separate game pieces of the game you are using.

Explain the rules of the chosen game to the students. As they remove pieces from the game that are marked with words from the memory passage, have them place the word in the blank on the poster board. If someone knocks down the tower, they are not out of the game if they can quote a least one complete sentence of the passage. Otherwise, they sit out one round until someone else knocks the tower down.

As students play, ask: **Who likes to go first when they play games? We all do. Why do you like to be first?** Allow students to answer and then discuss their answers. **Why is it hard to let someone else go first in this game?** (The structure is stable and the chance of it falling is not as great.) **Are there other times in your life when it is hard to let someone else go first? We may want to be first in line for a meal, so we don't worry about cleaning up or helping others. We might be hungry and so on. Look at the poster board. What does the memory passage say we should do if we want to be first?** (We should be a slave to all.) **That's interesting. Do any of you want to be a slave? No? But I thought you said you wanted to be first? Yes? How is it possible to be a slave and be first?** Discuss. **Today, we'll find out what Jesus said about being first.**

Classroom Supplies
- sour lemonade
- good lemonade
- cups

Curriculum Supplies
none

Why Grow Up?

Before class, prepare two jugs of lemonade or any other drink. One should taste very sour and the other should taste good.

Say: **Who wants lemonade? Ice-cold lemonade! Wow! Most of you want lemonade. Great! Who should I serve first? Who wants the lemonade first?** Serve the sour lemonade to the students who insist on being first. Serve half the class, then stop and ask them how it tastes. Students should say that the lemonade is sour. Smell the lemonade and comment about what might have gone wrong with it. Open the jug with the good lemonade and serve it to the rest of the class. When finished, ask them how it tastes. Students should say it is great! Say: **Wow! It's great that you guys let me serve the other half of the class first. They were able to tell me that the first pitcher of lemonade wasn't good. Because you waited, you got to drink the best lemonade.**

We all have the desire to be first. Why do we want to be first? Discuss. **We think it is the best. We think we won't get anything if we wait until last. God's Word has something to say about being first and last. What does it say?** Discuss. Have students find and read Matthew 19:30; 20:16; Mark 10:31; Luke 13:30. **We may think the best place is first, but Jesus said that the best place is last. We're going to find out what it takes to be last so that we might be first in Jesus' eyes.**

How to Grow Up

Before class, divide the poster board into two columns and twelve rows. Title one column "Attitudes" and the other "Blessings."

Have students find Matthew 5:1-12. Read it aloud as students follow along in their Bibles. Say: **We are going to list the attitude and blessing from each verse. We'll do one verse together, and then we'll break into groups.**

Read verse three again. Ask: **What is the attitude in this verse?** (Poor in spirit.) **What is poor in spirit? To be poor in spirit is to be the opposite of puffed up, arrogant, or conceited. It is knowing that you need Jesus. People who are puffed up, arrogant, or conceited might say something like this: "Thank you, God, that I am not a lowly sinner like other people." Or "Thank you, God, that I am so wise and so much better than these people." To be poor in spirit is to realize that you cannot be what God wants without his help. Someone who is poor in spirit might say, "O God, I need your forgiveness and help. I am unworthy of your grace."** Write "poor in spirit" in the first row under "Attitude."

Ask: **What is the blessing for those who are poor in spirit—those who know that they need Jesus?** (Theirs is the kingdom of heaven.) **What does this mean?** (They will be in Heaven someday.) Write "Theirs is the kingdom of heaven" in the first row under "Blessings."

Divide the class into small groups and assign each group one verse. Have the students read the verse and discuss its meaning. Students are to define the attitude and give examples of how it is displayed. Then they are to define the blessing. If students need help defining an attitude, have them look it up in a dictionary.

When all groups are finished, have each group discuss the attitude and blessing for their verse. Write the attitude in the "attitude" column and the blessing in the "blessing" column.

Point to the list of attitudes. Say: **These are the attitudes that Jesus wants us to have.** Point to the list of blessings. **These are the blessings we receive because of these attitudes. Are these blessings something that you would like to receive? Do you want to spend eternity in Heaven? Do you want to be comforted when you are sad? Do you want to be satisfied when you want what is right? Do you want mercy? Do you want to be with God? Do you want a reward in Heaven? Yes, these are all blessings that we want!**

We have two more attitudes and blessings to add to our list. Let's find and read Mark 10:43-45, our memory passage. What two attitudes are listed here? (Servant, slave.) **What two blessings?** (Great, first.) Write both attitudes and blessings on the poster board. **How do the attitudes in our memory passage match up to what Jesus teaches in Matthew 5?** (A person who has the attitudes listed in Matthew 5 will be a servant and slave. He will have the blessings of being great and being first.)

Point to poster board. Say: **Today's Scriptures teach us that our attitudes directly affect what happens to us. These attitudes are Jesus' attitudes; they bring blessings to us.**

Classroom Supplies
- Bibles
- paper
- pencils
- markers
- poster board
- dictionaries

Curriculum Supplies
none

Classroom Supplies
- napkins
- markers

Curriculum Supplies
none

Ready to Grow Up

Ask: **Why do we need to have Jesus' attitudes?** Discuss. **They are the tools we need to live like God wants us to live. I think we would all agree that we want the blessings of Jesus' attitudes. The question is this: how do we get Jesus attitudes? We are going to do what servants do.**

Drape a napkin over your arm similar to the way a waiter would. Say: **When I think of a servant, I think of a waiter who waits on customers in a restaurant. Have you ever seen a server at a restaurant drape a towel over his arm like this? A napkin is a good symbol for a servant. Since we're working this month on being servants, we are going to use napkins to help remind us of that. Each week we will look for opportunities to put others first. This week your assignment is to let others go first. Let's name some times when we can let others go first. When do you have to stand in line?** (Lunch, bathroom, drinking fountain, playground, and so on.) **What other opportunities do you have to let others go first? Think about situations at home or when your family is traveling or when choosing what to watch on TV. Is letting someone have first choice one way to have a servant's attitude toward them?** Distribute napkins. Have students write the following sentence on their napkins: "Let others go first." Students may need to practice writing on a napkin before they are able to do it smoothly.

Classroom Supplies
none

Curriculum Supplies
none

Growing Up Every Day

Say: **Drape your napkin over your arm like a servant. Remember this symbol of a servant. You are a servant in God's kingdom. Take your napkin home and each time you let someone else go first, make a check mark on the napkin.**

Lead students in prayer. Seek God's guidance in finding opportunities to let others go first in line. Ask him to create a servant's heart in each student. Close by leading the students in reading the memory passage.

Lesson 2

Growing in Attitude

Look Out For the Interests of Others

Philippians 2:1-8

Bible Focus

Jesus was a humble servant.

Life Focus

Identify Jesus' attitude.

Growing Up in the Word: Mark 10:43-45

Set up one or both of the following activities for students to do as they arrive. Greet each student and direct him or her to the activities to join in.

Memory Activity 1

Before class, write every two words of the memory passage on separate slips of paper. Scramble the papers face up on a table. Have the students unscramble the words and then read them aloud.

Say: **We're going to prepare a puppet show about a great man. Everyone knows about him because of the way he was a servant.** Have the students prepare the puppets for the children's story based on Luke 10:30-37, the Parable of the Good Samaritan. They will color the puppets, cut them out, and attach a craft stick. While they are working on the puppets, have one student read the story to everyone.

Say: **Who is the servant in this story?** After students answer ask: **Who are you more like when you see a stranger who needs help? Are you like the priest and Levite who were too busy or too proud to stop and help? Which one of these men was the servant? Which man is great?**

Have one student be the narrator and read the story from the Bible while other students are the puppeteers. Practice telling the story before going to your adopted class to share. Remind the students that these younger children look up to them, and they can be servants to them by showing God's love. Also remind them that they are being servants by helping the teachers.

Go to the class you have chosen to serve and have the students share their

Classroom Supplies
- paper
- markers
- craft sticks
- large table cloth
- scissors
- clear tape

Curriculum Supplies
- reproducible page 85 (stick puppets)

story. A table with a cloth draped over the front can serve as a puppet stage. Have the class read the memory passage before they leave.

Classroom Supplies
- pencils

Curriculum Supplies
- reproducible page 86 (word search)

Memory Activity 2

Before class, make one copy of the word search for each student. In class, distribute the worksheet and instruct students to look for words in the memory passage. They may work together. When they complete the page, have them recite the passage together.

Say: **Our memory passage tells us we must be servants in order to be great. Do you know any servants who are great? Name some great people that you know. Why are these people great?** Discuss. **What the world calls great and what Jesus calls great are not always the same. That is what the words "not so with you" mean. God doesn't measure greatness the way the world does. Would you rather be great in the world's eyes or would you rather be great in God's eyes? To be great in God's eyes, you must learn to be a servant. What do servants do?** Discuss.

Why Grow Up?

Before class, cut out several pictures of jewelry and/or precious stones. Attach them to a piece of paper and include the price of the gems with the picture. If a price is not listed, guess. Divide the memory passage into the same number of phrases as you have jewelry pictures. Write the phrases on the back the pictures in order from the lowest price to the highest.

Classroom Supplies
- magazines or newspapers with pictures of people and jewelry
- scissors

Curriculum Supplies
none

Also, cut out several pictures of people. Some should be popular, famous people, and some should be pictures of people doing something, such as a doctor examining a patient, someone raking, a secretary typing, and so on.

In class, have students put the jewelry pictures in order of greater value. This should be fairly easy since the prices are listed on the picture.

Next, have them do the same thing with the pictures of people—put them in order of greatness. When finished, ask students what criteria they used to rank the people.

Say: **Why is it harder to put people in an order of value? What kind of order would Jesus put these people in? He says those of us who want to be great must be servants and slaves.** Have students turn the pictures of jewelry over and read the memory passage. Then discuss how the people in the pictures are being servants. Say: **A servant looks out for the interests of others. Which of these people are looking out for the interests of others?**

Jesus is the greatest servant of all because he gave his life to look out for our interests. He did that by making a way for us to have eternal life. We are all certainly interested in eternal life!

How to Grow Up

Say: **We going to list the characteristics from Philippians 2:1-8 that tell us what kind of servant Jesus is.** Read through the passage verse by verse and list the characteristics on the chalk board. Then have students write a definition of a servant.

Next, distribute the articles or magazines for students to search. They should search to find one person who fits the description of a servant and one who does not. Ask: **Who is more Christ-like, the celebrities or the servants? What Jesus attitudes do each of the people you read about have? Who do we tend to follow? Why?**

It is very important for us to understand that Jesus was a servant, and he calls us to follow him and to be servants as well. A great person in God's kingdom is the person who is a servant.

Classroom Supplies
- Bibles
- magazine and newspaper clippings with articles of celebrities and servants (or gather a few copies of Sports Illustrated, Readers Digest, Voice of the Martyrs, and other magazines that interview people)
- pencils
- chalk board

Curriculum Supplies
none

Ready to Grow Up

Drape a napkin over your arm. Say: **Servants often wear a napkin over one arm. This month we are using a napkin as the symbol of a servant. We are using it to help us learn the attitude of a servant. Last week we had a servant assignment. Our assignment was to let others go first. Were you able to put many check marks on your napkin?** Ask the students to share about their experiences this past week.

Say: **Jesus is our best example of a servant. Our memory passage tells us that Jesus came to serve us. Jesus was a servant because he looked out for the best interests or needs of others. He looked out for my best interests and for your best interests. What needs do we have in common that Jesus looked out for?** Discuss. **We need eternal life, forgiveness of sins, and unconditional love.**

Your assignment this week is to serve by looking out for the best interests of others. When you and a friend are watching TV, you could look out for your friend's best interests by watching programs that have good, clean messages. What else might a friend's needs be? How can you look out for their needs or best interests? Discuss.

You could look out for you mom's needs by setting the supper table. Your mom works hard to put supper on the table, and it would serve her needs or best interests if you could help her do the things you are able to do. Even though it might not be very exciting to set the table, it is something that needs to be done. How else could you look out for your mom's needs? Discuss. Here are some additional ideas of how the students could meet another person's needs or look out for their best interests: sit by someone who is usually alone on the bus or at lunch; rake a yard; do housework; read a story to a younger brother or sister; send a card to someone who lives alone; visit a nursing home; take out the garbage; help your teacher clean up the classroom; pick up paper towels off the bathroom floor at school; brush the dog or cat.

Distribute napkins and markers. Have students write the following sentence on their napkins: "Look out for the interests of others."

Classroom Supplies
- napkins
- markers

Curriculum Supplies
none

Growing Up Every Day

Say: **Drape your napkin over your arm like a servant. Remember that you are a servant in God's kingdom. Take your napkin home and each time you look our for the interests of others, make a check mark on your napkin.**

Lead students in prayer. Seek God's guidance in recognizing what others need and serving them in that area. Ask God to create a servant's heart in each student. Close by having the class recite the memory passage.

Classroom Supplies
none

Curriculum Supplies
none

Lesson 3

Growing in Attitude

Consider Others Better Than Yourself

Luke 18:9-14

Bible Focus

Jesus taught us to be humble and meek.

Life Focus

Choose a way to grow in humility.

Growing Up in the Word: Mark 10:43-45

Greet students as they arrive. Show them to the following activity and encourage them to get involved.

Memory Activity 1

Provide materials and instruct student to make cards for the students in their adopted class. Students may choose or draw names, whichever works best for your class. Some students may have to make more than one card. Students should write a message in the card that reflects or summarizes the message of the memory passage. After the students have finished the cards, allow them to deliver them personally. Encourage the students to pray for the person they wrote to as the week goes on.

Say: **When we were the age of the students in our adopted class, most of us loved to get attention from someone older. That is one purpose of these letters: we are going to give someone younger some of our attention. How is giving attention to someone being a servant to them?** (We will help them feel special.)

Classroom Supplies
- memory passage poster board from lesson 1
- construction paper
- markers
- names of the students in your adopted class

Curriculum Supplies
none

Memory Activity 2

Before class, copy the reproducible page and cut the cards apart. Make one set for every five students.

In class, divide students into groups of five or fewer. Give each group a set of cards. One student draws the cards and asks the questions to the other four in the group. If using buzzer boards, the student who rings his buzzer first gets the first chance to answer. If no boards are available, have students raise their hands to

Classroom Supplies
- scissors
- buzzer boards (if available)

Curriculum Supplies
reproducible pages 87, 88 (questions and answers)

answer. As a student gets the answer right, he gets that card. Whoever has the most cards at the end is the winner. When the questioning round is completed, give students a chance to earn the memory passage cards by reciting the memory passage.

Say: **This game is one where you try to be first and the greatest by getting the answers right. Is it wrong to want to win? How can you be a winner without being un-Jesus-like in your attitude?** Allow discussion. Look for answers like these: You can be an encourager to the other players. You can help your team be a winner. It's not wrong to want to win, it is wrong to make that your only focus and to hurt others to get there.

Ask: **What does the memory passage say about being first?** (We are first when we are servants.) **We can be good at something and still serve others. We do that by considering others to be more important than ourselves. Today, we will find out what that means.**

Classroom Supplies
- ribbons
- metal
- award certificates
- trophies

Curriculum Supplies
none

Why Grow Up?

Display the awards where students can look at them. Ask: **Why do people receive awards?** Discuss. **Usually a person receives an award because he has a talent. What talents do you have? What are some awards you have received?** Discuss. **I'll bet you were proud of yourself. You should be. You worked hard to win the award.**

Are you better than other people because you do something well? Do you ever notice other people doing something and think that you are better? Is it wrong to be good at something? No, it's wrong to not have a humble attitude when you are good at something.

Who gives us our talents? Who should be exalted by our talents? God has blessed us with whatever talents we have. God wants us to use those abilities to exalt and glorify him. Do you know that we can become too proud of our talents? We can even consider ourselves better people than others because of our talent. God is not glorified when we use our abilities to put others down.

Jesus warns us about thinking we are better than others. Having Jesus' attitude of servanthood means that we don't consider ourselves better than anyone else.

How to Grow Up

Before class, write the following phrases on strips of paper to define the word self-exalted: "considers himself better than others"; "doesn't give God credit for who he is"; "puts others down to make himself look better"; "takes all the credit for his abilities"; ignores people who need help if he doesn't think they deserve it."

Write these phrases on strips of paper to define humility: "doesn't boast about his abilities"; "gives God glory for who he is"; "shows respect to all people regardless of who they are"; "associates with people"; "considers others better than himself."

Prepare two sets of Bible-times costumes. Pin the "self-exalted" definitions to different pieces of one set and the "humility" definitions to different pieces of the second set. Mix the sets of clothing together and put them in a basket.

Have students find and read Luke 18:9-14 silently. Say: **This passage is about two men: one man exalted himself and one man humbled himself. Show me how the man who exalted himself stood.** Have all students show you. **Show me how the man who humbled himself stood?** Have all students show you.

Ask a volunteer to read the words of the man who exalted himself. He should do so with a proud, arrogant voice. Then have a second volunteer read the words of the man who humbled himself. He should do so with a sad and sorrowful voice.

Choose two volunteers. One will represent the Pharisee—the man who exalted himself—and one will represent the tax collector—the man who humbled himself. Say: **We are going to dress these two students in Bible-times clothes. Each piece of clothing in this basket belongs to either the man who exalted himself or the man who humbled himself. You will be able to tell which piece is which by the message that is attached. We will read the message, decide who it belongs to, and place the article of clothing on the correct student.** Have the students take turns choosing an article of clothing and reading aloud the message attached to it. Students may help one another if needed.

Ask: **What does Jesus say will happen to the man who exalts himself?** Discuss. **What does Jesus say will happen to the man who humbles himself? Which one does Jesus tell us is the better attitude: exalting oneself or humbling oneself? Jesus teaches us to be humble. Would you rather have Jesus humble you or exalt you? What attitude does Jesus tell us to have in order for us to be exalted by him?** (A humble attitude.)

Classroom Supplies
- Bible
- newsprint paper
- markers
- pens
- two Bible-times costumes with five pieces each (robe, belt, hat, sandals)
- basket

Curriculum Supplies
none

Ready to Grow Up

Drape a napkin over your arm. Say: **This month we are using a napkin as our reminder to be a servant. We are using it to help us learn the attitude of a servant. Last week we had a servant assignment. Our assignment was to look out for the interests of others. Did you choose to do what a sibling or friend wanted to do over what you wanted to do? Were you ablet to put many check marks on your napkin?** Ask the students to share how they looked out for the interests of others.

Say: **When you served others by looking out for their interests, you were great people. Our memory passage tells us what it takes to be great.** Have a volunteer read Mark 10:43-45. **In today's Scripture, we looked at a man who thought he was great and a man who thought he needed help. Which one of the two men was really the great one?** (The one who was meek and humble; the one who knew he needed God's help.) **A servant is a person who is meek and humble. A servant is a person who considers others better than himself.**

Your assignment this week is to be a servant by considering others better than yourself. This week, congratulate your friends when they do a good job at something. Maybe they make a good grade on a test, or they score the winning point in the game. Focus on what your friends do and tell them what a good job they did. Look around you every day for times that you can say these things to others: "Great job!"; "You did a good job on that!"; "I like the way you played that song"; "I think it's great that you're so good in math"; "You

Classroom Supplies
- napkins
- markers

Curriculum Supplies
none

are really good at basketball." Don't talk about what you do well; talk about what they do well.

Distribute napkins. Have students write the following sentence on their napkins: "Consider others better than yourself."

Growing Up Every Day

Classroom Supplies
none

Curriculum Supplies
none

Say: **Let's drape our napkins over our arms. We are servants of God's kingdom. Take your napkin home to remind you to consider others better than yourself. Each time you compliment another person and focus on what they do well instead of what you do well, make a check mark on your napkin.**

It is natural for us to compare ourselves to other people. We want to be the best. The whole world compares people to measure greatness. And we all want to be great. But it is "not so with us." What does Jesus say about greatness? Let's say our memory passage together. Do so. **The person who is great is the person who serves others. A servant considers others better than himself.**

Lead the class in prayer. Ask God to open the eyes of the students to see ways that they can compliment others—ways to consider others better than themselves.

Lesson 4

Growing in Attitude

Serve With Mercy

Matthew 18:21-35

Bible Focus

Jesus taught us to be merciful.

Life Focus

Choose a way to grow in showing mercy and forgiveness.

Growing Up in the Word: Mark 10:43-45

Greet the students as they arrive. Direct them to one or both of the activities described below.

Memory Activity 1

Before class, attach the word "servant" to the sash, the word "great" to the crown, the word "first" to the badge, and the word "slave" to the hat.

As the students arrive, have them read the memory passage. Give students the prepared props. Ask them to use the props and add actions to help them memorize the verse. Students may also put the passage into skit form. If your class is large, divide the verse into sections and have each group work on a smaller piece of the passage.

Bring the groups together to share their ideas. Agree on one motion for each word or phrase and practice saying the verse together. When the motions or skit is complete, share it with your adopted class.

Examples: One student could stand big, bold, and tall while another student places the crown (great) on his head to say this phrase: "whoever wants to become great among you." Then the student would drop to his knees and start scrubbing the floor while the other student replaces the crown with the sash (servant) to say this phrase: "must be your servant."

Say: **Memorizing Scripture is fun and exciting when we add motions. Making up motions can seem silly, but it really can help us remember the passage so that we can apply it to life. Sharing it with our adopted class is another way that we will serve them. When we tell others what Jesus has done for us, we display a servant's attitude to them.**

Classroom Supplies
- memory passage poster made for lesson 1
- sash
- crown
- badge
- hat
- paper
- marker

Curriculum Supplies

none

Memory Activity 2

Display the poster board. Have the class sit in a circle and say the memory passage. The first person says the first word of the passage, the second student says the second word, and this continues around the circle until the group has said the entire passage. To add fun to the game, the students should stand when they say their word, then sit back down. Allow students to use the poster for help.

Classroom Supplies
memory passage poster made for lesson 1

Curriculum Supplies
none

Say: **One way to be a servant is to be a team player. Each of you had to do your part to quote the entire passage. As servants of God's kingdom, we must work together to let others know that Jesus was the greatest servant of all. How did Jesus serve us?** (He gave his life.) **What is a ransom?** (It is an exchange of one thing for another.) **What did Jesus exchange for us?** (His life.)

Why Grow Up?

If your class is large, divide the students into two groups and give each group a backpack. Give one student in the group the backpack to carry. Give the other members one each of the heavy items. These group members will form a line. As the student with the backpack moves down the line, each person should name a sin that needs to be forgiven such as "I lied," "I cheated," or "I stole." Each time a student says something, they add their heavy item to the backpack. After everyone has added something to the backpack, say: **Each one of us has been hurt by the wrong things that other people do. These heavy items in the backpack represent the sins of others that we need to forgive.**

Classroom Supplies
- one or two backpacks (depending on class size)
- rocks, books, or other heavy items
- paper
- marker

Curriculum Supplies
none

Ask the student carrying the backpack how he feels. **How would you describe these unforgiven sins that you are carrying?** Have the class discuss his answer. **Carrying a backpack full of heavy items is like carrying around unforgiveness for others. Unforgiveness weighs you down. How could you lighten your load?** Discuss.

Have the students carrying the backpacks go to each student in line and say, "I forgive you." As they do, the student takes one heavy item back out of the bag and lays it on the floor. At the end of the line ask again how the students feel.

Say: **Forgiveness is important. Not only does it lighten our load, but it guarantees that God will forgive us. Let's find out what Jesus said about forgiveness.**

How to Grow Up

Before class, make one copy of the reproducible page and cut it into parts. Place the parts in a container. Arrange an area of the room to look like a courtroom. Include a judge's seat, a witness stand, a jury box.

Set the scene for a classroom trial by having students draw for parts. Anyone not receiving a part will be the jury. After everyone knows his part, have students find and silently read Matthew 18:21-35.

Say: **A servant has been arrested. He is charged with being unmerciful. The trial hearing is about to begin.** Instruct the judge to take his place. The judge will call the hearing to order, call each witness one at a time to testify, and will ask questions. Students will speak in their own words. Allow some freedom of characters here. Help students walk through the recounting of the story in trial form. Prompt students as needed.

After the trial, say: **This servant is on trial for being unmerciful. What is mercy?** Discuss. **Mercy is kind and compassionate treatment of an enemy, an offender, someone under your authority, or someone who has a problem. Can you give me an example of mercy?** Discuss. **This servant deserved to be punished for what he owed his master. But the master showed mercy by forgiving the debt.**

Now that we understand what mercy is, it is time to come to a verdict. Jury, is Servant #1 guilty of showing no mercy? Allow time for discussion and answer, which should be yes. **What should his punishment be?** Discuss.

The unmerciful servant made a terrible mistake! His act of unforgiveness caused him to be unforgiven, too.

From this story, Jesus wants us to learn to avoid a terrible mistake. What is it? (He wants us to avoid being unmerciful.) **He wants us to be merciful. When we aren't merciful, we won't receive God's mercy.**

Classroom Supplies
- Bibles
- table
- chairs
- a gavel
- container

Curriculum Supplies
reproducible page 89 (character descriptions for the court scene)

Ready to Grow Up

Say: **The unmerciful servant wouldn't forgive a fellow servant who had the same problem he had—debt. We have people in our lives every day who need forgiveness for the same problems we have. God wants us to serve them by showing them mercy and forgiveness.**

Saying "I forgive you" is easy, but showing mercy and forgiveness is not as easy. Showing mercy and forgiveness is what Jesus has called us to do. He has called us to have the same attitude that a servant has.

Drape a napkin over your arm. Say: **We have been working to develop the habit of serving others. We are using a napkin to remind us about being servants. Last week your assignment was to consider others better than yourselves. How did you consider others better than yourselves? What compliments did you give to others?** Discuss.

Your assignment this week is to show mercy and forgiveness to others. We've been serving a younger class this month. Do you remember what it was like to be that age? Discuss. **Sometimes it is easy to be impatient with younger children. They are not very coordinated yet. They can bug you, follow you, and annoy you. They may spill their drinks, wander off, or interrupt you. These are all problems that you have or have had. You were that age at one time, and you did the same things that might irritate you now. We show mercy and forgiveness to these children when we are patient with them as they make mistakes while growing up. They have the same problems that you once had. How can you treat them with mercy and forgiveness?** Discuss. **We treat them with mercy and forgiveness when we are patient with them and show kindness for their stage in life.**

What about problems that people who are older than you have? You don't have the problems that your parents, grandparents, or teachers have. How

Classroom Supplies
- napkins
- markers

Curriculum Supplies
none

should you treat them when they irritate you? Discuss. **You are growing older and you will have the problems of those who are older one day. So you should also treat them with mercy and forgiveness. How can you treat them with mercy and forgiveness?** Discuss.

What about your teachers at school? Sometimes you may get angry with teachers because of difficult assignments or tests or because they talk about stuff you think is boring. Think about times when you or your classmates made it difficult for the teacher by not paying attention. Have you ever treated a substitute teacher poorly because she is new? How should you serve your teachers? Discuss. **Whether or not we like what our teachers say or do, we ought to show them respect and treat them with mercy and forgiveness.**

Distribute napkins. Have students write the following words on their napkins: "Show others mercy and forgiveness."

Growing Up Every Day

Classroom Supplies
none

Curriculum Supplies
none

Say: **Drape your napkin over your arm. Remember, we are servants of the kingdom of God. Take your napkin home to remind you to show mercy and forgiveness to those around you. Mercy and forgiveness are shown in the way we treat others. Each time you show mercy and forgiveness to someone, make a check mark on your napkin.**

Making an effort to be kind and nice to others is what a servant would do. And servants in God's kingdom truly are the great ones. Lead the class in prayer. Ask God to guide students in their assignment this week to show mercy and forgiveness. Close by reciting the memory passage.

Lesson 5

Growing in Attitude

Check Your Attitude

Matthew 19:16-26

Bible Focus
The rich young man did not choose to have a God-first attitude.

Life Focus
Give up a me-first attitude and replace it with a God-first attitude.

Growing Up in the Word: Mark 10:43-45
Greet students by name as they arrive. Encourage them to participate in one or both of the following activities.

Memory Activity 1
Before class, arrange for your students to serve a snack to your adopted class. Make copies of the memory passage printed in the introduction to this unit. Make one for each snack ingredient and each utensil. Attach a copy of the passage to each item.

In class, students will prepare a snack for their adopted class. Before they use each item, they must read the memory passage aloud. Have them prepare a snack tray of crackers topped with cheese or peanut butter. Have them also make juice from juice concentrate. When the snack is prepared, take it to serve to your adopted class.

As students work, ask: **Why is what we are doing a service to our adopted class? How are you feeling about doing this? Are you looking out for the needs of others? Are you letting someone else go first? How are you considering others better than yourself? Are you showing mercy and forgiveness? Who was the greatest servant of all time? How did Jesus serve us?**

Classroom Supplies
- snack crackers
- cheese
- peanut butter
- spreading knives
- serving tray
- napkins
- cups
- juice concentrate
- water
- pitcher
- clear tape

Curriculum Supplies
copies of the memory passage from the unit page

Memory Activity 2
Have the students test each other's knowledge of the passage by doing the following activity. Divide the students into groups of three or four. Have one student be the leader of his or her group to start. The leader should begin quoting Mark 10:43-45. Have the student pause whenever he wants to. Tell the leader to pause a total of seven times. When the leader pauses, the other students in the

Classroom Supplies
none

Curriculum Supplies
none

group must shout out the next word. The leader will give a point to the person who says the word first. The game continues until each student has been the leader for his group.

Ask: **When we are servants and slaves to others, who are we really serving?** (Jesus.) **Being a servant means having a God-first attitude. All of our activities this month have been in service to others, but really, we have served Jesus. We have traded a me-first attitude for a God-first attitude.**

Why Grow Up?

Before class, make a path in the room. Have tables or chairs along the way. On each table or chair place play money, jewels, or pictures of expensive things. At the end of the path have the cross and the garbage can. Have a helper at each of the stations.

Tell students that the path represents life. Instruct them to walk along the path. Stagger their start times so they will have time to stop at each station. As they walk, have the helpers at the stations offer them the valuables they have. Give the students even more than they can carry. Let them pick out the house and car they want. As the helpers offer the students various objects, they should say things similar to the following: "This is all you need to be happy"; "Do you want to be great? This is what you need"; "Here's the perfect thing for anyone who wants to be first"; "This will make you happier than anything else"; "Do you want to be famous? Then this is what you need"; "Do you want to be rich?"

Classroom Supplies
- play money
- fake jewelry
- small toy cars
- pictures of expensive things like houses, TVs, VCRs, computer games, CD players, etc.
- a clean garbage can
- a five- or six-foot cross (can be paper, wood or cardboard)

Curriculum Supplies
none

Have the person at the end of the path represent Jesus. When students arrive at the end, he should say the following: "Jesus is the way to true happiness. Throw down your worldly possessions and follow him." Most of the students will, but some may hesitate. If so, ask them why they want the stuff in their hands. Also quote parts of the memory passage.

As they finish, say: **How many of you thought a second before dropping your possessions to follow Jesus? How easy is it to get wrapped up in stuff instead of what is most important—Jesus? What things keep you from Jesus? It may be video games, music, friends.** Let the students share. **Today we will learn one of the hardest lessons yet. We will work on giving up our me-first attitudes—the attitudes that keep us from being the servants Jesus has called us to be.**

How to Grow Up

Have students find and silently read Matthew 19:16-26. Ask the students to list what the rich young man did right during his life. He did not murder. He did not commit adultery. He did not steal. He did not lie. He honored his mother and father. He loved his neighbor.

Ask: **Was the rich young man a good person? So, what did the rich young man do wrong?** Listen to their replies and then say: **Is it wrong to be rich?** (No.) **Is it wrong to love money more than Jesus?** (Yes.) **What did the rich young man lack?** Explain that the rich young man was too attached to his money and possessions and that is why he was sad. **The man lacked the kind of love for Jesus that would give up anything. He was not willing to give up his money. He had a me-first attitude.**

The disciples seemed discouraged because this man was a good person, but Jesus said he could not enter the kingdom of heaven because he was attached to his money. How does Jesus tell them they can conquer such attachments? (With God all things are possible.) **Do you know anyone who you think will never let God be in control of his life? According to Jesus' words, anyone can go to Heaven, but they have to let God be the one in control.**

The story of the rich young ruler is a very sad story. He was such a good person, yet he was not willing to give up the very thing that kept him from God. He did not choose to have a God-first attitude. Remember his example. Don't let a me-first attitude ruin your eternity.

Classroom Supplies
none

Curriculum Supplies
none

Ready to Grow Up

Before class, make one copy of the reproducible page for each student.

Say: **Last week your assignment was to show mercy and forgiveness to others. What happened this past week? How were you able to show mercy and forgiveness? How were you able to be patient with someone who didn't have the same skills you have?** Discuss.

Mercy and forgiveness are important attitudes of a servant. We're going to look at another important attitude of a servant. It's the God-first attitude. Distribute reproducible page. **Look at the items on the ruler. Do you own any of these things? Is there anything pictured that you hope to have someday? Is there anything not pictured that you own or want to own? These items are nice and they make life more enjoyable. But they should never get in the way of following Jesus.**

Do any of these things keep you from Jesus? The rich young ruler's attitude about money kept him from Jesus. Do you have an attitude toward one of these things that will keep you from Jesus? Do you ever stay home from church to watch TV, ride your bike, or play on a sports team? Then a me-first attitude is keeping you from Jesus.

Before we started this unit, we had our own ideas about how to be first and how to be great. Wanting to be first and wanting to be great are the attitudes that keep us from Jesus. They are me-first attitudes instead of God-first attitudes. Anytime you stay home from church to sleep or watch TV, you are showing a me-first attitude.

Are you willing to give up what Jesus asks you to give up? If so, you have a God-first attitude. Are you willing to give up your me-first attitude? When we have God-first attitudes, we still enjoy these things, but we see Jesus first. Have students cut out the crosses on the page and glue them over the items. **The items we like are still there, but we see Jesus first. Instead of me first, it is Jesus first.**

God-first attitudes bring blessings because they are the attitudes that lead us to salvation. If we have a me-first attitude, then we will miss the blessings.

Your assignment this week is to give up your me-first attitude and replace it

Classroom Supplies
- napkins
- markers
- scissors
- glue or clear tape

Curriculum Supplies
reproducible page 88 (ruler)

with a God-first attitude. Distribute napkins. Have students write the following sentences on the napkin: "I will give up my me-first attitude. I want a God-first attitude."

Growing Up Every Day

Classroom Supplies
none

Curriculum Supplies
none

Say: **Let's drape our napkins over our arms. We are servants of God's kingdom. We've spent this month learning to be servants like Jesus. I hope it has been fun. Do you know that you can be of service to all kinds of people but still have a me-first attitude? Our attitudes come from our hearts. They show us how we feel about the things around us. We can help with a younger class and really care about those kids. Or, we can just go through the motions and look like we are serving when we are actually thinking about ourselves. This week, use your napkin to remind you to pray for a God-first attitude to cover your me-first attitude. Put a check mark on your napkin each time you pray about your attitude.**

Lead students in a prayer seeking God's help in changing me-first attitudes into God-first attitudes. Then lead the class in reciting Mark 10:43-45.

The Good Samaritan

Luke 10:30-37

Traveler (before)

Traveler (after)

Levite

Priest

Samaritan

Innkeeper

Whoever Wants to Become Great

Find the words to Mark 10:43-45. Words can be found up, down, across, diagonally and backwards. When you find a word, circle it. Repeated words are only found one time.

Mark 10:43-45

Not so with you. Instead, whoever wants to become great among you must be your servant, and whoever wants to be first must be slave of all. For even the Son of Man did not come to be served, but to serve, and to give his life as a ransom for many.

S	A	S	Y	O	U	R	D	D	F	A	C
A	E	H	F	J	H	I	S	K	I	N	L
W	M	R	E	O	R	N	T	Y	W	D	S
A	O	U	V	I	R	S	O	H	P	C	O
V	C	B	N	E	M	T	O	A	M	S	N
D	E	V	E	N	D	E	F	G	A	H	O
K	B	L	W	E	V	A	R	G	N	G	F
T	Y	U	B	E	I	D	O	N	Y	I	M
M	P	G	R	E	A	T	C	O	V	V	A
B	U	T	E	F	I	L	B	M	N	E	N
M	A	S	S	D	S	T	N	A	W	F	G
H	R	K	T	L	W	O	L	E	I	S	R
T	O	Y	U	I	O	L	P	C	T	O	N
V	F	I	R	S	T	B	N	N	H	M	A
Y	S	D	E	F	G	H	A	N	D	K	L
O	W	R	N	O	T	V	E	R	T	Y	U
U	V	I	O	P	R	C	S	L	A	V	E
E	V	B	N	E	R	A	N	S	O	M	M
A	S	D	S	F	G	L	U	E	M	O	C

Card #1

Whoever wants to
become great among
you must be your what?

(answer: servant)

Card #2

Whoever wants to be
first must be what?

(answer: slave to all)

Card #3

Who did not come
to be served?

(answer: The Son of Man)

Card #4

What did the Son
of Man come to do?

(answer: serve)

Card #5

What did the Son of Man give
as a ransom for many?

(answer: his life)

Card #6

Who must be
your servant?

(answer: whoever
wants to become great)

Card #7

Who must be slave
to all?

(answer: whoever
want to be first)

Card #8

Who did the Son of Man give
his life as a ransom for?

(answer: many, you, me)

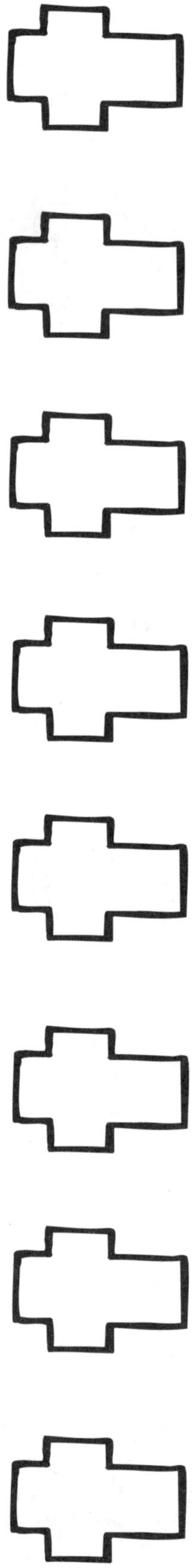

Card # 9

Who is the Son of Man?

(answer: Jesus)

Card #10

What is "not so with you?"

(answer: the measure of greatness)

Card #11

Recite Mark 10:43-45.

"Not so with you. Instead whoever wants to become great among you must be your servant, and whoever wants to be first must be slave of all. For even the Son of Man did not come to be served, but to serve, and to give his life as a ransom for many."

Card #12

Recite Mark 10:43-45.

"Not so with you. Instead, whoever wants to become great among you must be your servant, and who ever wants to be first must be slave of all. For even the Son of Man did not come to be served, but to serve, and to give his life as a ransom for many."

Judge

Oversees the trial, calls witnesses to testify, asks questions.

Servant #1

Will tell what servant #2 owed him (100 denarii) and explain that he has waited a long time to be repaid and needs the money for his own family. When reminded of what the master did for him, he will say that the situation is different because the master has a lot of money.

Servant #2

Will tell what happened when servant #1 asked to be repaid. He will admit he owes the money, but explain he doesn't have it. He will report that servant #1 tried to choke him.

Master

Will tell what he did for servant #1. He will state that servant #1 owed him 10,000 talents and was going to be sold into slavery along with his family since he could not pay. When he saw how upset the servant was, he was merciful and cancelled the debt instead of selling him.

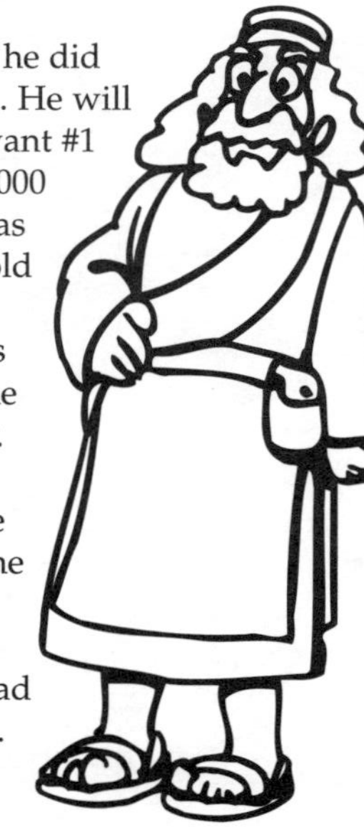

Witness #1

Works in the master's house. He was there when the master forgave servant #1. He then was on his way to the market and saw the incident with servant #2.

Witness #2

Was on the street at the time servant #1 tried to choke servant #2. He knows servant #2 and knows he is very poor, but is very generous.

Witness #3

Was on the street and heard screaming. She saw servant #2 try to run away, but he was caught.

The Jailer

Will say that servant #1 brought servant #2 into his jail. He will say that servant #1 was screaming and ranting about money.

UNIT 4

Growing in Worship

Unit Aims

Know:	Worship is honoring God for who he is and what he does and that the gift of salvation through Jesus is the greatest reason for worshiping God.
Feel:	Feel thankful for salvation.
Do:	Worship God for the salvation he offers through Jesus.
Memorize:	Matthew 1:20, 21

Why Grow In Worship?

The theme of these Christmas lessons paves a wonderful path for your students to experience God's greatest gift of all: Jesus. Activities, games, stories and songs pull back the curtain to reveal that this indescribable gift is addressed to them and provides for them the greatest reason for worshiping God. The unit's memory passage from Matthew 1:20, 21 declares clearly that Jesus came to save us. The Scriptures from Matthew and Luke fill in the details that surround the birth of Jesus Christ.

Building on the good news of the Christmas story is the undeniable response of the people this story touched. Zechariah prophesied about a Savior, angels visited shepherds, Mary and Joseph received heavenly instructions about names, and Magi came with precious gifts. Each character in these stories responded to the news that Jesus was the Savior in life-changing ways. Guide your students to move from knowing Jesus is born to worshiping him as the one who saves them from their sins.

Summary

Grow in the grace and knowledge of Jesus Christ by understanding the great gift of salvation we have through Jesus Christ and by worshiping God because of that wonderful gift.

- Worship God for the gift of salvation through Jesus (what salvation is).
- Praise and thank Jesus for being the Savior (why Jesus brought salvation).
- Praise and thank Jesus for the suffering he endured to bring salvation (how Jesus brought it).
- Worship God because Jesus is the only one who can save us.
- Thank Jesus for salvation by bringing him gifts of worship.

Lesson Aims

Scripture focus	Bible focus	Life focus
Lesson 1 Luke 1:57-75	Zechariah prophesied about Jesus being a "horn of salvation."	Worship God for the gift of salvation through Jesus (what salvation is).
Lesson 2 Matthew 1:18-21	The angel said, "Name him Jesus...he will save his people from their sins."	Praise and thank Jesus for being the Savior.
Lesson 3 Luke 2:8-18	The shepherds hear the angel say that Jesus is the "Savior...Christ the Lord."	Praise and thank Jesus for the suffering he endured to bring salvation.
Lesson 4 Luke 2:21-38	Simeon spoke of Jesus—"For my eyes have seen your salvation."	Worship God because Jesus is the only one who can save us.
Lesson 5 Matthew 2:1-12	Magi brought gifts of worship to Jesus, the king of the Jews.	Thank Jesus for salvation by bringing him gifts of worship.

Memory Passage: Matthew 1:20, 21

"After he had considered this, an angel of the Lord appeared to him in a dream and said, 'Joseph son of David, do not be afraid to take Mary home as your wife, because what is conceived in her is from the Holy Spirit. She will give birth to a son, and you are to give him the name Jesus, because he will save his people from their sins.'"

Classroom Supplies
- scissors
- glue
- envelope

Curriculum Supplies
reproducible page 116 (circles)

Memory Passage Review Activity

Copy the circles from the reproducible page. If possible, copy the page on heavy card stock paper. Glue the circles listed below back-to-back. Put the circles in an envelope. Students will unscramble the memory passage. When finished, they will turn the circles over and read the message, which is "Jesus saves." Encourage students to make up their own games using the circles.

J —"After he had considered this,
E —an angel of the Lord appeared to him
S —in a dream and said, 'Joseph son of David,
U —do not be afraid to take Mary home as your wife,
S —because what is conceived
S —in her is from the Holy Spirit.
A —She will give birth to a son,
V —and you are to give him the name Jesus,
E —because he will save
S —his people from their sins.'"

Lesson 1

Growing in Worship

The Gift of Salvation

Luke 1:57-75

Bible Focus

Zechariah prophesied about Jesus being a "horn of salvation."

Life Focus

Worship God for the gift of salvation through Jesus.

Growing Up in the Word: Matthew 1:20, 21

Prepare one or both of the following activities for your students. Greet students as they arrive. Play instrumental Christmas music as the students work.

Memory Activity 1

Before class, write Matthew 1:20, 21 on poster board and display it where your students can see it easily. Prepare sets of two name tags for each student. On one side of the first name tag write a common name (does not have to be students' names). On the other side write a word or portion of Matthew 1:20, 21. On the second tag write the name's meaning. Example: Write "Sarah" on the first name tag and "Princess" on the second name tag. Make enough name tag sets for each student in your class. For a large group prepare two sets of name tags. Color-code each set so teammates will recognize which group to work with. Give students more than one name if needed to complete the memory passage.

As students arrive show them the name they will be wearing and tape it to the front of their shoulder. Tape the name's meaning to the student's back. Be sure they don't see this! Students are to discover the meaning of the name they are wearing by gathering clues from their classmates. As students guess their name's meaning, they may untape the front name tag and turn it over to discover a portion of the memory passage. Encourage students to work together to put the passage in order. When the passage has been put together, instruct the students to read it aloud as a group.

Say: **Names are special. Parents can spend many hours choosing a name for a new baby. Our memory passage tells us about a special baby that was to be born to Mary and Joseph. Mary and Joseph didn't have to spend hours deciding on a name for the baby. The angel told Mary and Joseph to name their**

Classroom Supplies
- construction paper
- name tags
- tape
- poster board
- marker
- book of baby names with meanings

Curriculum Supplies
none

baby Jesus! Jesus means "the Lord saves." That's why Jesus is so special. He came to earth to save us from our sins. Being saved from our sins means being forgiven for all the wrong things we do. When we worship, we recognize and proclaim praise and thanks for who God is and what he has done. Jesus' name helps us recognize both: it shows that he is the Savior, the one who saves us. We can worship God because he saves us through Jesus.

Memory Activity 2

Classroom Supplies
- marker board or chalkboard
- marker or chalk
- eraser

Curriculum Supplies
none

Before class, write Matthew 1:20, 21 on the marker board or chalkboard. Ask for a volunteer to read the memory passage aloud. Ask the class to say the verse aloud together. Allow the volunteer reader to choose one word of the memory passage to erase. Be sure the word is erased completely. Ask the class to repeat the passage, this time inserting from memory the word that is missing. Continue in this manner until all the words have been erased. Encourage students to recite the verse from memory when the board is completely erased.

For a shorter amount of time, erase a phrase, more than one word, or all the words that are the same such as "a," "to," "the," and so on. To add variety as the class reads aloud, suggest using different voices such as deep, high, sleepy, excited, loud, and soft or suggest differing tempos such as walking, marching, waltzing, walking, and running.

Say: **Our memory passage tells us that an angel had an important message for Mary and Joseph. Mary and Joseph were going to be parents to a baby that was so special that an angel was sent to be sure Mary and Joseph gave him the right name: Jesus. The name Jesus means "the Lord saves." Jesus was coming to bring salvation—to save his people from their sins. What a great reason to worship!**

Classroom Supplies
- glass jar with label removed and tight-fitting lid
- water
- red food coloring
- eye dropper or tablespoon
- bleach

Curriculum Supplies
none

Why Grow Up?

Before class, fill jar with tap water leaving approximately an inch of space at the top. Replace lid.

Display jar to class. Say: **What do you see?** Allow students to respond. **When we are born we don't have many decisions to make. Someone who takes care of us decides what we will eat, what we will wear, and where we will go. As we become older, we begin to make these decisions for ourselves. That means we're growing up! We choose what to wear, what to eat (sometimes!), what to read, who to talk to, and what music we want to listen to. I hope the decisions you make about these things are good ones.**

Sometimes we make decisions that aren't good, such as disobeying our parents, being hurtful to a friend, and gossiping or lying. These bad decisions stain us and make us dirty. They stain us with sin. Our lives are no longer clean. Hold up clear jar. **But they are stained and dirty.** Add a dropper of red food coloring to the jar.

Say: **Jesus wanted to give us a way to make our lives clean again. He wanted us to be forgiven of our sins and to live with him forever. That's what the gift**

of salvation is: Jesus forgiving our sins and making us clean. Add a dropper or tablespoon of bleach to the red water. **Jesus can take a life that is dirty and stained with sin and make it clean again.** Allow class to observe the water slowly becoming clean.

Say: **This month we are learning to grow in worship. Worship is a word that means telling God how special he is. The story of Jesus' birth, the birth of the Savior, is one of the most special reasons why we worship God. Even though we do things to make our lives dirty with sin, God gave us a way to be forgiven: through Jesus. Let's pray together right now and thank God for saving us from our sins.** Ask students to quietly bow their heads. Ask them to think about something they've done that they need to ask God's forgiveness for. Pray: **"Thank You, God, that you love us even when we do wrong things. Please hear all of our prayers for forgiveness and make our lives clean and new again. Help us to stop doing wrong things and live our lives so that everyone will know how much we love you. In Jesus' name, amen."**

How to Grow Up

Classroom Supplies
- sheets
- fabric for belts and head coverings for Bible costumes
- doll baby
- baby blanket
- small writing tablet
- blank paper

Curriculum Supplies
reproducible page 117 ("His Name Is John" skit)

Before class, make a copy of the script for each student. Assign parts and distribute costume materials. Arrange students in a theater-in-the-round, that is a stage set in the center of the auditorium. Distribute Bibles to the townspeople or those students not having a speaking part. Direct these students to locate Luke 1:57-75. Ask them to follow along in the Bible as the story is acted out.

Have students present the skit. After the skit, say: **Having a baby is an exciting time for parents. How much more exciting do you think it was for Zechariah and Elizabeth, since they were older than most people who have babies?** Allow students to respond. **It was so exciting that when Zechariah had the chance to respond to God's message—by obeying God and calling his son John—he was suddenly able to speak, and the first thing he did was to praise God. Zechariah recognized that God had done something great—he gave Zechariah and Elizabeth a son when they were old—so he worshiped God for what he had done. This Scripture passage also includes a prophecy about Jesus saving his people from their sins. How does it make you feel that Jesus came to save us?** (Glad, happy, relieved, thankful.) **When we recognize what God has done for us, like providing our salvation or allowing Zechariah and Elizabeth to have a son, we ought to worship God.**

God does many things for us every day, and we need to look for those things and recognize them. Then we need to worship God for who he is and what he has done. During Christmas, it's easy to be thankful for things that God has done, and it's easy to remember that God sent Jesus as a little baby. But just as Zechariah's prophecy looked forward to God sending salvation to his people, we need to look forward to our future in heaven with God because of the salvation that Jesus has provided for us. Jesus brought us salvation by dying on the cross, and when we recognize what God has done, we can worship him for who he is and for what he has done.

Ready to Grow Up

Classroom Supplies
- used Christmas cards
- hole punch
- yarn or ribbon
- pen or marker
- scissors
- Christmas tree

Curriculum Supplies
none

Each week during this unit, students will be given the opportunity to create an ornament for the classroom Christmas tree. Each week students will need sufficient materials to make two ornaments. This is to provide students the opportunity to make an additional ornament to put on their tree at home or to give to someone with whom they could share what they have learned in that week's lesson.

Before class, set up a Christmas tree in the classroom that can be used all month. Write the following on the chalkboard: "Salvation is a gift from God."

Distribute Christmas cards to students. Instruct students to choose a scene, picture, or group of words to cut from a card. Explain that these cut-out pictures will be used as gift tag ornaments that will hang on the tree. When each student has had the opportunity to cut out a tag, ask them to copy the phrase from the chalkboard on the blank side of the gift tag. Underneath this, each student should letter the following: "To: (student's name)" and "From: Jesus."

Punch a hole in the end of each tag and thread yarn or ribbon and tie. Students should make two ornaments. When students have completed the name tag ornaments, invite them to gather around the classroom tree. Ask: **How do you feel when you receive a gift?** Allow students to respond. **Usually we are happy to receive gifts. Think about the best gift you would like to receive. How would you feel if someone promised to give you that gift? Would it be easy to wait to receive it? If you knew you were definitely going to get that special gift for Christmas, how much more excited would you be each day as Christmas got closer? Show me how you would act when you finally received that gift.** Allow students to react. **Wow! Some of you are going to be really happy to get that special gift. That's exactly why Zechariah praised God when he could finally speak. God promised him a son, and he finally had a son! Not only that, but God promised to send the Messiah! It's no wonder Zechariah worshiped God.**

One at a time, have students place one ornament on the classroom tree. Students will save their second ornament to use at home. Say: **When you hang this ornament on your Christmas tree at home or when you give it to a friend, remember how excited Zechariah was when he received the gift God promised. Think about how exciting it is that God has given us the gift of salvation through Jesus.** Lead the class in singing "Lord, I Lift Your Name on High."

Growing Up Every Day

Classroom Supplies
- thank you notes
- pens
- second ornaments from "Ready to Grow Up"

Curriculum Supplies
none

Say: **Not only do we react in a happy and excited way when we receive a gift, but we also react in a thankful way to the person who gave us the gift. One of the things many people do when they receive a gift is to write a thank-you note to the person who gave them the gift. Not only can we worship God because of giving us salvation through Jesus, but we can thank God for that as well. Let's write a thank-you note to Jesus for the wonderful gift that he's given us!** Distribute thank-you notes and pens. Give the class several minutes to complete their notes. Ask for volunteers to read their notes aloud.

Say: **This week at home, use your second ornament to remember that Jesus gave you the gift of salvation. Many times when we wear a sweater that some-**

one has given us or play with a game or toy we received as a gift, we remember the person who gave us the gift. Choose a special place at home to display your ornament so that whenever you look at it, you will remember the gift that God gave us. It may be on your family's Christmas tree. Before you place your ornament, read the message you have written on it. As you place the ornament, say a prayer of worship and thanks to God for that wonderful gift.

Close today's session by asking students to repeat Matthew 1:20, 21.

Lesson 2

Growing in Worship

Jesus Is Our Savior

Matthew 1:18-21

Bible Focus

The angel said, "Name him Jesus…he will save his people from their sins."

Life Focus

Praise and thank Jesus for being the Savior.

Growing Up in the Word: Matthew 1:20, 21

Prepare one or both of the following memory activities for your students. Greet students by name as they arrive. Play instrumental Christmas music as students work.

Classroom Supplies
- chairs
- cassette player
- Christmas music cassette
- self-stick notes

Curriculum Supplies
none

Memory Activity 1

Arrange one chair for each student in a large circle. Assign each chair a number by writing a number on a self-stick note and attaching it to the back of each chair. Write Matthew 1:20, 21 on the chalkboard so that it can be seen easily.

Begin this activity by asking students to read Matthew 1:20, 21 aloud as a group. Explain that they will be playing Christmas Chairs. As you begin the music, students will walk around the inside of the circle of chairs. When the music stops, students are to sit in the chair they are in front of. The teacher will then choose a number to call and that student will respond by reading the memory passage. After the verse has been read twice, begin erasing sections of the verse. Continue erasing until students are reciting Matthew 1:20, 21 from memory.

Option: Choose a number and let that student recite the first part of the passage. Call a second number to allow a different student to continue. Choose several numbers for students to recite in tag-team fashion until the entire passage has been recited.

Say: **Our memory passage tells us why Jesus was born. Why?** (He will save his people from their sin.) **This is the same reason why Jesus brought us salvation: our sin. In our activity today, each of you recited the memory passage when your number was called. Do you know that Jesus calls each one of you to salvation?**

Memory Activity 2

Before class, write Matthew 1:20, 21 on the chalkboard. Divide the class into teams. This activity will work in groups of many sizes: pairs, individual, or large groups. Explain that they will be creating their own memory passage poster by replacing as many words and phrases as they can with pictures or words from the media you have provided. For example, the phrase "angel of the Lord" could be a picture of an angel from a Christmas card or old visual aid material. The word "considered" could be constructed one letter at a time from words found in magazines, advertisements, or newspapers.

Encourage your students to be imaginative. Give them a time limit and let them create! When the time limit has been reached, invite each group or individual to share its poster with the entire class. Encourage the class to read aloud together. At the end of the activity, ask your students to recite Matthew 1:20, 21 from memory. Display memory posters on a wall or hallway outside your classroom. Be sure the artists sign their work!

Say: **We all wonder what angels look like. An angel of the Lord spoke to Joseph in a dream. What do you think that was like for Joseph?** Discuss. **What do you think Joseph thought of the dream?** Discuss. **We know that Joseph believed because he obeyed the instructions of the angel.**

Classroom Supplies
- old magazines
- Christmas cards
- old Christmas visual aids
- advertisements
- newspapers
- large piece of poster board or butcher paper
- scissors
- glue
- markers or crayons

Curriculum Supplies
none

Why Grow Up?

Distribute lunch sacks to students. Display the container of goodies. Say: **These special treats are for special people! In order to receive these treats, you must ask yourself the following questions:**

1. **Have you ever lied?**
2. **Have you ever disobeyed your parents?**
3. **Have you ever been unkind to a friend?**
4. **Were you ever jealous of someone else?**
5. **Have you ever cheated at school?**
6. **Have you ever been lazy about doing chores around the house?**
7. **Have you ever gossiped about someone you didn't like?**
8. **Have you ever said words you know you shouldn't say?**

Ask: **How did you answer these questions?** Let students think about this for just a minute. **If you answered "no" to all these questions, you might be perfect. Only perfect people—those who've never done anything wrong—can have some of these special treats. Anyone who is perfect may come forward, and I will share my treats with you! However, if only perfect people can have these treats, that means I can't have any! I'm not perfect. I've done many things I've needed to be forgiven for. As a matter of fact, that's true of all of us. We've all done and said things that are wrong—things we wish we hadn't said or done.**

God knows that we are not perfect. He knows we have a tough time with sin. But when we accept Jesus as our Savior, he will forgive us for all our sins! Isn't that great? That means that even though we have sinned, we can be forgiven! Even though none of us are perfect, I will still share my treats! Ask students to line up with their sacks and share with each one. When everyone has

Classroom Supplies
- assorted treats (bubble gum, balloons, pencils, mints, boxes of raisins, bite-size candy)
- see-through container
- lunch sacks

Curriculum Supplies
none

received a treat, ask: **How do you feel about getting treats even though you know you don't really deserve them?** Guide students into a discussion about being thankful. **This is just like our salvation. Even though we don't really deserve to be forgiven of our sins, God still provided a way for us to be forgiven: Jesus. How much more thankful should we be about receiving forgiveness when we don't deserve it?** Allow students to respond. **When we worship God, we can be thankful that Jesus is our Savior and praise him for that.**

How to Grow Up

Classroom Supplies

- Bibles
- butcher paper
- markers
- crayons
- old Christmas cards or visuals
- glue

Curriculum Supplies

none

Before class, divide a length of butcher paper into eight sections by drawing vertical lines on the paper. Label the first section Matthew 1:18. The next section will be blank. The third section should be labeled Matthew 1:19 and the next section will be blank. Continue labeling every other section with Matthew 1:20 and 1:21 leaving the section in between blank. For large groups, prepare more than one mural.

Direct your students to locate Matthew 1:18-21. Encourage volunteers to read the verses aloud. Display the prepared mural for your students. Explain that it will be their job to illustrate or tell the story that they have just read about in the Bible. Students should be assigned or may volunteer to illustrate the various sections of the mural. Some students may prefer to letter the verses in the labeled spaces while others will illustrate those verses using the art and materials provided.

Say: **While you are preparing this mural, remember that the story you are illustrating is an important and wonderful one! Think carefully about what people will learn when they see your story.** When the mural is complete, ask each group to read their portion of the Scripture passage aloud. Attach it to a classroom wall for the remainder of the unit.

Ask: **What are some of the unusual events that surrounded Jesus' birth?** (Even before Mary and Joseph were married, Mary was going to have a baby; the baby was from the Holy Spirit.) **After reading this Scripture passage, what are you thankful for?** (That Joseph didn't disobey God and divorce Mary; Jesus saves us from our sins!)

Say: **This must have been a really tough time for Joseph. He and Mary were not married yet, but Mary was going to have a baby. How do you think he must have felt?** Allow students to respond. **He was probably pretty angry, upset, or confused. That's when God sent the angel to help him understand what was going on. The angel helped Joseph understand that even though things were not happening the way he thought they should, this was God's plan. God showed Joseph that what was happening was through God's power, power so great that everybody's sins would be forgiven! Joseph still might not have understood completely, but he obeyed God and did not divorce Mary. The son that Mary and Joseph would have would be the Savior of everybody. That's a big promise, but since Joseph was a righteous man, he trusted and obeyed God. Joseph recognized God to be faithful and righteous, so he obeyed God, which is another way we can worship God.**

Even though we know that we have sinned, we can be forgiven through

Jesus, the Savior. When we recognize that Jesus is the Savior who forgives us when we have sinned, we can worship him thankfully for our forgiveness by trying to obey him. When we try to stop sinning and live in obedience to God, we are worshiping him everyday.

Ready to Grow Up

Before class, photocopy heart patterns so that each student will have one.

Ask: **Did you use your name tag ornament to worship Jesus this past week?** Discuss. **It's important that we remember what Jesus has done for us. We're going to make another ornament today.**

Distribute black and white paper or felt, scissors, and patterns to each student. Remember to distribute enough materials for each student to prepare two ornaments. Direct students to trace and cut two black hearts and two white hearts. Place one black heart and one white heart back to back and punch a hole through the top center of both. Students will then glue the hearts together and thread with yarn or string for hanging. Use permanent marker to write students' initials or name on the white side. Show a completed ornament to the class.

Say: **This ornament reminds me of a gift! Before I knew Jesus, my heart looked like the black side of this ornament. I was a sinner and did things I knew I shouldn't do. But when Jesus came to earth, he came to forgive my sins. When he forgives me, my heart looks like this.** Turn to the white side.

Ask students to place one of their ornaments one at a time on the classroom tree. Begin this time by putting your own ornament on the tree. Say: **While I hang this on the tree I'm going to ask Jesus to forgive me for something that I've done wrong. And then just like we do when we open our Christmas gifts I'm going to say thank you, Jesus!** Close by leading the class in singing "Lord, I Lift Your Name on High."

Classroom Supplies
- black and white construction paper or felt
- scissors
- glue
- hole punch
- string or yarn
- fine-tip permanent marker
- pencils

Curriculum Supplies
reproducible page 118 (heart patterns)

Growing Up Every Day

Say: **Jesus brought us salvation because each one of us is a sinner. Without forgiveness for our sins, we would be hopeless and lost. God knew we needed his forgiveness. So he sent Jesus to make it possible for us to be forgiven. This week at home, place your second ornament with the ornament from last week. Before you place your ornament, hold the black side and tell God about a sin that you need forgiveness for. As you place the ornament, turn it to the white side and thank him for his forgiveness. Then whenever you see your ornament, you can remember that you are a sinner who is forgiven by Jesus and that by living in obedience to God, you are worshiping him.**

Ask for volunteers to recite Matthew 1:20, 21. After the passage has been recited ask students to say the passage aloud together replacing the words "his people" with their own names and the word "their" with "his" or "her." Ask a volunteer to pray or lead the class in prayer thanking Jesus for his gift of salvation.

Classroom Supplies
- second ornament from "Ready to Grow Up"

Curriculum Supplies
none

Lesson 3

Growing in Worship

Jesus Died for Our Salvation

Luke 2:8-18

Bible Focus

The shepherds hear the angel say that Jesus is the "Savior…Christ the Lord."

Life Focus

Praise and thank Jesus for the suffering he endured to bring salvation.

Growing Up in the Word: Matthew 1:20, 21

Prepare one or both of the following memory activities for your students. Greet student by name as they arrive. Play instrumental Christmas music as students work.

Memory Activity 1

Before class, print Matthew 1:20, 21 on the four pieces of colored poster board or construction paper. The memory passage will be printed four times. Cut each poster board into various-sized pieces and place them on the walls around the classroom. Place tissue paper around the flashlights and secure with rubber band (one color per flashlight). For large groups increase the number of colors and flashlights used.

Divide the class into four groups. Instruct each group that when the room is darkened they are to search for the pieces of poster board that match the color of their flashlight's light. They may use only their flashlight to see. When all the pieces have been found, groups should put together their passage. Turn lights on when all groups have completed their puzzle and have groups recite the memory passage.

Say: **We've filled this room with several colors of light today. These colors were pretty. The night that Jesus was born, God's glory shone around the shepherds. That must have been beautiful. What would it have been like to have been surrounded by God's glory?** Discuss. **What a wonderful way to announce the birth of the one who would save his people from their sins.**

Classroom Supplies
- four flashlights
- four sheets of colored tissue paper
- four pieces of corresponding colored poster board or construction paper
- rubber bands
- marker

Curriculum Supplies
none

Memory Activity 2

Classroom Supplies
- Bibles
- assorted Christmas wrapping paper
- chalkboard
- clear tape

Curriculum Supplies
none

Before class, choose several different patterns of Christmas wrapping paper. Write the entire memory passage on the white side of each pattern. Then cut the paper into puzzle-style pieces. Paper clip the pieces of each pattern together. Make one puzzle for each team.

Begin this activity by asking for volunteers to write Matthew 1:20, 21 on the chalkboard. Let volunteers share by writing several words before passing the chalk to another student. When the verse has been completed, read it aloud as a group.

Divide class into teams (one team per wrapping paper design). Distribute wrapping paper pieces. Have each group place the Scripture pieces face down on the table in front of them. At your signal, each group should turn the pieces over and place them in the correct order. As groups finish constructing the memory passage, they may simply turn the pieces over and move to a different pattern to try again. When finished, groups may tape the pieces together.

Say: **An angel announced to Mary that she would be the mother of Jesus. An angel also announced to Joseph that he should take Mary as his wife and that he should name her baby Jesus. Today, we'll see a third time that angels gave an announcement about Jesus' birth.**

Why Grow Up?

Classroom Supplies
- envelopes
- play money (bills)

Curriculum Supplies
reproducible pages 119, 120 (role cards)

Before class, copy the reproducible pages and cut them into six cards. One set serves as name tags for six volunteers. These may be taped or hung as a necklace.

Place various amounts of play money (not much!) in six different envelopes to hand to the volunteers playing the above roles. Ask for students to wear the name tags and assume the character roles. Ask for six additional volunteers to serve as members of the class court. You will need one more volunteer to be the class jailer. Designate a section of the classroom to be the jail. Seat the court members in front of the rest of the class. Hand each court member one of the crime cards from this lesson's activity pages.

Say: **Today the court of the class of (add your church's name) will come to order. Court, please call the first case to trial.** As the court member reads the case name, that volunteer should step forward to face the jury. The court member will read all the information on the card including the fine that is to be paid. Although each defendant has cash in an envelope, none of them will have enough to pay the exorbitant fines the court imposes. As each one is unable to pay, the jailer will escort him to jail.

When each card has been read and all the defendants are jailed, say: **The crimes our defendants committed were silly things and not worth the money the court wanted them to pay. But there are things all of us do that cost a lot. We call these things sin. When we lie, cheat, disobey, steal, gossip, or become jealous we hurt others and ourselves. There is nothing we can do or say that makes that sin go away. That's why Jesus is called our Savior. He came to save us from our sins. He did that by dying on a cross. He gave his perfect life for our sinful ones so that we could find a way to "get out of jail!"** Ask the students who are in jail to come join the rest of the group. Ask your class to pray thanking God for giving Jesus to be our Savior. Ask for volunteers to pray aloud.

How to Grow Up

Classroom Supplies
- Bibles
- construction paper shapes
- poster or marker board
- markers
- paper grocery sack
- cassette tape recorder
- cassette tape

Curriculum Supplies
none

Before class, cut five Christmas shapes from construction paper so that each student will have one. (Example: stars, trees, bells, angels, manger, and so on.) Place shapes in a grocery sack.

Say: **At Christmastime, we usually just think about Jesus' birth. There are many songs that have been written about Jesus' birth, and we like to sing them at this time of year. When we sing these songs, we are worshiping God, thanking him and praising him for the great gift of Jesus. But how much more important is it to remember that Jesus didn't simply come to be a baby in a manger; he came to save us from our sins. When we worship God at Christmas by singing songs about Jesus' birth or by celebrating his coming, we can also praise God for the salvation that came to all people through this baby born in a manger.**

On the chalkboard draw the five shapes large enough to letter in. In the first shape write "8 & 9"; in the second write "10 & 11"; in the third write "12 & 13"; in the fourth write "14 & 15"; and in the last write "16, 17, & 18."

Locate Luke 2:8-18 with your class. Read this aloud together or ask for volunteers to read individual verses.

Pass the grocery sack among your students. Ask them to choose one shape from the sack. Instruct students who have the same shape to group themselves together. Using the shapes on the board as a guide, each group is to choose a familiar song tune such as a Christmas carol or other praise song and write words that tell the message of their particular verses.

Set a time limit on the song writing. When everyone has finished, bring the groups together for a concert! Begin by asking the first group to sing their composition. Let each group share in turn. Ask them to practice one more time so that you can record their song on tape. Play it for the group to enjoy.

Say: **The message the angels brought to the shepherds and the praises they gave to God must have been beautiful. It announced the birth of Jesus. Jesus was born so that he could save us. Jesus brought us salvation through his birth and through his death. Jesus is our Savior.**

Ready to Grow Up

Classroom Supplies
- dowel rods or twigs or sticks
- twine or coarse string
- small eye hooks
- glue
- ribbon

Curriculum Supplies
none

Before class, gather enough materials for each student to make two ornaments.

Ask: **Did you use your heart ornament to worship Jesus this past week?** Discuss. **It's important that we remember what Jesus has done for us. We're going to make another ornament today.**

Break the rods or sticks into two- and three-inch pieces or have students break their own pieces. Instruct students to form a cross shape with one two-inch piece and one three-inch piece. Wind the string or twine around the cross section of these two pieces in an X motion until pieces are secure. Secure string with glue. Insert a small eye hook into the top of the cross and thread a piece of ribbon through it.

Ask for a volunteer to recite the unit memory passage. Say: **The last part of Matthew 1:20, 21 tells us that Jesus will save his people from their sins. We know Jesus is the Savior, and we know that we need him to save us! This cross that we've made to hang on our tree reminds us how Jesus saved us. It reminds us of what he did to take all our sins away. He died on a cross even though he had done nothing wrong. He took our place so that we could be forgiven. How could Jesus take away our sins?** Allow students time to respond. **Jesus could take our sins away because he was a perfect sacrifice. In the Old Testament law, God required that sin be paid for through a sacrifice of an animal without defect or some other similar sacrifice. We know that Jesus became a sacrifice on the cross, but sometimes we forget that he was a perfect, blameless sacrifice. We think of Jesus as a baby at Christmastime, and we think of Jesus as a sacrifice and risen Savior at Easter, but the fact that Jesus lived on earth for more than thirty years as a man, just like one of us, shows just how special a sacrifice he was. We know we have sins, even if they are just little ones that sometimes happen because we just aren't thinking. Jesus didn't have any sins. When he died on the cross, he was without any sins. Jesus' whole life was worship to God because he knew that God was worthy of his obedience, even if it meant dying on the cross.**

Allow students to hang their ornament on the tree one by one. Ask for a volunteer to chose a song to sing as the ornaments are being hung or lead the class in singing "Lord, I Lift Your Name on High."

Growing Up Every Day

Classroom Supplies
- second ornament from "Ready to Grow Up"

Curriculum Supplies
none

Say: **This week at home, use your second ornament to remember how Jesus brought you salvation. Place the ornament with the other ornaments that you have made. Before you place your ornament, remind yourself that the cross is where Jesus took your place. As you place the ornament, say a pray of worship and thanks to God for sending Jesus to die for your sins. Also, remember that for Jesus to take our place, he had to live a perfect life in obedience to God. Jesus worshiped God every day by being obedient. When you look at the cross ornament, keep that in mind as you try to make your life a model of worship through obedience.**

Close by having the class recite Matthew 1:20, 21 followed by prayer.

Lesson 4

Growing in Worship

Jesus Is the Only Way

Luke 2:21-38

Bible Focus

Simeon spoke of Jesus—"For my eyes have seen your salvation."

Life Focus

Worship God because Jesus is the only one who can save us.

Growing Up in the Word: Matthew 1:20, 21

Prepare one or both of the following memory activities for your students. Greet student by name as they arrive. Play instrumental Christmas music as students work.

Memory Activity 1

Classroom Supplies
- Bibles
- Christmas bells
- chalkboard

Curriculum Supplies
none

Before class, print Matthew 1:20, 21 on the board. Separate it into the following phrases: "After he had considered this,/ an angel of the Lord/ appeared to him in a dream/ and said, 'Joseph son of David,/ do not be afraid/ to take Mary home as your wife,/ because what is conceived in her/ is from the Holy Spirit./ She will give birth to a son,/ and you are to give him the name Jesus,/ because he will save his people/ from their sins.'" Depending on the ability of your class, use shorter phrases.

Direct the class to form a circle. If your class is large, consider forming more than one circle. Hand the Christmas bells to a student. Ask this student to say the first phrase of the passage, jiggle the bells, and pass them to the student on his right. This student will repeat the first phrase and add the second. He will then pass the bells to a third student and so on until the passage has been completed.

At some point begin to erase selected words from the phrases written on the board, encouraging students to say the verse without additional help. Challenge them by completely erasing the board. Vary this activity by increasing the tempo with a drumbeat or shakers.

Say: **The Jews knew that a Messiah was coming. They didn't know when he would come. But God told one man that he would not die until he had seen the Lord's salvation. This man's name was Simeon. He saw Jesus—the one who would save his people from their sins—before he died.**

Classroom Supplies

- Bibles
- index cards
- butcher paper
- markers

Curriculum Supplies

none

Memory Activity 2

Before class, copy segments of Matthew 1:20, 21 onto index cards. Make several sets. You may wish to let your students locate Matthew 1:20, 21 in their Bibles and choose a short memory segment themselves. Assist the class in forming small groups or choosing partners. If you have a very small class you may choose to make this an individual activity.

Have the groups choose one index card. Distribute lengths of butcher paper and markers. Explain that students are to rewrite their portion of the memory verse as a rebus puzzle. Students will replace key words with pictures that sound like the words in their memory phrases, or they will create word addition and subtraction problems. For example, the word angel could be presented as the following: "and - d + cage - ca + l." Give the groups a time limit and when time is called ask each group to present their puzzle to the rest of the class. As each segment is worked out correctly, that group or individual should be placed with their puzzle in the order of the verse. When all puzzles have been solved and everyone is standing together, ask each group to read aloud their portion of the memory verse in order.

Say: **Before Mary and Joseph were to be married, Joseph learned that Mary was pregnant. Joseph must have been angry and confused about this. He decided to divorce her quietly. But an angel of the Lord gave Joseph a little help so that Joseph wouldn't be afraid to take Mary as his wife. Not only had God chosen Mary to be the mother of Jesus but also he had chosen Joseph to be the earthly father of Jesus.**

Classroom Supplies

- poster board
- markers
- blank
- lined paper
- pencils

Curriculum Supplies

none

Why Grow Up?

Ask: **What do Alexander Graham Bell, Robert Fulton, and Thomas Edison have in common? They were inventors! These men all made things or invented items that improved our world: the telephone, the steamboat, and the light bulb.** Divide the class into groups. If you have a small class you may wish to allow students to work in pairs or individually. Distribute paper and pencils. Explain that every group will have five minutes to make a list of wonderful things people have either made, discovered, or invented that made our world a better place to live. Allow students to brainstorm. After the allotted time, gather the group around the poster board. Ask students to share their ideas. Write each item on the left side of the board and the way that it is valuable on the right side. For example, you could write "penicillin" on the left and "makes people well" on the right.

Leaving one space at the top of the board, write several of the students' ideas. When you have finished, ask for volunteers to tell which invention or discovery was the best. When everyone has had an opportunity to share, write the word "Jesus" at the top of the list. Beside "Jesus," write "saves us from our sins."

Say: **There are many wonderful things that people have done or invented or discovered. Some of them changed our world. Some even helped to save lives! Sometimes we honor those people by remembering them every once in a while. But only one person can save us from our sins: Jesus. Only he has the power to do that. Because of that, we need to remember every day to worship God.**

How to Grow Up

Classroom Supplies
- Bibles for every student
- lined paper
- pens or pencils

Curriculum Supplies
none

Make sure every student has a Bible. Direct the class to locate Luke 2:21-38. Ask for volunteers to read the Scripture verses aloud. When all the verses have been read ask: **Where did Mary and Joseph take Jesus?** (Jerusalem.) **Why did Mary and Joseph take Jesus to Jerusalem?** (To present him to the Lord.) **What sacrifice should Mary and Joseph have offered?** (Two pairs of doves or two young pigeons.) **What was Simeon promised he would see before he died?** (The Christ.) **How did Simeon know who the baby Jesus was?** (The Holy Spirit was upon him.) **Who else spoke to Mary and Joseph about Jesus in the temple?** (Anna the prophetess.) **To what other people did Anna speak?** ("To all who were looking forward to the redemption of Jerusalem.") **Why do you think she told other people?** Allow students to respond. **I'd say that with great news like what she had just heard, she'd just have to tell other people.**

Distribute paper and pens to your students. Say: **You have just been hired to write a newspaper column for the Jerusalem Times. Your assignment is to report on the events that happened the day Mary and Joseph took baby Jesus to the temple to be presented to the Lord. Just as Anna told everyone around her about the Savior she had just seen, we also ought to worship God by expressing our praise and thankfulness to other people.** Encourage them to include interviews, eyewitness accounts, and quotes from the main characters. When students have finished, ask for several volunteers to share their newspaper articles. Display all the articles in the classroom for everyone to read.

Say: **God told Simeon that he would see the Savior. God pointed Simeon directly to Jesus and to no other. God revealed Jesus to Simeon as the Savior. Jesus is the only one who can save us.**

Ready to Grow Up *

Classroom Supplies
- scissors
- glue
- white chenille wires
- red construction paper

Curriculum Supplies
reproducible page 118 (candy cane pattern)

Before class, make a copy of the candy cane pattern for each student.

Ask: **Did you use your cross ornament to worship Jesus this past week?** Discuss. **It's important that we remember what Jesus has done for us. We're going to make another ornament today.**

Distribute candy cane patterns, red construction paper, pencils, scissors, glue and white chenille wires. Give your students the following instructions:

1. Cut two candy canes from the red construction paper.
2. Cut the chenille wires into sections that are as wide as the candy cane and glue them onto the candy cane shapes to make a stripe effect.
3. When the stripes have begun to dry, punch a hole in the bottom of the ornament so that when it is hung on the Christmas tree, it will resemble the letter "J" rather than the candy cane shape.
4. Distribute ribbon for students to tie onto their ornaments.

Ask students to hold their ornaments up by the ribbon. Ask: **What does this ornament remind you of? The letter "J"!** Encourage your class that when they hang this ornament on the tree they will remember that "J" stands for Jesus, the only one who can save us from our sins!

Give students the opportunity to hang one of their ornaments on the classroom tree at this time. Say: **As you hang your "J," thank Jesus for being your Savior!** Close this time by singing "Lord, I Lift Your Name on High."

Growing Up Every Day

Say: **When it's Christmastime many of us are busy thinking about gifts, time off from school, decorations, parties and food! Sometimes it's easy to forget the real reason we celebrate Christmas. It's easy to forget about Jesus. Maybe this will help you remember.**

Give each student a wrapped Life Savers brand candy and an adhesive bandage. Say: **This week at home, use this Life Saver candy and bandage along with your second ornament to remember that Jesus is the only one who can save you. Before you place your ornament, use the bandage to remind you that you do wrong things that hurt God, others, and yourself. You sin. As your place the ornament, use the Life Saver candy to remember that Jesus was born to save you from your sins. He's the only one who has the power to do that. He is your lifesaver. Then say a prayer of worship and thanks to God for Jesus.** Have students put the Life Savers brand candy covered by the bandage on the back of the ornament.

Close by repeating the memory passage aloud together. Raise hands in the air when you come to the part of the passage that says, "because he will save his people from their sins."

Classroom Supplies
- individually wrapped Life Savers brand candies
- adhesive bandages
- second ornament from "Ready to Grow Up"

Curriculum Supplies
none

Lesson 5

Growing in Worship

Gifts of Worship

Matthew 2:1-12

Bible Focus

Magi brought gifts of worship to Jesus, the king of the Jews.

Life Focus

Thank Jesus for salvation by bringing him gifts of worship.

Growing Up in the Word: Matthew 1:20, 21

Prepare one or both of the following memory activities for your students. Greet students by name as they arrive. Play instrumental Christmas music as students work.

Memory Activity 1

Classroom Supplies
- large index cards
- marker

Curriculum Supplies
none

Before class, prepare two sets of index cards. For both sets, write each word of the memory passage on a separate index card. Write Matthew 1:20, 21 on a chalkboard.

Divide the class into two teams. Have students read the memory passage from the chalkboard. Place the first verse of both sets of cards face down on the floor in between the two teams. At your signal, members of the teams are to run to the center area, retrieve one card and bring it back to their team's area. If a team member retrieves a duplicate card, he must return the card to the center area and choose a different card until all the correct cards have been chosen. As soon as the team places the cards in the proper order, the team should stand up and say it aloud. Challenge the team to say the passage from memory. Repeat this process for each verse of the memory passage. If you have a large group use different teams for each verse of the memory passage.

Say: **Whenever a baby is born, we celebrate. How do we celebrate?** (We usually have a baby shower.) **What happens at the baby shower?** (Gifts are given to the baby.) **Jesus was the most important baby ever born because he came to save us from our sins. He received some expensive gifts from some important people. What gifts and what important people?** (Gold, incense, and myrrh from the Magi.)

Classroom Supplies
a copy of Matthew 1:20, 21

Curriculum Supplies
none

Memory Activity 2

Recite Matthew 1:20, 21 aloud together as a class. Choose a member of the class to be "It." "It" must move about the room trying to tag and freeze his classmates. Once a student is frozen, he must remain frozen until the teacher asks him to recite Matthew 1:20, 21. If the student is able to successfully recite the memory passage, he is unfrozen and becomes "It." If the student is unsuccessful in reciting the memory passage, he should be given a copy of the verse to study while frozen. The teacher will attempt to unfreeze him a second time. Continue in this manner for the time allotted for this activity.

Say: **Being frozen is like being unsaved. A person who is unsaved is frozen in sin. We don't have to remain frozen in our sin. We can have God's forgiveness through Jesus, the one God sent to save his people from their sins. Thank God that he sent Jesus!**

Classroom Supplies
- small slips of paper
- pencils
- envelopes
- chalkboard

Curriculum Supplies
none

Why Grow Up?

Ask your group to think of a person who is special to them. Ask: **When you want to tell this person how special they are, what kind of things do you say? What kind of things do you do for them?** Allow students to respond. **We've been learning about how special Jesus is. Today we want to worship him. Worship is another way of saying we want to tell him how special he is. Let's think of some ways we can worship Jesus.** Write group's ideas on the board such as sing, pray, thank him for saving us, giving an offering, and so on.

Distribute slips of paper and pencils to your students. Explain that each of them is to write what gift of worship they will give to Jesus today. Direct them to write their gift on a slip of paper provided and place the slip in an envelope. Ask each student to write his name on the envelope. Collect all envelopes for use during "Ready to Grow Up."

Classroom Supplies
- Bibles
- microphone prop
- clipboard
- Bible-times costumes
- chairs

Curriculum Supplies
copies of the "Good Morning Bethlehem" script printed here

How to Grow Up

Before class, make copies of the script and cut them apart so each actor has his section. Prepare cue cards for the stagehand with the following on them: Matthew 2:2; Matthew 2:6; Matthew 2:8; Matthew 2:12.

Choose students for the following roles: Katie Christmas (talk-show host), Rachel Levi, King Herod, Mr. Silas (chief priest), Mr. Scribe (teacher of the Law), Mary, Wise Man 1, Wise Man 2, Wise Man 3, and Stagehand. If you have a smaller class, combine some of the roles such as Mr. Silas and Mr. Scribe and also Wise Men 1, 2, and 3.

Seat Bible characters and host in front of the class in talk-show style with guests in order of appearance. Direct rest of class to locate Matthew 2:1-12 in their Bibles. Explain that the class will be following along in their Bibles as the guests are interviewed. The audience should listen for this cue: "Audience, may I have a direct quote on that?" This is the audience's cue to read aloud from the Bible passage.

Good Morning, Bethlehem

Katie: Hello and welcome to "Good Morning, Bethlehem!" We have some interesting guests who are here to talk with us today concerning the recent miraculous events in Bethlehem and Jerusalem! We have heard from our sources within the palace that foreign diplomats have been summoned to attend a summit with King Herod. We're speaking now with Rachel Levi, a resident of Jerusalem. During a shopping expedition, Rachel had an encounter with some of these mysterious visitors from the East. Tell us, Rachel, what happened during your encounter with the Magi?

Rachel: Well, Katie, I have to tell you, they certainly weren't your typical tourists asking for directions! It was all very exciting!

Katie: Did they speak to you directly? What were they looking for?

Rachel: From what I could gather, they were looking for someone very important. They wanted to find him so they could worship him.

Katie: Thank you, Rachel. Audience, may I have a direct quote on that?

(Stagehand displays cue card #1. Class reads Matthew 2:2 from their Bibles.)

Katie: Thank you, audience. Our next guest works very closely with palace officials. Having been a part of the King's advisory board for many years we've invited Mr. Silas and Mr. Scribe to speak with us today. Mr. Silas, can you tell us what King Herod is feeling right now?

Mr. Silas: Katie, I can tell you that King Herod is very anxious to know why these men are looking for a new king. I think he is very interested to know what they find.

Katie: Can you tell us what your involvement is in all of this?

Mr. Silas: King Herod called a meeting of all his most important advisors—of course, I was a part of that—to pool all the information we could give him about where the new king was to be born.

Katie: Mr. Scribe, were you able to give him any direction on this matter?

Mr. Scribe: Anyone who is familiar with the writings of the prophets would be able to tell you that Bethlehem is the expected birthplace of the Messiah.

Katie: Audience, may I have a direct quote on that?

(Stagehand displays cue card #2. Class reads Matthew 2:6.)

Katie: It is our belief that King Herod finally took matters into his own hands and secretly summoned the visitors to meet with him. Our next guest is here to talk with us about these wonderful events is King Herod himself. Welcome, King.

King Herod: Thank you.

Katie: King, tell us how you felt when you heard that these men were looking for the King of the Jews?

King Herod: First let me make it clear that I am the King who rules over the Jews. So all this talk understandably was very disturbing.

Katie: What action have you taken to control this situation?

King Herod: We had a meeting, a very quiet meeting of course. There's no sense in getting all of Jerusalem in an uproar!

Katie: What was your goal for this meeting? Did you accomplish anything?

King Herod: I think the meeting was very successful. I discovered when this star appeared, and I made these wise men promise me that when they found this so-called baby king they would come back and tell me where he is.

Katie: Why are you so interested in finding this baby?

King Herod: No comment at this time.

Katie: Audience, may I have a direct quote on that?

(Stagehand displays cue card #3. Class reads Matthew 2:8).

Katie: Next, let's talk with a person very close to this situation—the baby's mother, Mary. Mary, welcome to our show.

Mary: Thank you.

Katie: Mary, tell us about your first encounter with these wise men from the East.

Mary: When they visited, they had been traveling for a long time following a star that showed them how to find us. They were overjoyed that the star had stopped, and they had finally found what they were looking for.

Katie: What was the reaction of these men when they first met your son Jesus?

Mary: They bowed down and worshiped him. They had brought gifts with them—treasures, really. They opened them and presented them to Jesus.

Katie: What gifts did they bring?

Mary: Gold, incense, and myrrh.

Katie: Thank you, Mary, for sharing your incredible story with us today. Our last guests today are three of the wise men who were involved in the search for Jesus. What was your reaction when you found the baby Jesus?

Wise Man 1: We were overjoyed. We had found the new King!

Katie: Why did you search for the King in Bethlehem?

Wise Man 2: It was actually King Herod who gave us that information. He consulted with all his advisors and told us Bethlehem was the place!

Katie: Maybe you can tell us, then, in light of all the help King Herod gave you, why did you disregard his request to return and tell him where the baby was?

Wise Man 3: After we had seen the child we had a dream. The dream warned us that we should not tell King Herod what we knew. We decided to go home a different way—out of the way of King Herod!

Katie: Audience, may I have a direct quote on that?

(Stagehand displays cue card #4. Class reads Matthew 2:12).

Classroom Supplies
- red and green construction paper
- scissors
- pencils
- tape
- yarn or ribbon (white)
- metal ornament hangers
- clear tape

Curriculum Supplies
reproducible page 264
(cube pattern from unit 10)

Ready to Grow Up

Before class, copy the cube pattern for each student. If possible copy the cube on red and green paper. Each student will need two.

Ask: **Did you use your "J" ornament with the Life Saver candy and bandage to worship Jesus this past week?** Discuss. **It's important that we remember what Jesus has done for us. We're going to make another ornament today.**

Distribute copies of the reproducible page, construction paper, pencils, and scissors to the students. Instruct them to trace the gift box pattern onto the colored construction paper. Demonstrate how to fold the pattern into a box shape by folding on the dotted lines and securing with tape. Before students tuck in the last flap to close the gift box, distribute envelopes with students' names from the "Why Grow Up" section of this lesson.

Say: **What is in your envelope is your gift of worship to God. Just as the wise men brought Jesus precious gifts, our worship and praise is precious to Jesus. The reason the wise men brought precious gifts to Jesus is because Jesus is worthy of receiving special gifts. That's what worship is, expressing that someone is worthy of special attention or gifts.** Ask the students to take the small piece of paper from their envelopes and place it in their gift boxes. After this step, students may complete the box by securing the last flap with tape. Leave the second ornament open. Students may wish to tie their gift with ribbon or yarn. Attach a metal ornament hook to the ribbon and invite the class to join you around the Christmas tree. Have students hang their ornaments.

Growing Up Every Day

Before class, copy one heart for each student. Gather your class around the Christmas tree. Ask for volunteers to locate ornaments they have created in past sessions. Encourage students to tell about the ornaments and what they help us learn and remember about Jesus and why he was born.

Say: **Today we've made a gift for Jesus. Each of us has chosen something to give. What do you think Jesus wants most from us?** Discuss. **What Jesus wants most from us is a heart that worships him.** Distribute one heart to each student. **This week at home, place this second ornament with the rest of your ornaments from this month. Before you place the ornament, take out the heart and write your name on it. Put it back in the gift box and tape the box shut. Tie the ribbon around it. As you place the ornament, pray and tell God that you are giving him the gift of your heart.**

Close today's session by first reciting this unit's memory passage. Then sing "Happy Birthday, Jesus" or "Lord, I Lift Your Name on High."

Classroom Supplies
- classroom Christmas tree with this month's ornaments
- second ornament from "Ready to Grow Up"

Curriculum Supplies
small heart from reproducible page 118

J

E

S

U

S

S

A

V

E

S

After he had considered this,

an angel of the Lord appeared to him

in a dream and said, "Joseph son of David,

do not be afraid to take Mary home as your wife,

because what is conceived

in her is from the Holy Spirit.

She will give birth to a son,

and you are to give him the name Jesus,

because he will save

his people from their sins." Matthew 1:20, 21

Characters: Elizabeth, Zechariah, Neighbor 1, Neighbor 2, Neighbor 3, Relative 1, Relative 2, Narrator 1, Narrator 2.

Narrator 1: In the town of Judah lived a woman named Elizabeth. She was going to have a baby. Her husband's name was Zechariah. Zechariah was unable to talk after a conversation with an angel several months earlier. Zechariah and Elizabeth were elderly. Elizabeth had a cousin whose name was Mary. Mary was also going to have a baby.

Narrator 2: When it came time for Elizabeth to have her baby, she gave birth to a boy.

Neighbor 1: Elizabeth has just had a baby boy!

Neighbor 2: We must go see Zechariah and Elizabeth and tell them how happy we are that they have been blessed with a child.

Narrator 1: Eight days after the child was born, the neighbors and relatives came to visit Elizabeth and Zechariah.

Relative 1: The child will be named Zechariah after his father!

Elizabeth: No! He is to be called John.

Relative 2: There is no one among your relatives that has that name.

Neighbor 3: *(signs to John with hands)* What name do you want this child to be called?

Zechariah: *(writes on tablet)* His name is John.

Narrator 2: As soon as Zechariah wrote these words, he was able to speak again. He praised God.

Neighbors and Relatives: *(excited, happy, praising God)* This is wonderful! Do you believe it? How amazing! Praise God!

Narrator 1: Then Zechariah was filled with the Holy Spirit. He began to tell about the wonderful things that were going to happen.

Narrator 2: God gave Zechariah a message about the baby that was going to be born to Mary and Joseph. God wanted everyone to know how special the baby Jesus was going to be. This is what Zechariah said . . .

Zechariah or entire class: "Praise be to the Lord, the God of Israel, because he has come and has redeemed his people. He has raised up a horn of salvation for us in the house of his servant David (as he said through his holy prophets of long ago), salvation from our enemies and from the hand of all who hate us—to show mercy to our fathers and to remember his holy covenant, the oath he swore to our father Abraham: to rescue us from the hand of our enemies, and to enable us to serve him without fear in holiness and righteousness before him all our days."

Jack Graybill
Age 42
Occupation: Attorney

Katherine Allwell
Age 19
Occupation: Professional Baby-sitter

Vanessa Mild
Age 32
Occupation: Travel Writer

Jordan Bank
Age 28
Occupation: Chef

Walter Hitch
Age 51
Occupation: Ice Cream Delivery Man

Amy Maybe
Age 60
Occupation: Interior Designer

Katherine Allwell
Crime: Burned dinner.
Fine: $165.00

Jack Graybill
Crime: Wore an ugly tie!
Fine: $150.00

Jordan Bank
Crime: Drove a dirty car.
Fine: $99.00

Vanessa Mild
Crime: Overshopped
Fine: $275.00

Amy Maybe
Crime: Forgot to water her plants.
Fine: $175.00

Walter Hitch
Crime: Forgot to mow his lawn.
Fine: $110.00

UNIT 5

Growing in Discipleship

Unit Aims

Know: Understand what it means to be a disciple.
Feel: Feel eager to follow Jesus.
Do: Demonstrate being Jesus' disciple—to help someone else be a disciple.
Memorize: Matthew 28:16-20

Why Grow in Discipleship?

The focus of this unit is discipleship: accepting the call, learning to be a good disciple, and growing as a Christian by following the example of Jesus Christ. Children can understand the challenges faced by the first Christian disciples and can identify with the feeling of being chosen. They want to be a part of teams and activities involving others; they also want the independence to choose for themselves to accept invitations for such involvement. The lessons of this unit offer students the chance to become members of Jesus' team—a hard working, loving, caring, enthusiastic winning team whose success is not measured in numbers but in growth. Use this unit to invite your students to become a part of a winning team, not just for a season or two but forever.

The memory passage for this unit is both a summary and an acclamation of the unit focus. In Matthew 28:16-20, Jesus commissions his followers to take all they have learned and seek to make disciples of all people. This unit will expand their understanding of the importance of making a commitment to answer Christ's call to "go and make disciples of all nations."

Summary

Grow up in every way to be like Christ by following his example and teachings about discipleship.

- Choose to be a disciple and to make disciples.
- Be salt and light to those you are discipling.
- Love enemies to help them become disciples.
- Be a servant to those you are discipling.

Lesson Aims

Scripture focus	Bible focus	Life focus
Lesson 1 Matthew 4:18-22; 9:9-13	Jesus invited people to follow him and learn how to make disciples.	Follow Jesus by choosing to make disciples.
Lesson 2 Matthew 5:13-16	Disciples are like salt on bland food and light in the darkness.	Choose a way to be salt and light for someone this week—to help them be a disciple.
Lesson 3 Matthew 5:38-48	Disciples love enemies.	Choose a way to love an enemy—to help them be a disciple.
Lesson 4 Matthew 20:20-28	Disciples become great through serving others—to help them be disciples too.	Choose a way to be a servant—to help all people be disciples.

Memory Passage: Matthew 28:16-20

"Then the eleven disciples went to Galilee, to the mountain where Jesus had told them to go. When they saw him, they worshiped him; but some doubted. Then Jesus came to them and said, 'All authority in heaven and on earth has been given to me. Therefore go and make disciples of all nations, baptizing them in the name of the Father and of the Son and of the Holy Spirit, and teaching them to obey everything I have commanded you. And surely I am with you always, to the very end of the age.'"

Classroom Supplies
- two poster boards
- markers
- scissors
- a large envelope
- glue
- small pictures of sports equipment such as a soccer ball, football, baseball, volleyball, basketball, tennis racket, hockey stick, golf club, running shoe

Curriculum Supplies
none

Memory Passage Review Activity

Divide one poster board into three columns and ten rows. Label the columns as follows: sport, equipment, skill. Label the rows as follows: soccer, volleyball, baseball, tennis, basketball, hockey, track, golf, Matthew 28:16-20.

Cut the second poster board into 24 cards. Make eight sets of three cards related to the different sports: one card for the name of the sport, one with picture of a piece of equipment, and one with a skill needed to play the sport. For example, one set could include the word "Soccer," a picture of soccer ball, and the word "Kicking." Then, divide the memory verse into 24 phrases and write a phrase on the back of each card in the order shown by the chart.

To play, students organize the sports cards on the poster grid. When finished, students turn over all the cards and read the message from Matthew 28:16-20. Ask: **What is Jesus telling the members of his team to do?** Then have students mix up all the cards and arrange the phrases of the memory passage without organizing the sports words first!

Lesson 1

Growing in Discipleship

A Disciple Follows Jesus

Matthew 4:18-22; 9:9-13

Bible Focus
Jesus invited people to follow him and learn how to make disciples.

Life Focus
Follow Jesus by choosing to make disciples.

Growing Up in the Word: Matthew 28:16-20
Set up one or both of the following activities for students to do upon arrival. Greet students by name and encourage them to welcome others as they arrive.

Memory Activity 1
Before class, write the following words on separate slips of paper: mountain, worshiped, doubted, heaven, earth, nations, baptizing, teaching, commanded, always. Write the memory passage on the poster board with blanks where there words listed above should be. Adjust the number of words on the slips and the corresponding number of blanks in the memory passage according to the number of students in your class. One word/blank is needed for every two students.

Divide class into pairs of students and have them choose one slip of paper. Direct each pair to create an action that represents their word.

As the passage is read aloud, pairs fill in the blank by performing their action. The others try to identify the word. When the correct word is identified, the pair can write the word in the blank.

When all the blanks have been filled in, have the students read the complete passage again, this time with everyone demonstrating the actions that were created for the missing words.

Say: **Who was Jesus talking to in this Scripture passage? Who were some of the eleven disciples who were with Jesus in Galilee? Today we are going to find out how these people and many others came to be disciples of Jesus.**

Classroom Supplies
- jar
- paper
- poster board
- marker

Curriculum Supplies
none

Memory Activity 2
Before class, use the stencils to make the word "disciple." Divide the memory passage into eight phrases. Include the reference with the last phrase. Beginning

Classroom Supplies
- large alphabet stencils
- scissors
- construction paper
- marker
- tape

Curriculum Supplies
none

with the letter "D," write each phrase on the letter, following its shape. (The path of the words will form the shape of the letter.)

In class, tape the letters to the wall in scrambled order. Have students turn to Matthew 28:16-20 and read it aloud. Choose one student to find the letter with the first phrase and place it in first position. Continue until all phrases have been identified and the word "disciple" is unscramble.

Say: **Matthew 28:16-20 contains an important command. What is it?** (To make disciples.) **What makes this command important?** (Jesus gave it. It is the way people will be saved.) **Who is Jesus talking to in this passage?** (His disciples, all believers everywhere.) **Our goal this month is to be a disciple ourselves by making more disciples. Our goal is to obey Jesus' command to make disciples.**

Why Grow Up?

Classroom Supplies
- plain paper plates
- markers or crayons

Curriculum Supplies
none

Say: **Imagine that I am working on a special project and I need helpers. Would it be a good idea to choose a person who is shy to be my helper? Who can show us how that person might respond when picked? Show me the person's response. How might those who think they are the best at everything act when chosen?** Have the whole class demonstrate their answers at the same time. **What about children who are afraid or who think they might not be able to do what I ask? How might someone who is not usually asked to be a helper respond? What might be the answer of someone who is having a terrible day?** Allow adequate time for one or more students to act out the possibilities.

Focus attention on the fact that people respond differently. Say: **We are all different. We have different feelings and different moods. We have different strengths—things we are good at doing—and different weaknesses—things we are not so good at doing. But when we are called to help someone, does it really matter if we are the best or the strongest or the fastest or the smartest?** Allow students to respond. **What does matter most when we are called upon to help someone?** (That we say yes and try to help as best we can.)

Distribute the paper plates and markers to the students and ask them to draw a smiling face and the word "YES!" on one side and a frowning face and the words "NO WAY!" on the other.

Say: **Now let's imagine some situations where we might be called to follow someone. Use the faces on your plates to show your answers. What should your answer be if you were going shopping with your parents and they said, "We're going this way, follow us"?** Allow students to respond by holding up their plate faces. **Suppose you were on a scout hike and your group leader said, "Follow me"? What if one of your friends said, "Here's how to steal candy from the drug store; follow me"? What if your pastor says, "Let me tell you what we're doing at the church next Sunday; follow me"? What would be your answer if someone you know said, "I can show you a place where we can smoke cigarettes; follow me"?**

We make choices every day about who to follow. Choosing to follow Jesus is the most important decision we will ever make.

How to Grow Up

Say: **Let's take a look at how some people in the Bible responded when Jesus called them.** Divide the students into two groups. Assign one group Matthew 4:18-22. Assign the second group Matthew 9:9-13. Instruct the groups to carefully read their assigned passages, then create a skit that illustrates what the disciples in these passages might have thought or said to one another when Jesus called them to follow him. Direct the students to create dialogue that shows what characteristics the disciples might have seen in Jesus and their feelings about being called. Perhaps they were confused, afraid, eager, curious, or amazed. Encourage the students to use their imaginations to place themselves in the situations of the disciples as they were called.

After an adequate amount of preparation time, allow each group to present their skit. Make positive comments about the presentations and encourage applause for each group.

Say: **In today's Scriptures, ordinary people said yes to the call of Jesus. They stopped what they were doing, sometimes good things, sometimes not-so-good things, and chose to become followers of Jesus. They chose to change their lives by putting Jesus ahead of everything else. Close your eyes for a moment. Imagine Jesus standing in front of you, just as he stood before Simon, Matthew, and the others. Picture him calling you be his follower, his disciple. What will your answer be?**

Classroom Supplies
Bibles

Curriculum Supplies
none

Ready to Grow Up

Before class, copy the handout for each student.

Say: **Of course our answer to Jesus' call is yes! We want to be his followers. We want to be his disciples. One of the many wonderful things about being a disciple of Jesus is that we are not alone. Jesus is always with us and all the disciples of Jesus continually pray for and support one another.** Invite the students to form a circle and to place their right hand lightly on the shoulder of the person to their right. Set a serious, prayerful mood. **Let's take a few minutes to remember our answer to Jesus' call and to promise to help one another remain true followers of Jesus.**

Address one of the students. Say: **(Student's name), Jesus says to you, "Follow me, (student's name)." What is your answer?** Allow time for the student to respond. Address the student on whom the first student's right hand rests. **(Student's name), Jesus says to you, "Follow me, (student's name)." What is your answer?** After this person has responded, go back to the first student and ask: **(First student's name), will you help (second student's name) grow as a faithful follower of Jesus?** When this student has answered, proceed in the same way, asking each student his answer to Jesus' call, followed by asking the previous person if he will help the classmate on whom his hand rests to grow as a faithful disciple. When everyone has provided an answer to the call of Jesus and pledged to help a classmate grow in discipleship, have the students return to their seats.

Say: **We have all accepted the call to become disciples of Jesus. We have all promised to help one another remain true to this call. Now let make some-**

Classroom Supplies
- markers or crayons
- scissors
- pencils
- glue
- one shoelace per student
- four wooden beads per student (large enough to thread onto the shoelace)
- pencils

Curriculum Supplies
reproducible page 139 (Yes! Beads)

thing to help us remember to keep those promises!

Distribute handout. Ask the students to color the three "Yes!" strips and to cut them out. When all students have the three strips colored, say: **On the back of the first strip, write a one-sentence promise to Jesus about answering his call. On the back of the second strip, write a one-sentence prayer for the person you promised to help grow as a faithful follower of Jesus. On the back of the last strip, write a one-sentence thank you message to Jesus for calling all people to be his disciples.** Allow a few minutes for completion of this task.

Demonstrate how to roll and glue the strips into beads. With the colored "Yes!" side of the strip down, begin rolling the strip onto a pencil. When the strip is wrapped around the pencil once or twice, apply a thin line of glue down the center of the remainder of the sentence-side of the strip then continue rolling. When the entire strip has been rolled on the pencil, carefully slide the pencil out and a cylindrical bead remains. Proceed in the same way to make two more beads. On the shoelace, have students thread a wooden bead, a "Yes!" bead, a wooden bead, a "Yes!" bead, and so on. Center the beads on the shoelace and tie a knot near each end.

Say: **Use these beads as a necklace or arm band, hang them in a prominent place, use them as a light pull cord, tie them to a jacket or backpack, use them as a bookmark. Most of all, use them to remember that you are a disciple of Jesus Christ.**

Growing Up Every Day

Classroom Supplies
pencils

Curriculum Supplies
reproducible page 139 (Yes! Beads)

Before class, make additional copies of the "Yes!" bead strips. Separate them into strips so that each student will have one. Direct the students to again write on the back of the bead strip the name of the fellow student who they said they would help follow Jesus.

Say: **Take this bead strip home this week. Use it to remind you to pray for who is listed there. Use it to remind you to encourage who is listed there to be a disciple of Jesus. When you have done so, make the strip into a bead and add it to your shoestring of beads we made today.**

Being a follower of Jesus is the choice Christians have been making for more than 2000 years. Today we have all said yes to the call of Jesus and have all promised to help one another to grow as faithful disciples. Our "Yes!" beads will help us remember our promises.

Lesson 2

Growing in Discipleship

A Disciple Lights the World

Matthew 5:13-16

Bible Focus

Disciples are like salt on bland food and light in the darkness.

Life Focus

Choose a way to be salt and light for someone this week—to help them be a disciple.

Growing Up in the Word: Matthew 28:16-20

Set up one or both of the following activities for students to do upon arrival. Greet students by name and encourage them to welcome others as they arrive.

Memory Activity 1

Distribute reproducible page 140 and direct the students to fill in the words missing from the memory passage and use the numbered letters to fill in the matching numbered spaces on the candle.

When students are finished filling in the puzzle, have them color and cut out the candle, then tape the edges to make a standing candle. Have students write the puzzle answers on separate index cards and tape one card to separate candles. If you have less than seven students, make extra candles. These will be used during "Ready to Grow Up."

Say: **This sheet has our memory passage printed inside the outline of a candle. What do you think being a disciple and a candle have in common?** Discuss. **What are candles used for?** (Light.) **Jesus compares his disciples to light because of the way that they affect the world. The puzzle answers tell us some of the things Jesus' disciples do that create light or goodness in the world. What are they?** (Puzzle answers: generosity, compassion, patience, faith, good deeds, mercy.) **In today's lesson, we'll use our puzzle answers to help us find out how we can be the light of the world.**

Classroom Supplies
- Bibles
- pencils
- clear tape
- scissors
- crayons or markers
- index cards

Curriculum Supplies
reproducible page 140 (Yes, I Will Shine)

Memory Activity 2

Before class, write the individual words of the memory passage on pieces of wide masking tape and arrange them in a circular trail on the floor.

Classroom Supplies
- a flashlight for each person
- wide masking tape

Curriculum Supplies
none

Divide the class into five groups. Assemble each group at a different beginning word of the five verses of the memory passage—"then," "when," "then," "therefore," or "and." Provide each student with a flashlight and darken the room. Invite the students to shine their lights on the word at which they are standing.

Direct each group of students to slowly walk the trail, reading the words of the memory passage in order as they shine their lights on them until they reach the place where they began. At the conclusion of the activity, turn on the lights and collect the flashlights.

Say: **Could you have followed the trail of the memory passage without light? How many sources of light can you name? Do you think a person could ever be considered a light? Jesus calls his disciples light? Why do you suppose he compares us to light?** Discuss. **We'll find out more in today's lesson.**

Why Grow Up?

Classroom Supplies
- salted and unsalted pretzels
- salted and unsalted potato chips
- salted and unsalted saltine crackers

Curriculum Supplies
none

Ask: **How many of you have eaten potato chips before? Pretzels? Crackers? It is not a surprise that nearly everyone has eaten these foods. Think about how these foods taste before you try some here today.** Invite the students to sample one or more of the unsalted items without mentioning that they are unsalted. **How do these snacks taste? Does anyone notice anything different about them? Is there anything that might give them more flavor or make them taste better to you?**

Your students will probably discern that the salt is missing from these popular snack foods. Say: **Most of us are accustomed to eating these foods salted rather than unsalted.** Offer the students the salted varieties of the same three snacks. **Try these. What do you think? It doesn't matter whether you like the salted or unsalted snacks better. What does matter is that you recognize salt and know that salt is used to add a certain flavor to foods.**

Salt is a seasoning that was popular when Jesus lived on earth, too. Salt is also used to preserve food. Salt is important to us. We need it to survive. Jesus said his disciples were like salt.

How to Grow Up

Classroom Supplies
- Bibles
- large clear pitcher
- large spoon
- 1/8 teaspoon table salt
- small paper cups

Curriculum Supplies
none

Direct the students to open their Bibles to Matthew 5:13. Invite the class to read this verse aloud with you. Ask: **In what ways do you think followers of Jesus are the salt of the earth?** (Found everywhere, important for life, add flavor to life by sharing the love of God with others, make a difference.)

Say: **We all know the strong flavor of salt, but this flavor can also be lost or changed.** Invite a volunteer to pour the table salt into the pitcher of water and begin stirring. **What is happening to the salt in this pitcher?** (It is mixing with the water, becoming diluted, making the water taste somewhat salty by losing its original form and strength.) **If we stir this water long enough, what will happen to the grains of salt?** (They will disappear.) Invite a volunteer to taste the water. **We know there is salt mixed into this water, but how is the flavor different from the flavor of the salted snacks?** (It can barely be tasted anymore.) **Yes, the flavor of the salt is nearly gone.**

If Jesus' disciples lose their saltines, what could happen to our world?

Discuss. **Evil would rule. Being like salt is important for Jesus' disciples.**

In the next three verses Matthew 5:14-16 Jesus compares his followers to something else which is also common but important. Read these verses. **What other common but important thing does Jesus call his followers?** (Light.) **In what ways do you think the followers of Jesus are the light of the world?** (They spread the gospel message, share God's love with others, and live lives of good example.)

If Jesus' disciples don't shine their lights, what could happen to our world? Discuss. **Darkness (evil) would rule. Shining our lights is important for Jesus' disciples.**

Ready to Grow Up

Before class, copy enough yes! bead strips so each student has one. Write the following words on separate index cards: laziness, anger, greed, selfishness, jealousy, violence, bitterness. If Memory Activity 2 wasn't done today, make seven copies of reproducible page 140 without the puzzle and write the following words on separate candles: generosity, compassion, patience, faith, good deeds, mercy. Form the pages into candles.

Classroom Supplies
- pencils
- notebook paper
- index cards
- scissors
- clear tape

Curriculum Supplies
- reproducible page 139 and 140 (candle and Yes! Beads)
- candles from Memory Activity 2

Say: **The theme of all the lessons of this unit is saying yes to Jesus' call to be his disciple and growing in discipleship by becoming the best followers of Jesus that we can be. Last week we took this first step by saying yes and by promising to help others remain faithful disciples as well. Did you remember to pray for and encourage a classmate?** Discuss.

Our lesson today gives us another important way to help others be disciples of Jesus. Ask the students to form groups of two or three members. Give each group one of the index cards. Set the paper candles in view. Say: **On each card is written a word that describes how people live without Jesus. These actions are actions of the darkness. On each of these candles is written a word that describes how people live with Jesus. These actions are actions of the light. Look at your card and look at the candles. Which action written on the candle is the light that covers the action written on your card?** Give students a minute to decide. Define words and give examples as necessary. Then ask the groups to roll up their cards and place them inside the tube of the paper candles.

Say: **Jesus calls his disciples the salt of the earth and the light of the world because godly actions outshine evil actions. Disciples of Jesus are light because they bring light to the darkness. Disciples of Jesus are salt because they bring flavor to a flavorless world.**

This week, think of someone you know who could really use the salt of the earth and light of Christ because they are sad, lonely, sick, or because they are someone who needs an invitation to church.

How can you be salt or light for this person? How about taking them a little candle or making them a candle of colored paper with a pretty colored flame? You could take them a package of microwave popcorn or invite them over to share some popcorn and fellowship with you. Perhaps you can think of a better way to be the salt and light for this special person. You decide. Be the salt and light for someone you know this week, and we'll take time during our

next lesson to hear about how you chose to say yes to being a disciple of Christ.

Give each student one "Yes!" bead strip. Say: **Write the person's name and what you will do on the back of your "Yes!" bead strip. When you have done what you've promised to do, make this strip into a bead and add it to your shoestring of beads we made last week.**

Growing Up Every Day

Classroom Supplies
- flashlights for each person
- recording of "This Little Light of Mine"

Curriculum Supplies
none

Distribute the flashlights and invite the students to create a light show to the song "This Little Light of Mine." Before darkening the room, ask the students to point and freeze their lights on the words "this," "light," and "mine," then move the lights without stopping on the words "I'm gonna let it shine." Practice once or twice before darkening the room and creating the light show.

Say: **You used real light to create a beautiful show in the dark to help you remember to be the light of Christ for others. Now we're back in the light of day, and it's time to put our words into action!**

Lesson 3

Growing in Discipleship

A Disciple Loves His Enemies

Matthew 5:38-48

Bible Focus
Disciples love enemies.

Life Focus
Choose a way to love an enemy—to help them be a disciple.

Growing Up in the Word: Matthew 28:16-20
Set up one or both of the following activities for students to do upon arrival. Greet students by name and encourage them to welcome others as they arrive.

Memory Passage Activity 1
Write the memory passage in a single line along a length of adding machine tape. Trim to eliminate any extra tape. Roll up the strip.

Ask the students to arrange themselves standing in a single row. Give the rolled up memory passage to the first student and direct this student to maintain a hold on the beginning of the passage. Unroll the strip and pass it along to the left. When the last student is holding the end of the strip, ask all the students to slide their hands along the strip so that their hands are touching one another. Have students read the part of the passage that appears between their hands. Have students move from a straight row into a circle so that they can all see the entire verse on the strip inside their circle and read the passage aloud in unison.

Say: **You had to work together to make the memory passage visible to everyone. Working together is not always easy. Have you ever had trouble working with others, perhaps on a project or chore at home? Did you solve the problem and get the job done? What happened? Jesus has some advice for us today about how we are to treat those who are difficult to get along with.**

Classroom Supplies
- adding machine tape
- marker

Curriculum Supplies
none

Memory Activity 2
Before class, write phrases of the memory passage on the masking tape. You will need one phrase per student. Distribute the pieces of masking tape as the students arrive. Direct the students to stick the masking tape strips across the toes of their left shoes and read the phrase to themselves several times.

Classroom Supplies
wide masking tape

Curriculum Supplies
none

Say: **It's time to step together to create our memory passage! Stand together so that Matthew 28:16-20 appears in order on the tops of your shoes. The person with the first words of the passage should stand with his left foot forward.** Invite the person with the next phrase to place his left foot next to that of the first student. Proceed in this way, being aware that students may need to hold on to one another to maintain their balance.

When the entire verse is visible across the toes of the students, choose several students to reverse their feet, putting their right toes into the line instead of their left. Ask: **What happened?** Discuss. **When something or someone makes the message of the Scripture more difficult for us to see, does that mean the message is no longer there?** Allow time for students to respond and encourage them to express assurances that the Scripture message is constant in spite of whatever obstacles or roadblocks might come up. **Sometimes it can be very difficult to do what we want to do or what we know is right because others insult us, make fun of us, or treat us as their enemies. Sometimes people steer us away from what Christ wants us to do, or they keep us from seeing how God calls his people to live. Today we are going to learn how Jesus wants his disciples to deal with their enemies.**

Why Grow Up?

Classroom Supplies
a large supply of scrap wood blocks, paper cups, or any other readily available items that students can easily use to build towers

Curriculum Supplies
none

Direct students to arrange themselves in a circle on the floor. Place the building materials in the center of the circle.

Say: **I am sure that you have built many different kinds of towers, buildings, castles and similar structures since you were very small. Your goal is to be the first one to build a tower ten pieces high. Use any of these items, but there is one catch: whenever you have five or more pieces arranged, anyone else in the room may knock down your tower or simply take any building block you are using that they want. Of course, you may do the same to keep others from getting ahead of you. Ready? Start building!**

Allow students to select materials, build, knock down each other's structures, and steal building materials from one another. If someone actually accomplishes building a ten-piece structure, stop at that point. If not, watch carefully to make sure that the activity does not get out of hand and stop it after several minutes.

Say: **Wow! How did you feel when someone knocked down your tower or took some of your building materials? Did you do the same to them? How did you feel when you destroyed someone else's work? Did you feel differently about taking materials from someone who had taken them from you rather than someone who had not? Why did you choose not to knock down or take from this person's tower?**

Retaliating against someone who has hurt or offended us in some way is called taking an eye for an eye and a tooth for a tooth. These words are found in the Old Testament. Do you think this is a fair way of dealing with those who wrong us? Do you think it is a good idea? Let's find out what Jesus has to say about the eye for an eye idea.

How to Grow Up

Direct students to Matthew 5:38-48 in their Bibles. Ask them to follow along silently as you read the passage. Take care to pause briefly between each example Jesus gives in this passage to emphasize the numerous situations where Jesus applies his teaching.

Classroom Supplies
- Bibles
- several cassette tape recorders with a blank cassette tape for each

Curriculum Supplies
none

Say: **This passage clearly tells us that Jesus does not want his followers to take an eye for an eye or a tooth for a tooth when they are wronged. Look how many different examples Jesus gives us for how his disciples should treat their enemies! What does Jesus say to do if someone strikes you? Turn the other cheek. Of course Jesus does not mean that you should stand there and allow someone to continue to hurt you. What do you think he means?** (To not strike back, to leave the situation, to show no hatred or violence back to the person who attacks you in any way.)

What did Jesus say to do if someone wants to take your tunic? (To give him your cloak too.) **What do you think this means?** (Not to get involved with silly disputes; settle disagreements quickly and simply; not to place material possessions ahead of living in peace.)

What did Jesus say to do if someone forces you to walk a mile with him? (Walk two miles instead.) **What did Jesus say his followers should do when someone asks for help or needs to borrow something from you?** (Give, lend.)

Jesus also said that loving our friends and neighbors and greeting those we know is not enough for those who seek to be his disciples. What else does Jesus expect his followers to do? (Love those who are our enemies, greet strangers, be kind to all even if the kindness is not returned.)

What do you think Jesus means when he tells us to be perfect? Can any of us truly be perfect? Guide students toward understanding that Jesus is telling his followers to keep God in mind as our example for everything we do and to never stop trying to treat others with the same never-ending love God has for us.

Divide the class into several groups depending on the number of cassette recorders available. Say: **Every day there are hundreds of radio commercials and programs that help people learn how to deal with problems. Let's put the messages of today's Scripture passage in a radio commercial. In your commercial, talk about how people can apply Jesus' teachings to situations in today's world. Write a commercial that encourages people to say yes to being a disciple of Jesus. When you have a commercial you like, record it so we can all listen to it together.** Allow ample time for the students to work on this project. Circulate among the groups to keep them on task and provide assistance as needed.

Ready to Grow Up

Say: **Last week we talked about being the salt and light of Christ for others. Did you bring light to someone this week? What did you do?** Allow students to respond.

Say: **You did a wonderful job of saying yes to bringing the light of Christ to**

Classroom Supplies
- pencils
- crayons or markers
- clear tape
- small, smooth stones (one per student)

Curriculum Supplies
reproducible pages 141, 142 (game board and pyramid)

others last week! Let's continue to grow in discipleship and continue bringing the light of Christ to others every day. This week we will be thinking about how we can love an enemy or a stranger in order to help them become disciples of Jesus.

Distribute handouts. Explain that students are going to create a board game. First, direct students to create move forward and move back spaces. Say: **Move forward spaces remind us that we are following Jesus' commands.** Have them include several of these bonus spaces. For example, one space might say, "Forgave the kid who made fun of you—move forward three," or "Walked away from a gossiping group—move forward five," or "Took the first step to welcome a new student—move forward two," or "Loaned your allowance to someone to buy lunch—move forward four."

Say: **Move back spaces are needed to remind us that sometimes we don't follow Jesus.** Have them include several of these move back spaces. For example, one space could read as follows: "Refused to accept an apology—move back six" or "Retaliated against someone—move back four."

When students have designated their move forward bonus spaces and move back penalty spaces, ask them to do the following: color two spaces on the trail solid blue, color one space solid red, write the word "yes" in the remaining spaces on the trail and color, and create a name for their game related to the yes theme of this unit such as "Say Yes to Jesus."

Distribute pyramids and follow the instruction on the page to construct. Have students select a stone to be their playing piece and to choose partners. Allow the partners to play the game twice, if time permits, once using each game board.

Classroom Supplies
pencils

Curriculum Supplies
reproducible page 139 (Yes! Beads)

Growing Up Every Day

Before class, make one copy of a yes! bead strip for each student.

Say: **Today, we've considered many ways to treat others—especially our enemies—with kindness. We know that we need to be Jesus' disciples not only to those who love us and are kind to us, but also to those who are not so friendly to us. We especially want to concentrate on a person who may not like us or that we may not like. If you don't have anyone that fits this description, concentrate on someone that doesn't get much attention at school. Write that person's name on the back of your "Yes!" bead strip. Make a pledge to speak to or smile at that person every time you see him this week. At the end of the week, if you have shown kindness by speaking to and smiling at the person on you bead, then make your bead strip into a bead and add it to the shoestring of beads we made two weeks ago.**

Invite the students to form a circle, cross their arms in front of them, then join hands. Join the prayer circle as well and lead the prayer. Say: **Please repeat each line of this yes prayer after me.**

Yes, Lord, I have answered the call to be your follower. Pause while students repeat. **Yes, Lord, I want to be a light to the world for you.** Pause. **Yes, Lord, I promise to serve those who are my enemies or who hurt me in some way.** Pause. **Yes, Lord, I am your disciple.** Pause. **Yes, Lord, I put following you ahead of everything else in my life. In Jesus' name, amen.**

Lesson 4

Growing in Discipleship

A Disciple Is a Servant

Matthew 20:20-28

Bible Focus

Disciples become great through serving others—to help them be disciples too.

Life Focus

Choose a way to be a servant—to help all people be disciples.

Growing Up in the Word: Matthew 28:16-20

Set up one or both of the following activities for students to do upon arrival. Greet students by name and encourage them to welcome others as they arrive.

Memory Activity 1

Classroom Supplies
- large old light colored T-shirts (available for next to nothing at thrift stores, Goodwill stores, and similar outlets for clean, inexpensive clothing)
- permanent marker

Curriculum Supplies
none

Divide the shirts into two equal sets. If you have an odd number of students in your class, plan to be on one of the teams yourself. Write a portion of the memory passage on all the shirts of each set. When students arrive, have the shirts turned inside out and arranged in two piles. As an alternative to shirts, attach yarn to large cards so that students will have to slip the cards over their head and wear like a necklace.

Divide the students into two teams. Explain that at the signal, each team will head for one of the piles of shirts. Each team member needs to choose a shirt, turn it right side out, and put it on so that the portion of the memory passage printed on the shirt appears in the front. Then all members of the team need to line up in a row so that the words of the verse appear in the proper sequence. The first team to present the verse in the proper sequence wins. Shuffle the teams and play again as time permits.

Say: **I noticed that many of you were helping one another with getting the shirts turned right side out and put on the right way. Some of you were also helping your teammates find their proper place in the row to make the verse appear properly. Helping and serving others is an important part of being a disciple of Jesus. What have we learned so far about how to be a good disciple?** Allow students to recall several examples from previous lessons. **Can you think of any occasions when Jesus was a servant?**

Classroom Supplies
ball of yarn

Curriculum Supplies
none

Memory Activity 2

Gather the students in an open area or hallway in a loose circle. Tie the end of a ball of yarn loosely around your wrist and unravel some of the yarn from the ball. Explain that you are going to pass or toss the yarn ball to someone else, who is to say the first word of the memory passage, wrap the yarn around his wrist, arm, ankle, or waist, unravel more of the ball, and pass or toss it to another student who will say the next word of the verse and do the same. Continue in this way until the entire verse has been recited and the entire class is connected by a giant yarn web.

Say: **Look at us! What does all of this look like to you?** Responses will vary. **Why do you think we did this? Can you think of any ways this web connecting all of us relates to the Scripture passage you recited while making it? The Word of God is for everyone. We are linked together by what Jesus says in this passage that all his disciples are to do. Followers of Jesus are one family in the body of Christ. We are called to work together in bringing Jesus to others. For several weeks now we have been talking about what it means to be a disciple of Jesus and what it is that he expects his followers to do. What are some of the things we have already learned about being a good disciple?** Allow several students to recall examples from previous lessons. **Today we will see what else Jesus has in mind for his disciples.**

Classroom Supplies
- Bibles
- odorless hand lotion

Curriculum Supplies
none

Why Grow Up?

Have the students get their Bibles, arrange their chairs in a semicircle, and sit down. Say: **While we are talking and learning more about being disciples of Jesus, I am going to do something nice for you.** While you proceed with the lesson, walk along the semi circle and massage a small amount of hand lotion on each student's hands.

Say: **I am thinking of a story Jesus told about a traveler who comes across someone who is hurt and takes care of him, even though he is not from his same country and is a stranger to him. Does anyone remember the name of this story?** (The Good Samaritan.) Find this story in Luke 10:30. Invite a volunteer to read the story aloud. **Who would you say is the person who best serves the Lord in this story? How does he do it?** (By serving the man in need.)

I am thinking of an occasion when the disciples were arguing about who is the greatest. Does anyone remember what Jesus said? (If anyone wants to be first he must be last.) Find this story in Mark 9:33. Invite a volunteer to read the story aloud. **What did Jesus say the one who would be first must be?** (A servant to all.)

I am thinking of the night before Jesus died. He gathered with his friends for a meal, but before they ate, Jesus did something special for them. Does anyone remember what he did? (Washed his disciples' feet.) Find this story in John 13:12. Invite a volunteer to read the story aloud. **Why did Jesus say that he washed the feet of his disciples?** (To show them how to serve others as he has served them.)

How did it feel to have lotion rubbed into your hands while we have been talking? Why do you think I did this for you? (To do something nice for us, to make us feel good, to demonstrate service.)

How to Grow Up

Say: **Does anyone know what it means when someone says that your vision is 20/20? Yes, it means you can see perfectly, and that is a great way to remember the message of today's Scripture. These words of Jesus will help you have 20/20 perfect vision of what Jesus wants his followers to do.**

Please find Matthew 20:20 in your Bibles. Suggest that you will serve as the narrator and invite volunteers to take the parts of Jesus, Zebedee's sons, and their mother for reading Matthew 20:20-28 aloud.

Say: **All parents want good things for their children. What was this mother asking for her sons?** (To be the most important followers of Jesus.) **What did Jesus say to her that meant that she was asking for the wrong thing?** (You do not know what you are asking.) **What did Jesus say that the brothers could do with him on earth?** (Share his cup.) **Who did Jesus say decides all the places in his kingdom?** (His Father.)

How did all the other apostles feel about it when they heard that the mother of James and John had been asking for special favors for the two? (They were indignant.) **What does indignant mean?** (Furious, outraged, offended.) **Jesus took great care to try to explain to his followers that he and they were nothing like earthly rulers and teachers. How did he say that the earthly rulers treated people?** (They lord their power over others and make sure that everyone knows that they are the boss.) **How did Jesus say that his disciples were to treat people?** (As if the disciples were the servants of the people.)

Today we talked about some ways people served others in Bible times. What does it mean to serve others in our world today? Allow ample time for responses and examples from the students. **Let's look at some real-life situations to see how we can put Jesus' words into action.**

Classroom Supplies
Bibles

Curriculum Supplies
none

Ready to Grow Up

Before class, make one copy of the situations and cut it into six sections. Copy one "Yes!" bead strip for each student.

Invite the students to share their experiences of the past week with greeting and smiling at an enemy or a stranger. Encourage students to share the details of both their successes and failures in connecting with others. Help the students develop alternate strategies for opening doors with those who continue to resist their attempts at friendship.

Say: **Being a disciple of Jesus is an important job because it brings light to those who live in darkness. Being kind to an enemy brings light. So does being of service to others.** Divide the class into six groups. Distribute the situations from the handout. Assign each group one of the scenarios to study.

Say: **Read each situation then talk about it in your group. Perhaps your group will agree that the best thing to do in this situation is one of the choices listed. Maybe you have a better idea for acting in a way Jesus would expect from his followers.**

Allow several minutes for groups to consult, then allow each group to present their opinions. If time permits, ask the students to think of other situations where they are faced with decisions about serving others or to recall and share

Classroom Supplies
- pencils
- scissors

Curriculum Supplies
reproducible pages 143 and 139 (What You See and Yes! Beads)

times when they have been served.

Have the students think of at least one way they can be of service to someone this week. Suggest that they serve by being the last in line. Distribute the "Yes!" bead strips and pencils. Say: **On the back of this bead strip, write down one way you will be of service to someone this week. When you have done what you have promised to do, roll this strip into a bead and add it to your "Yes!" bead collection.**

Growing Up Every Day

Classroom Supplies
ball of yarn

Curriculum Supplies
none

Say: **At the start of our class today, we joined together in reciting the Scripture memory passage for this unit. Now this unit has come to and end and it is time for us to put the words of the memory passage into action. However, we know that this is not always easy, as we just talked about in sharing our stories about trying to reach out to others. That is why as we try to do as Jesus asks, we also help one another and pray for one another and all other followers of Jesus each day. This time as we pass the ball of yarn around, say a silent prayer of thanks for the person who hands it to you and a silent prayer of blessing for the person to whom you pass it on.** Silently begin the activity as during Memory Activity 2 but with quiet reverence.

When everyone is connected and part of the yarn web, ask the students to recite the memory passage together aloud once more.

YES!
YES!
YES!
YES!
YES!
YES!
YES!
YES!
YES!
YES!
YES!
YES!
YES!
YES!
YES!
YES!
YES!
YES!
YES!
YES!
YES!
YES!
YES!
YES!
YES!

YES!
YES!
YES!
YES!
YES!
YES!
YES!
YES!
YES!
YES!
YES!
YES!
YES!
YES!
YES!
YES!
YES!
YES!
YES!
YES!
YES!
YES!
YES!
YES!
YES!

YES!
YES!
YES!
YES!
YES!
YES!
YES!
YES!
YES!
YES!
YES!
YES!
YES!
YES!
YES!
YES!
YES!
YES!
YES!

YES! BEADS

What You Need
scissors
pencil
glue
crayons or markers

What You Do

1. Color and cut out each strip.
2. With the "Yes!" side of the strip down, begin rolling the strip onto a pencil.
3. When the strip is wrapped completely around the pencil once or twice, apply a thin line of glue down the center of the remainder of the inside of the strip.
4. Continue rolling. When the entire strip has been rolled around the pencil, carefully slide the pencil out.

Yes! I Will Shine

1. Fill in the missing words of Matthew 28:16-20
2. Transfer the numbered letters to the blanks below.
3. Cut out the candle.
4. Join and tape the edges so the candle will stand.

Then the _1_ _ _ _ _ _ disciples went to

_2_ _ _ _ _ _ _ _, to the _3_ _ _ _ _ _ _ _

where Jesus had told them to go. When they saw him,

they worshiped him; but some _4_ _ _ _ _ _ _.

Then Jesus _5_ _ _ to them and said, "All

_6_ _ _ _ _ _ _ _ _ in _7_ _ _ _ _ and on

earth has been given to me. Therefore go and make

disciples of all _8_ _ _ _ _ _ _, baptizing them

in the name of the _9_ _ _ _ _ and of the

_10_ _ and of the _ _ _11_ _12_ _ _ _ _ _, and

_13_ _ _ _ _ _ _ _ them to _14_ _ _

_ _ _15_ _ _ _ _ _ _ _ I have commanded you.

And surely _16_ am with you always, even to the very

end of the age.

Ways We Can Shine!

_ _ _ _ _ _ _ _ _ _
2 1 8 1 15 14 10 16 13 11

_ _ _ _ _ _ _ _ _ _
5 14 3 12 6 10 10 16 14 8

_ _ _ _ _ _ _ _
12 6 13 16 1 8 5 1

_ _ _ _ _
9 6 16 13 7

_ _ _ _   _ _ _ _ _
2 14 14 4   4 1 1 4 10

_ _ _ _ _
3 1 15 5 11

YES! GAME

PYRAMID BLOCK & INSTRUCTIONS

What You Need
- a marker for each player (stone, button, coin)
- pyramid block
- "Yes!" game board

How to Play

Place markers on start. Take turns tossing the pyramid block. Move the number of spaces shown on the bottom of the pyramid.

Players follow the directions given on the board. If a player lands on a solid blue space and can recite Matthew 28:16-20 from memory, the player automatically wins the game. If a player lands on the red space, he must return to start. The first player to reach the finish wins.

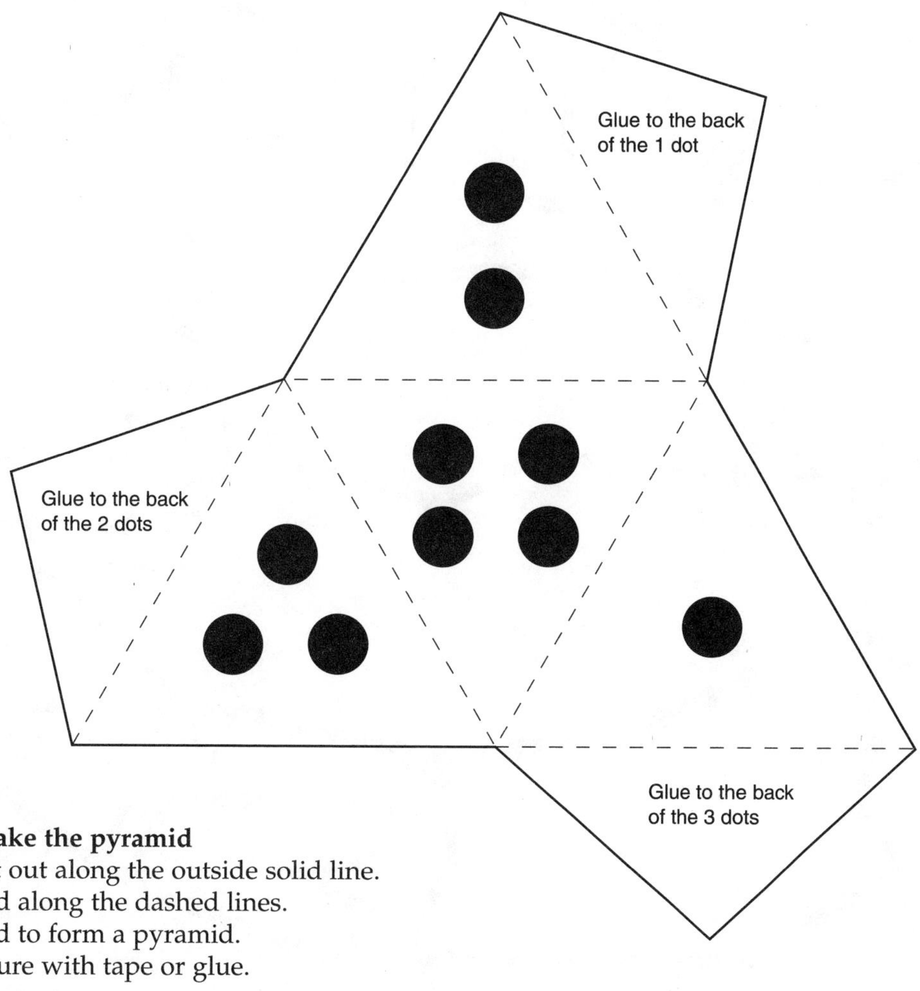

To make the pyramid
1. Cut out along the outside solid line.
2. Fold along the dashed lines.
3. Fold to form a pyramid.
4. Secure with tape or glue.

START
FINISH

What Will You Do About What You See?

Read each scene; then look at the options. If you think the best thing to do is one of the options shown, check the box next to it. If you can think of a better thing to do, check the box next to *Other* and write in your answer.

WHAT YOU SEE: One piece of pie remains. Your mom saved it for you because you had a soccer game right after dinner and missed dessert. You hear your dad ask your mom, "Is there any more of the great pie left?"

WHAT YOU DO:

__ Run to the kitchen and eat the pie; after all, it is yours!
__ Offer to split the last piece with your dad.
__ Ask your mom to bake another pie for your dad.
__ Other: ____________________
____
____
____
____

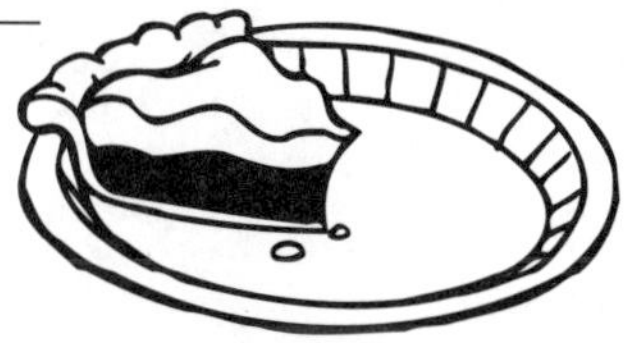

WHAT YOU SEE: Your sister accidentally missed the trash can when she threw some candy wrappers away on her way out the door, and now the dog has gotten into them and left sloppy shreds of paper all over the kitchen.

WHAT YOU DO:

__ Tell your mom what happened, making sure she knows you were not the one who caused it.
__ Yell at the dumb dog.
__ Clean up the mess.
__ Other: ____________________
____
____

WHAT YOU SEE: The crankiest old man in the neighborhood opens his front door wearing his pajamas to get his newspaper. It rolls off his front porch under a shrub covered with snow as you are walking by his house on the way to school.

WHAT YOU DO:

__ Walk by his house quickly, looking the other way as you always do.
__ Walk by laughing.
__ Pause and point to where the newspaper landed.
__ Other: ____

WHAT YOU SEE: You and your family have been working in the yard all afternoon. Everyone is really tired. Your mom goes to the kitchen to make dinner.

WHAT YOU DO:

__ Ask if you could set the table or help in some other way.
__ Watch TV until dinner is ready.
__ Hide in your room.
__ Other: ____________________
____
____
____

WHAT YOU SEE: You score the winning point in your ice hockey game, but your team's goalie is named the most valuable player.

WHAT YOU DO:

__ Congratulate the goalie and be happy that your team won.
__ Take the coach aside and say you think this is not fair.
__ Ask the other team members what they think of this decision.
__ Other: ____
____

WHAT YOU SEE: You've done all your chores perfectly, and your dad says you can go out to play. Your older sister, who likes to tease you, still has to sort out a basket of the family's socks and to study for a big test.

WHAT YOU DO:

__ Yell, "Have fun with the socks!" as you head outdoors.
__ Say, "Gee... it's a shame you have all those socks to sort."
__ Leave her alone and go play.
__ Other: ____________________
____
____

UNIT 6

Growing in Prayer

Unit Aims

Know:	Identify/explain what Jesus taught about prayer.
Feel:	Feel a desire to be close to God through prayer.
Do:	Pray to God in a regular planned time.
Memorize:	Matthew 6:9-13

Why Grow in Prayer?

As Christians, there is no other action that has the potential for changing our lives and the lives of others as prayer. If we help young people catch the vision early, what great things can they accomplish for Christ by the time they are our age? If young people learn how to pray and discipline themselves to pray regularly, prayer will become as natural to them as breathing. And breathing is definitely an essential part of life!

During this month's focus on prayer, students will learn how Jesus prayed, why they should pray, and who they should pray for. Students will keep a prayer journal at home as well as a "prayer concern" and an "answered prayer" list in the classroom. Both will serve to help students develop a personal prayer life.

Summary

Grow up to be like Christ by following his example and teachings about prayer.

- Follow Jesus' example of praying regularly (why pray). Work to establish a pattern of praying daily through this unit.
- Follow the pattern of Jesus' model prayer (how to pray).
- Use the right attitudes; be persistent (how to pray).
- Pray for self, close friends, all believers (who to pray for).

Lesson Aims

Scripture focus	Bible focus	Life focus
Lesson 1 Matthew 14:23; Mark 1:35; 6:46; Luke 3:21; 5:16; 6:12; 9:18, 28; 22:41	Jesus prayed on special occasions and on a regular basis.	Choose a time to pray regularly for the next thirty days.
Lesson 2 Matthew 6:9-13; Luke 11:1-4	Jesus' disciples asked him to teach them to pray.	Pray using the pattern of Jesus' model in a regular prayer time.
Lesson 3 Matthew 6:5-8; 7:7-11; Luke 11:5-13	Jesus taught us to keep asking God for what we need.	Pray with right attitudes in a regular prayer time.
Lesson 4 John 17:1-26	Jesus prayed for himself, for his disciples, and for all believers.	Pray for yourself, others, all believers in a regular prayer time.

Memory Passage: Matthew 6:9-13

"This, then, is how you should pray: 'Our Father in heaven, hallowed be your name, your kingdom come, your will be done on earth as it is in heaven. Give us today our daily bread. Forgive us our debts, as we also have forgiven our debtors. And lead us not into temptation, but deliver us from the evil one.'"

Memory Passage Review Activity

Classroom Supplies
- Bibles
- unruled index cards
- permanent markers
- envelope

Curriculum Supplies
none

Print each word of the memory passage on an index card along with any punctuation that goes with it. The Scripture reference should be on a separate card. Write the entire verse and reference on the front of the envelope to store the cards.

For one player: Shuffle the cards and put the verse in order. Try to beat your time.

For three to six players: One player shuffles the cards and gives each player an equal number of cards face down in front of them. Save enough to put in a drawing pile. Put these cards face down as well.

The first player places one card face up in the center of the playing area. The player to his right tries to put a word card from his pile before or after the card played. If a player does not have a playable word, he may exchange one card with the drawing pile. He may play that card if it works. If he still cannot play, he passes to the next player. The game continues until one player plays all his cards or until no one can play another word card. The winner is the one who played all or most of his cards when play stops. Complete the verse and say it.

Lesson 1

Growing in Prayer

P Is For Praise

Matthew 14:23; Mark 1:35; 6:46; Luke 3:21; 5:16; 6:12; 9:18, 28; 22:41

Bible Focus
Jesus prayed on special occasions and on a regular basis.

Life Focus
Choose a time to pray regularly for the next thirty days.

Growing Up in the Word: Matthew 6:9-13
Set up the following activities for students to begin as they arrive. Greet each student by name. If available, play Christian music quietly during activities that do not require heavy concentration.

Memory Activity 1
Before class, write the first phrase of the memory passage on the board: "Our Father in heaven, hallowed be your name."

Have students sit in a circle. If you have a large class, create multiple circles to play simultaneously. Place groups far enough apart so that they won't be too distracting to one another. Distribute the handout. Groups must work together to reverse each word, starting with the last word and working toward the beginning. When finished, have students read the verses aloud.

Say: **This is a familiar passage of Scripture. What do we call it?** (The Lord's Prayer or the model prayer.) **Where is this passage found in the Bible?** (Matthew 6:9-13.) **Who is speaking here?** (Jesus.) **Jesus gave us this prayer as an example of how we should pray. We're going to look at it piece by piece to help us when we pray.**

Look at the first phrase: "Our Father in heaven, hallowed be your name." This phrase addresses and praises God, the Father. What are some other words that have a similar meaning to the word "hallowed"? (Holy, set apart, respect, worship, praise, awesome.) **All of these words describe the greatness of God's name. God's name is great and holy because God is great and holy.**

Today let's see how many ways we can praise God for who he is, what he's made, or who he's given to us. We will start with the letter "A" and work our

Classroom Supplies
- pencils
- chalkboard
- chalk

Curriculum Supplies
reproducible page 163 (Reverse the Verses)

way through the alphabet. Each person must say all of the words that came before his letter and add a praise that starts with the next letter. We will say: "Our Father in heaven, hallowed be your name because you ________." We'll finish the sentence with a praise for who God is, what he created, or who he's given to you. For example, "Our Father in heaven, hallowed be your name because you are almighty, you made bananas, you made the colors," and so on. Let's see if we can do the whole alphabet! We definitely have a lot to praise and thank God for.

Classroom Supplies
- Bibles
- pencils
- chalkboard
- chalk

Curriculum Supplies
reproducible page 163 (Reverse the Verses)

Memory Activity 2

Distribute the reproducible page and have students follow the directions given there. When finished, have students read the passage together.

Divide the group into two teams. Instruct each team to make a list of words that they could substitute for the word "hallowed." If teams have trouble, instruct them to turn to the book of Psalms and skim the pages for words that David used to praise and describe God. When lists are finished, check each one, looking for far-fetched or wrong ideas.

Next, instruct teams to play a modified version of Hangman. Teams will take turns presenting one word from their list by drawing one blank for each letter on the chalkboard. The opposing team will take turns guessing letters to fill in the blanks. If a letter is guessed correctly, it is put in the correct blank. If not, the letter is written to the side and the team earns a letter from the word "hallowed." Teams have until they have spelled "hallowed," which is eight misses, to guess the word. Teams take turns as long as time permits.

Say: **This is a prayer that Jesus gave to his disciples and to us so that we would know how to pray. The first part of this prayer tells us that we should praise God. What line in this prayer is a praise to God?** ("Our Father in heaven, hallowed be your name.") **Hallowed means holy, so this prayer praises God for being holy. Which of the words that we used in our game today is your favorite way to describe God?**

Classroom Supplies
- blindfold
- masking tape

Curriculum Supplies
none

Why Grow Up?

Before class, use the masking tape to create a simple maze on the floor that is wide enough to walk through.

Say: **This maze looks simple. Who thinks they can get through it easily?** Now pull out the blindfold. **Now, who will try it blindfolded?** Blindfold a volunteer and send him through the course. Have the rest of the class remain quiet as the volunteer tries to walk the maze.

Now, let's try it again. Only this time our volunteer won't have to do it alone. Let the first volunteer choose a partner this time. Have the partner direct the blindfolded volunteer through the maze. The partner will tell the volunteer when to turn left or right, when to keep walking straight, and when they have reached the end. If you have time, allow other pairs to try the maze.

Ask: **Why was the maze easier to do with a partner?** (The partner saw what was ahead and gave directions.) **Sometimes we can feel like we are walking through the maze of life with a blindfold on because we can't see what is**

ahead. Wouldn't it be nice if there was someone who saw what was ahead of us and gave us directions along the way? Yes, we do have someone who knows what is ahead. Who is it? Our God knows what is ahead for each one of us. We need his directions.

How to Grow Up

Before class, write the following Scriptures sets on separate index cards:

1. Luke 3:21; Luke 5:16; Luke 6:12
2. Luke 9:18; Luke 9:28; Luke 22:41
3. Matthew 14:23; Mark 1:35; Mark 6:46

Divide students into three groups. Assign each group one set of Scriptures.

Say: **God has given us all of the directions we need for life. How can we know God's directions for our lives? Where can we find them? Read your verses and decide what they have in common. Write one word on the back of your cards that describes an action of Jesus in all of your verses.** Offer guidance if needed. After each group is finished, have them fold the card and put it in the sack.

Choose one person from each group to draw a card from the bag and read the word written there. Each card should have some form of the word "pray" on it. Say: **One way to know God's directions is through prayer. Our not knowing what is ahead and God's knowing what is ahead is a great reason why we should talk to God every day. We need to keep in touch with God through prayer.**

Who was doing the praying in each of your verses? (Jesus.) **Jesus sets an important example for us and our need to pray. As God's Son, Jesus prayed often. In fact our verses tell us several times Jesus prayed. When were they?** (Morning, evening, all night.) **We also discover several places where Jesus prayed. Name some.** (Mountainside, baptism, private place, alone.) **Did Jesus make time to pray?** (Yes.)

Something that was so important to Jesus that he did it all of the time must be very important for us to do as well. Jesus knew that he needed a partner who could direct his steps through life, and he kept in close contact with that partner. Who was his partner? (God.)

Classroom Supplies
- Bibles
- pencils
- index cards
- a paper sack

Curriculum Supplies
none

Ready to Grow Up

Say: **Jesus prayed regularly, finding private time to talk to God. Where and when can you find time to talk to God?**

Divide students into two to four teams. Taking the slips of paper, each team must write down simple words or phrases about where and when they can pray. Write at least six ideas. When complete, fold the slips of paper and place them in the paper sack. Teams will take turns picking from the other team's bag of ideas. Team members take turns acting out those ideas for their teammates to guess. Set a time limit for each charade and use a stopwatch or timer to regulate it.

Say: **Jesus prayed anywhere and anytime. Our charades show us that we can pray anywhere and anytime, too. It is also important for us to pray regularly. The Bible shows us that Jesus prayed regularly. Today, we want to set a time to pray regularly during this month. Think about a time that you could pray every day while we make our prayer journals.**

Classroom Supplies
- pencils
- paper sacks
- slips of blank paper
- timer or stopwatch (optional)
- string or hinged rings
- index cards
- markers
- hole punches

Curriculum Supplies
reproducible page 164 (prayer journal cover)

Many people use prayer journals to remind them to pray and to keep a record of the way God answers those prayers. If possible, share the benefits you have received from keeping a prayer journal.

Give each student a copy of the prayer journal cover, prayer check up, and eight index cards. Students should cut out the cover, color it, and glue it to an index card. They should do the same with the prayer check up and glue it to the back of the same card. Students should prepare seven more index cards for the coming week. Along the top of one side of each card, have students write the word "Date" and the words "My Prayer." On the reverse side of each card, have students write the word "Date" and the words "How This Prayer Was Answered." Students will write one prayer on the front of the card and the date when they began the prayer. They will write the answer to the prayer and the date on the back of the same card. When cards are prepared, students should punch a hole in the upper left corner of each card and tie them together with string or yarn or with a hinged metal ring.

Growing Up Every Day

Classroom Supplies
- poster board
- chalkboard
- chalk

Curriculum Supplies
none

Before class, prepare the poster board by dividing it into two columns. Label one column with the words "Prayer Requests" and the other column with the words "Prayer Answers." This poster board will be used each week.

Say: **We're going to write our first prayer for the week now. It will be a prayer of praise. Remember, the Lord's Prayer shows us that we should praise God when we pray. What part shows us that?** ("Our Father in heaven, hallowed be your name.")

Let's use this formula. As you explain the format for the praise prayer, write it on the chalkboard. Have students write the prayer on one of their index card journal pages.

"Dear God, You are (praise for who God is). I'm glad you created (name of what God made). Thank you for giving me (name of someone God's given you). In Jesus' name, amen."

Tomorrow, pray this praise prayer again. Add other praises to your prayer journal—at least one every day. If other prayers are answered, write them down as praises. Write how praying this prayer makes you feel.

We are also going to keep a list of prayer concerns for our class. Is someone you care about sick? Do you have a big test coming up? Are you very sad about something right now? Is there a problem that just won't go away? Do you have a bad habit that you want to break? Are you fighting a lot with your brother, sister, or parents? Share prayer concerns. Write them down on the poster board for the classroom. Save room for each week's new concerns. Now, pray for each concern mentioned. Have a student volunteer read the memory passage at the end of the prayer while everyone is still quiet.

Ask: **At what time will you pray every day?** Have students share when they have decided to pray every day. **Great! Remember, you can pray about anything, anywhere, anytime just as Jesus did. Hold on to your prayer journals. Let's see what happens when you remember to pray every day and write down what happens. Don't miss out on this opportunity to see God work right before your very eyes!**

Lesson 2

R is for Repent

Luke 11:1-4; Matthew 6:9-13

Bible Focus
Jesus' disciples asked him to teach them to pray.

Life Focus
Pray using the pattern of Jesus' model in a regular prayer time.

Growing Up in the Word: Matthew 6:9-13
Set up the following activities for students to begin as they arrive. Greet each student by name. Play Christian music quietly during activities that do not require heavy concentration.

Classroom Supplies
- Bibles
- drawing paper
- crayons or markers

Curriculum Supplies
none

Memory Activity 1
Divide Matthew 6:9-13 into sections so that each student or group of students receives one section. Students will design pictures or symbols to represent their part of the passage. For example: "Our Father in heaven" could be represented by clouds with the word "Dad" written among them.

When all sections are designed, let students take turns guessing what each symbol or picture represents. Then line up the artwork in order. Let the class identify what each symbol or picture represents. Then point to each picture one by one and recite the passage.

Say: **Jesus gave us this prayer to teach us how to pray. In his example, Jesus prays to God. We pray to God as well. Look at the prayer and name some reasons why we would pray to Jesus' father?** (He lives in heaven. He provides our food. He can forgive our sins. He is the one who can deliver us from evil.) **God is powerful, and he is in charge of all there is. It's awesome that our powerful God cares for us!**

Memory Activity 2
Before class, copy the following memory passage sections and suggestions for actions. Cut them into separate strips.

1. "This, then, is how you should pray." *Wag the pointer finger at the class and then fold hands to pray.*

Classroom Supplies
none

Curriculum Supplies
memory passage
phrases listed here

2. "Our Father in heaven." *Extend arms wide, to include the whole group, and then point to heaven.*
3. "Hallowed be your name." *Bowing, perhaps with arms extended in front of you.*
4. "Your kingdom come." *Place hands on head as a "crown" and then motion with a "come here" gesture.*
5. "Your will be done on earth as it is in heaven." *Look up, extend arms up and then down to earth.*
6. "Give us today our daily bread." *Cup hands together, holding them out in front of you as if waiting for someone to give you something, and then pretend to eat.*
7. "Forgive us our debts, as we also have forgiven our debtors." *Use two people for best results. The first person should look up, look sorrowful, and bow head. Then the second person walks up, looks sorrowfully at the first person, and bows her head. The first person extends her arm, pats the second person's head or shoulder, and smiles.*
8. "And lead us not into temptation." *Cover your eyes with one hand and act like you're pushing or pulling away from something with your other hand.*
9. "But deliver us from the evil one." *Act like you're picking something up and carrying it quickly away.*

Assign parts to individual students or to small groups of students to pantomime the memory passage. Section seven needs two people if using the suggested action. Give students time to decide what actions they will use to demonstrate their section of the memory passage. Arrange students in order, and have all of the students recite the memory passage while performing the actions. If time permits, have each individual or group teach their actions to the rest of the class.

Say: **Jesus prayed so much that his disciples wanted to learn to pray. So Jesus used this prayer to teach them how to pray. Look at the prayer and name some things that we should include in our prayers.** (We should tell God that he is great. We should ask him to provide the things we need. We should ask for forgiveness of sins and deliverance from evil.)

Why Grow Up?

Classroom Supplies
pencils

Curriculum Supplies
reproducible page 164
(Break the Code strips)

Make one copy of the reproducible for each student. Cut off the code key from the bottom half of the copies. The top puzzle portion will be handed out first. The bottom code key portion will be handed out later. Do not give students the verse reference or any clues at first.

Ask: **Can you break this code?** Hand out the copies, and let students work on it a few minutes. **How's it going?** Allow answers. **Would it help to have a clue?** Tell them one code clue.

Ask: **Did that help?** Allow answers. **Would you like another clue?** Give another clue or hand out the code key next. At some point, hand out the code key. The puzzle answer follows: "Lord, teach us to pray" (Luke 11:1).

Say: **Sometimes it's fun to try to figure out a puzzle with no clues or only a few clues. After all, a puzzle is only a game. However, it's not much fun to try to figure out life without a clue. Isn't it great that God gives us more than clues? He hands us the answers. Sometimes we find the answers in the Bible. Sometimes we find the answers in prayer. Not only did Jesus show us that he prayed regularly, he told us how to pray.**

How to Grow Up

Before class, write the acrostic for the word pray on the board.

P—Praise God
R—Repent
A—Ask for needs
Y—Yield to God's will

Divide the class into two groups. Assign one group Luke 11:1-4 and the other group Matthew 6:9-13. Instruct each group to look at the actual prayer and, using the acrostic, see how their assigned passage divides up under those four categories. If you have a large class, divide evenly into more groups, giving out the Luke and Matthew passages equally. For discussion, pair up one Luke passage group with one Matthew passage group until all groups are matched to compare their findings.

As an option, make copies of the Luke and Matthew Scripture passages and hand them out to the designated group. Have students circle and label the section that fits under each category.

Praise God: Luke 11:2, "hallowed be your name"; Matthew 6:9, "hallowed be your name."

Repent: Luke 11:4, "forgive us our sins, for we also forgive everyone who sins against us"; Matthew 6:12, "Forgive us our debts, as we also have forgiven our debtors."

Ask: Luke 11:3, "Give us each day our daily bread"; Matthew 6:11, 13 "Give us today our daily bread" and "lead us not into temptation, but deliver us from the evil one."

Yield to God's Will: Luke 11:2, "your Kingdom come"; Matthew 6:10, "your Kingdom come, your will be done on earth as it is in heaven."

After the groups have compared their passages, discuss the findings together. Ask: **Do you think Jesus meant for us to pray using the exact words he used here?** Discuss. **No, he wanted us to follow the pattern, not to use his exact words. Did you see a pattern in the prayers that you read?**

What part of the passages fit under "Praise"? Discuss. **What are other words we can use to praise God?**

What part of the passages fit under "Repent"? Discuss. **What are debts?** (Sins.) **Think about your life this past week. Now don't answer aloud, but think of at least one sin that you need to ask God to forgive.** Allow quiet moment. **God wants us to recognize and admit our sins.**

What part of the passages fit under the "Ask" category? Discuss. **What are other needs we can ask God for? Think of physical, emotional, and spiritual needs.**

What parts of the passages would fit under "Yield to God's Will"? Discuss. **What does "yield" mean? Yielding is knowing that God's way is not always our way and telling him that we will accept his answer to our prayer, even if it is "no" or "not now." Yielding is an important part of prayer. When we yield to God, we let him know that we trust his answer for our lives.**

Classroom Supplies
- Bibles
- paper
- pencils
- chalkboard
- chalk

Curriculum Supplies
none

Classroom Supplies
- index cards
- markers
- hole punch

Curriculum Supplies
none

Ready to Grow Up

Say: **How was your prayer time this past week? Did you keep your regular prayer time and pray every day? Did you use your prayer journals? What did you pray about? What prayers were answered?** Share your prayers and answers too. **Our God is a powerful God. He always hears and answers our prayer.**

Last week we wrote a prayer of praise in our journals. Did you pray your praise prayer again? Did any of you write a new praise prayer? The model prayer Jesus gave us—or the Lord's Prayer—shows that we should praise God when we pray. What part shows that? ("Hallowed be you name.")

The model prayer also shows us that we should admit our sins to God and ask for his forgiveness. Remember what the prayer says? "Forgive us our debts as we forgive our debtors." Let's write a prayer of repentance. Distribute one index card to each student. Have students write the prayer on one of their index card journal pages. As you explain the prayer, write the formula on the chalkboard.

Say: **Let's use this formula: "Dear God, I'm sorry that I disobeyed again this week. I know you were disappointed when I (admit what you did wrong). I don't want to keep disobeying you. Help me stop doing (what you did that was wrong). Thank you for loving me so much that you forgive me, even when I mess up again. In Jesus' name, amen."**

Lead students to prepare six more index cards for their prayer journals. Do so according to the instructions given with lesson one of this unit. When cards are prepared, have students add them to the book of cards made last week.

Classroom Supplies
classroom prayer and answer list

Curriculum Supplies
none

Growing Up Every Day

Say: **It's time to update our classroom prayer list. First, let's review what we've written here.** Review last week's prayer concerns and ask for updates concerning each one. Ask: **Are there any answers to these prayers?** Write those under the answer column of the poster board.

Ask: **Who has a prayer request to add to our list?** Write each new prayer concern on the same list as last week's list.

Choose students who are willing to pray aloud for specific items. Have the designated students mention the prayer requests in order, exactly as they are written, when it's their turn.

Say: **Keep up your prayer journals this week. Write your prayers in your prayer journal. Keep track of the answers to your prayer requests. You may miss how God is answering your prayers if you don't pay attention. Pray regularly and see what happens.** Ask a volunteer to read Matthew 6:9-13. **Let's say the memory passage as our volunteer reads it.**

Lesson 3

Growing in Prayer

A Is for Ask

Matthew 6:5-8; 7:7-11; Luke 11:5-13

Bible Focus

Jesus taught us to keep asking God for what we need.

Life Focus

Pray with right attitudes in a regular prayer time.

Growing Up in the Word: Matthew 6:9-13

Set up the following activities for students to begin as they arrive. Greet each student by name. Play Christian music quietly during activities that do not require heavy concentration.

Memory Activity 1

Before class, write the following attitudes on separate index cards: loving, disrespectful, shy, pushy, angry, surprised, happy, sarcastic, humble, proud.

In class, distribute index cards. Instruct students to keep the content of their cards a secret. Students will read the memory passage in a manner that communicates the attitude written on their card. Give students time to think about how their assigned attitude sounds. Give suggestions as necessary. When ready, have students take turns reading the memory passage with the "attitude." Other students guess the attitude.

Say: **We've just seen a lot of attitudes. Which of these attitudes are appropriate ones for prayer? God tells us that he wants us to pray with a humble attitude. When we have a humble attitude, we know that we need God. Today, we'll learn more of what God has to say about our attitudes when we pray.**

Classroom Supplies
- index cards
- marker

Curriculum Supplies
none

Memory Activity 2

Before class, write the memory passage on separate index cards. Make two sets. Remove the same ten key words from each set. Suggested words to remove include: hallowed, name, kingdom, bread, forgive, debts, lead, temptation, deliver, evil. With these removed cards, set up a word bank. During the game students will give definitions to the banker, which is you, in order to receive the

Classroom Supplies
- index cards
- marker

Curriculum Supplies
none

words that are missing from their passage.

In class, divide the students into two teams. Give each team one set of the memory verse cards. At the signal, the groups put the index cards in order. When the groups discover the ten missing words, they are to send one student at a time to the word bank to collect a word. Students do this by asking for the missing word by definition. Students may not use the word in the definition. The word banker then gives the student the word he has described. The student returns to his group, and places the word in its correct place. At that time, the next player goes to the word bank. Continue until each group has collected all ten missing words.

Say: **Asking is an important skill in life. If we want something, we usually have to ask for it. How do your parents know what you want?** (You ask.) **If you want a snack, you ask. If you want a scooter, you ask. If you want your back rubbed, you ask. What parts of our memory passage ask God for something?** (Give us our daily bread; forgive us; lead us not into temptation; deliver us from evil.) **When we need something from God, he wants us to ask him for it.**

Classroom Supplies
treats

Curriculum Supplies
none

Why Grow Up?

Place the plate or container of treats in plain view of the class. Now start talking about the treats. If you baked the treats, tell the class where you bought the ingredients, where you found the recipe, how you made the treats, and so on. If you bought the treats, tell the class where you shopped, how you decided on this treat, what your favorite treat is, and so on.

If someone asks you for a treat at this point, jump to the asterisked dialogue, do as it says, then come back to where you left off, continuing the line of questions until everyone has asked for a treat. If no one has asked you for a treat yet, go on with these questions: **What's your favorite snack? Do you like to have snacks? What do you think these snacks smell like? What do you think they taste like? Are you feeling hungry? Do you think these treats would taste good?**

If no one has asked for a treat by now, continue with these questions: **Why do you think I brought these treats? Who do you think they are for? How do you think you could get one?**

*If at any time during the previous discussion, someone asks if he can have one of the treats, first ask: **What's a polite word to use when you're asking for something?** If he says "please," hand that student a treat and go on with the discussion. When the rest of the class catches on, others will begin to ask politely for a treat. Stop and give out the treats to each one who asks politely, one to a customer, however. After each student has asked for a treat, stop the questions, and then discuss the following:

Say: **I had these treats here just waiting for you. What did you have to do to get one?** (Ask politely.) **What could have happened if you didn't ask?** (May not have received the treat.) **Was it hard to ask?** Allow comments. **Let's find out how we should ask God for what we need.**

How to Grow Up

Divide the class into three groups. Give one group Luke 11:5-13, the second group Matthew 6:5-8, and the third group Matthew 7:7-11.

Each group will read and then illustrate their portion of the Scripture. Students may divide their poster board into sections to illustrate two or more ideas if they wish. Set a time limit and let students know when half the time is up and when time is almost up. Each group will then explain what their illustration represents, and then one person from that group will read the group's Scripture.

Ask: **What do we learn about prayer from this passage? In the Luke passage, we learn that persistence or boldness is honored and that we must ask. In the Matthew 6 passage, we learn that God does not approve of prideful praying and that he wants prayers to be real, private, and for him, not for the approval of others. In Matthew 7, we learn that we must ask to receive, that everyone who asks will receive, and that God wants to give us good gifts.**

Classroom Supplies
- Bibles
- poster boards
- colored markers

Curriculum Supplies
none

After all presentations and conclusions are discussed, continue with the following: **All three passages teach us that we must ask for what we want or need. God knows what we need before we ask, so why must we ask at all?** Allow comments. **Asking reminds us who is giving us what we need; it shows that we trust God to provide what we need; and it reminds us of who owns it all anyway!**

What attitude must we have for God to answer our prayers? (Respectful, humble, knowing who we are praying to.)

What does God want us to ask him for? Discuss. **We can ask God for anything but mostly he wants us to ask for a relationship with him. He wants us to ask for the Holy Spirit.** Read Luke 11:13.

Ask: **Should we give up on praying if God doesn't seem to answer our prayers the first time?** (No.) **Perhaps God wants to see that we are sincere and persistent with our prayers. Your prayer journal will help you understand that as you keep it over time. I wonder what we have missed because we haven't asked?**

Ready to Grow Up

Classroom Supplies
- pencils
- index cards
- hole punch

Curriculum Supplies
reproducible page 165 (Asking Game)

Say: **How was your prayer time this past week? Did you pray every day? Did you use your prayer journals? What did you pray about? What prayers were answered?** Share your prayers and answers too. **Our God is a powerful God. He always hears and answers our prayers—in his own time.**

Last week we added a prayer of repentance to our journals. Did you pray your repentance prayer again this past week? Did any of you write a new repentance prayer? The model prayer Jesus gave to us shows us that we should admit our sins to God and ask forgiveness when we pray.

The model prayer also shows us that we should ask God for what we need. Let's practice asking for what we need.

Before distributing the handouts, fold them in half. Give the class these instructions: **Everyone will begin at my signal. These handouts have a list of statements that you must have other students sign if they can fulfill it. Have each person sign his name by the statement that he fulfills. Try to use each person's name at least once. Only use a name twice if you must.** Distribute handouts and give the signal to begin. Set a time limit and when time is up, see who has the most signed statements.

If your class is small, consider combining with another class for this activity, or visit other classes even adults, asking permission ahead of time for their participation.

Ask: **How did you find out who fit each statement?** (We had to ask.) **Did you get all of the names by asking just one time?** (No, we had to ask several times.)

This game is another reminder of what happens when we ask and what happens when we don't ask. Of course, this is just a game, but what good gift might you be missing out on if you're not asking God regularly and respectfully for what he already has planned for you?

Let's write an asking prayer this week. Distribute index cards. **Write your prayer on the index card.** As you explain the formula for the asking prayer, write it on the board.

Say: **Let's use this formula: "Dear God, thank you for being my friend. I pray that your Spirit will always stay with me. Today I ask you for (fill in area of need). Thank you for hearing my prayer and answering it in your own way, which I know is always best for me. In Jesus' name, amen."**

Distribute six more index cards to each student to add to their prayer journals. Have students prepare them as described in lesson one of this unit. When cards are prepared, have students add them to their prayer journals.

Growing Up Every Day

Classroom Supplies
none

Curriculum Supplies
none

Ask: **What are some of the good gifts that are mentioned in the Luke and Matthew verses?** Allow comments. **What are some other good gifts that you have?** Allow comments. **Good gifts can be many things: health, peace, a clear mind, food, a place to sleep, and friends.**

It's time to update our classroom prayer list. What good gifts are we going to ask for today? What do we need to pray about this week?

Write the prayer concerns and answers for today on the classroom list, saving room for next week's concerns. Review previous concerns and any answers to prayer. Pray for each new or recurrent concern mentioned. Let designated students pray about the specific concerns, then you close.

Have a student read the memory passage. Ask the rest of the class to say it along with the reader. Say: **Before you go, answer this question: What must you do to receive what God has for you?** (Pray or ask!)

Lesson 4

Growing in Prayer

Y Is for Yield

John 17:1-26

Bible Focus
Jesus prayed for himself, for his disciples, and for all believers.

Life Focus
Pray for yourself, others, all believers in a regular prayer time.

Growing Up in the Word: Matthew 6:9-13
Set up the following activities for students to begin as they arrive. Greet each student by name. Play Christian music quietly during activities that do not require heavy concentration.

Memory Activity 1
Instruct students to rewrite Matthew 6:9-13 in one of the following forms: make it rhyme, set it to music, say it as a radio announcer would, or read it dramatically. Let students choose which method they prefer. Limit the number per group, however, and create a new group if needed. That group may use the same forms if they wish.

Classroom Supplies
- paper
- pencils
- cassette tape recorder and cassette tape (optional)

Curriculum Supplies
none

If you have deaf interpreters available, ask them to teach a group how to sign the passage. Do you have a student or adult who speaks another language? Let them read the passage in that language, teaching the class key words like "pray," "Jesus," and "Father in heaven." When students are ready, let them present their work.

Say: **By putting Matthew 6:9-13 into another form, you helped it to be understood better by someone. That's kind of like translating it into another language. Does anyone know what languages the Bible was originally written in?** (Hebrew, Aramaic, and Greek.) **How did we get the Bible in our language?** (Someone had to translate it for us.) **It's a big job to translate the Bible into another language. Did you know there are still many people who do not have the Bible in their own language? Bible translators are busy working to translate it and even to create written languages for some people.**

It is God's will that everyone come to know him. When we pray for the work of Bible translators, we are praying for God's will. Let's pray for the

Bible translators who are working to bring God's word to everyone. If you know any Bible translators, pray for them specifically.

Memory Activity 2

Classroom Supplies
- chairs
- cassette tape
- cassette tape recorder
- paper
- marker
- tape

Curriculum Supplies
none

Before class, record the memory passage on a cassette tape. Speak clearly and in a rap-style rhythm. Make a sign that reads "Yield."

In class, set up a chair for all students minus one. Tape the "Yield" sign to one chair. Play this version of musical chairs. Gather students around the chairs. Play the memory passage recording. Have the students say the words along with the tape. Shut the tape off at some point. At this time the students must scramble to find a seat. One will be left out and one will sit in the chair marked yield. The person in the yield chair will give up (yield) his chair to the person who did not find a chair. The person who yielded will then sit out the next round. For the second round, remove a chair. The student who sits in the yield chair may give his place either to the person without a chair or to the person who was put out of the game in the first round. In the third round, the student in the yield chair will have a choice of three students to give his chair to. Continue in this manner until one student is left.

Say: **While playing this game, we learned the definition of the word "yield." What does the word "yield" mean?** (Give up what you want or have for someone else. Let someone else go first.) **Yielding is a part of praying. Our memory passage contains a phrase that shows us what yielding to God is. What is that phrase?** ("Your kingdom come, your will be done.") **When we give up our will or what we want to do God's will or what God wants, then we are yielding to God. Yielding means we accept how God answers our prayers.**

Why Grow Up?

Classroom Supplies
- a clear glass
- an egg (hard-boiled or not)
- water
- spoon
- measuring tablespoon
- salt

Curriculum Supplies
none

Before class, try this at home with the glass you intend to use in class to make sure you don't need more salt than is called for here. Glass size can make a difference.

Fill the glass half full of water. Keep the egg in a safe place nearby, along with other supplies.

Say: **We've learned a lot about prayer in the past weeks. We know we should pray regularly and respectfully if we hope to let God guide our lives. Did you ever wonder how your prayers can help someone else, though?**

Let's say that this egg represents someone you love. Think of his or her name. Who does this egg represent? Allow a few answers. Put the egg in the glass of water. **What happened to the egg?** (It sank.) **No one must be praying for (names of people students offered). Who will help me pray for them?**

Let your volunteer add two tablespoons of salt to the water and stir the water carefully until all of the salt dissolves.

Ask: **Now what happened to the egg?** (It floats.) **The salt represents the prayers we pray for each other. God can really lift you up when you are down. He hears the prayers of his people. Did you know that Jesus prayed for you and me when he was on this earth? Jesus lifted us up!**

How to Grow Up

Before class, make one copy of the reproducible for each student. In class, have students read John 17:1-26 silently before handing out the worksheet. Let students work separately, as pairs, or as groups to complete the page.

Ask: **Who is praying during the whole passage?** (Jesus.) **How many times does a form of the word "pray" appear on the worksheet?** (Five, not including the title.)

What is Jesus praying about in this passage? Jesus is praying for eternal life for his disciples and all believers. Look at the phrases you underlined. What are some of the things that Jesus prayed about his followers? (He prayed for their protection from the evil one. He asked that God sanctify them by the truth so that the world may believe.) **How are we to be sanctified?** (By the truth.) **What does sanctified mean?** (Set apart for holy use or for God's use.) **Where do we find the truth?** (God's Word.) **Where can we find God's words today?** (The Bible.)

Where did you put the star? What did Jesus pray about for you and me as believers? Read verses 20, 21, which say: "those who will believe in me." **Jesus prayed for you to believe and to tell others about him way back when he walked this earth! How cool is that?**

How does God feel about those who believe in his Son? (He wants them to be with him in Heaven to see his glory.)

This prayer of Jesus' shows us that we should pray for ourselves, for others, and for believers everywhere.

Classroom Supplies
- Bibles
- pencils
- markers

Curriculum Supplies
reproducible page 166 (Jesus Prays)

Ready to Grow Up

Say: **How was your prayer time this past week? Did you keep your regular prayer time? What was your attitude when you prayed? Did you use your prayer journals? What did you pray about? What prayers were answered?** Share your prayers and answers too. **Our God is a powerful God. He always hears and answers our prayers in his own time.**

Last week we added an asking prayer to our journals. Did you pray your asking prayer again this past week? Did any of you write a new asking prayer? The model prayer Jesus gave to us shows us that we should ask God for what we need when we pray. We should especially ask to have a relationship with him.

The model prayer also shows us that we should yield to God when we pray. When we ask for God's will to be done, we are yielding to God. When we pray for what God wants, then we are yielding to God. We give up what we want for what God wants. Can you think of another time when Jesus yielded to what God wanted? (In the Garden of Gethsemane the night before he was crucified, Jesus prayed for God's will.) Read Matthew 26:39-44.

Say: **In the prayer we read today, Jesus prayed for what God wants. Jesus prayed for himself, for his disciples, and for all believers. Jesus yielded to what God wants.**

Let's write a yielding prayer this week. Distribute index cards. **Write your prayer on the index card.** As you explain the formula for the yielding prayer,

Classroom Supplies
- index cards
- pencils
- hole punch

Curriculum Supplies
none

write it on the board.

Say: **Let's use this formula: "Dear God, I love you and want what you want. I pray for myself that I will yield (name area where you will yield to God). I pray for (name of friend) that he will yield (name area where he will yield to God). I pray for all believers that they will yield (name area where all believers will yield to God). In Jesus' name, amen."**

Distribute six more index cards to each student to prepare for their prayer journals. When cards are prepared, have students add them to their prayer journals.

Growing Up Every Day

Classroom Supplies
- a globe or map of the world
- pictures or names of the missionaries you know or support
- classroom prayer list
- marker

Curriculum Supplies
none

Say: **It's time to update our classroom prayer list.** Discuss the prayer concerns and answered prayers. Add any new answers to prayers. Say: **We are going to add our missionaries to our prayer list.** Take the list of missionaries and locate where they are serving on the map or globe of the world. Also have students choose a missionary to specifically pray for this week. Students should make a prayer journal card for this missionary.

Lead students in prayer. Begin by having students pray for the missionaries. Thank God that Jesus prayed for us before we were even born. Ask God to help the students trust him and see what happens when they pray continually, each day, and in the right way. Pray they will notice God's answers and thank him for them. Thank God for the students and pray that they will always love Jesus.

Say: **We've had many prayer requests and answered prayers this month. We have followed Jesus' example for our prayers. We've set a time to pray every day. We've learned a formula for prayer: Praise, Repent, Ask, Yield. We've prayed for ourselves, for others, and for believers everywhere. It's been a great month! Now that our unit on prayer is over, let's not stop praying.** Have everyone recite Matthew 6:9-13 together to close the session.

Reverse the Verses

Reverse each word, starting with the last word of the passage and working backward. The last word will be the first word and so on.

“.eno live eht morf su reviled tub ,noitatpmet otni ton su dael dnA .srotbed ruo nevigrof evah osla ew sa ,stbed ruo su evigroF .daerb yliad ruo yadot su eviG .nevaeh ni si ti sa htrae no enod eb lliw ruoy ,emoc modgnik ruoy ,eman ruoy eb dewollah ,nevaeh ni rehtaF ruO”

Write your translation below. Include the punctuation too.

Break The Code

"

___ ___ ___ ___ ,   ___ ___ ___ ___ ___   ___ ___

■ ☆ ✳ ❖ ,   ✢ ✿ ✠ ❁ ☞   ● ✪

___ ___   ___ ___ ___ ___ ."

✢ ☆   ✖ ✳ ✠ ☛

Code Key

A = ✠	C = ❁	D = ❖	E = ✿
H = ☞	J = ▲	L = ■	O = ☆
P = ✖	R = ✳	S = ✪	T = ✢
	U = ●	Y = ☛	

Prayer Check Up

- I pray regularly.
- I pray with the right attitude.
- I ask God for what I need.
- I pray for others.
- I truly believe God hears me when I pray.
- I accept whatever answer God sends.
- I thank God often.
- I praise God often.
- I look for God's answers every day.

ASKING GAME

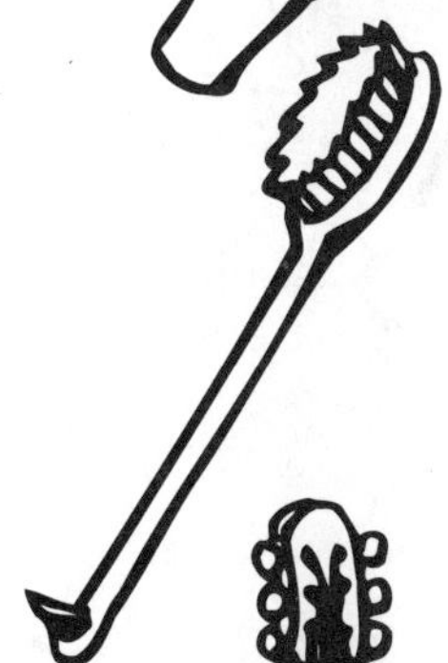

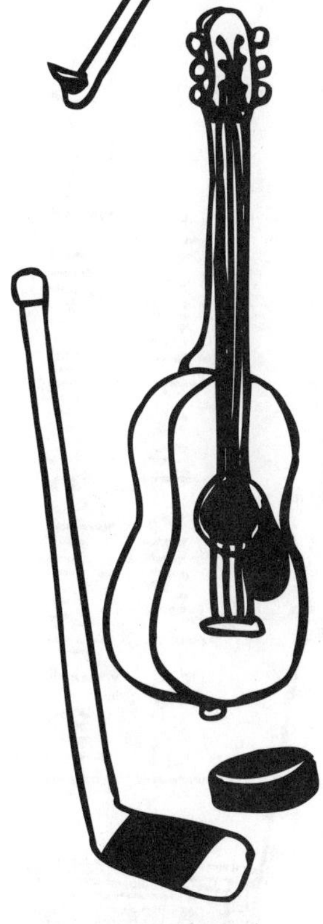

Find a person to fit each one of these statements. Ask that person to sign his name.

1. Loves to wrap gifts. ____________________
2. Prayed at least once today. ____________________
3. Has a birthday soon—when? ____________________
4. Writes in his or her prayer journal. ____________________
5. Will whistle "Jesus Loves Me" now. ____________________
6. Learned to pray as a small child. ____________________
7. Says the alphabet backward to you. ____________________
8. Recites Matthew 6:9-13 from memory to you. ____________________
9. Shows you that Star Trek "Spock" thing with his or her fingers. ____________________
10. Tells about an answer to a prayer. ____________________
11. Likes to eat broccoli. ____________________
12. Tells you two things about prayer. ____________________
13. Has not brushed teeth yet today. ____________________
14. Tells who the speaker is in Matthew 6:9-13. ____________________
15. Plays guitar or another stringed instrument. ____________________
16. Names one true thing that God does not want us to do when we pray. ____________________
17. Likes to play hockey. ____________________
18. Brought Bible today. ____________________
19. Knows how to skateboard. ____________________
20. Promises to pray about today's prayer concerns this coming week. ____________________

Jesus Prays for Himself, His Disciples, and All Believers

(John 17:1-26)

- *Circle all forms of the word pray.*
- *Underline all phrases where Jesus prays for his followers.*
- *Put a star by Jesus' prayer for you.*

Jesus Prays for Himself

Read John 17:1-5. Fill in the missing words.

Now this is eternal life: that they may _________ you, the only true God, and Jesus Christ, whom you have sent.

Jesus Prays for His Disciples

Read John 17:6-19. Fill in the missing words.

I pray for ______________. I am not praying for the ___________, but for those who you have given me, for they are yours. . . . Holy Father, _______________them by the power of your name—the name you gave me—so that they may be one as we are one. . . . My prayer is not that you take them out of the world but that you protect them from the _________ _________. They are not of the world, even as I am not of it. Sanctify them by the ___________; your __________ is truth.

Jesus Prays for All Believers

Read John 17:20-26. Fill in the missing words.

My prayer is not for them alone. I pray also for those who ___________believe in me through their message, that all of them may be one, Father, just as you are in me and I am in you. . . . Father, I want those you have given me to be ________ me __________ I am, and to see my _____________, the glory you have given me because you loved me before the creation of the world.

UNIT 7

Growing in Goodness

Unit Aims

Know: Identify thoughts, actions, and attitudes that are good.
Feel: Feel a desire for the things that are good.
Do: Choose one way to grow in goodness.
Memorize: Philippians 4:8, 9

Why Grow in Goodness?

Helping children grow in goodness in today's world is a challenge. Many influences around them contradict and mock goodness. The world portrays goodness as unpopular, weird, nerdy, and wrong. Sadly, children are confused about how to respond to choices between good and evil. A child's exposure to glamorous evil narrows the distinction, in their thinking, between good and evil. What is evil becomes cool. These elementary years are crucial because children are forming their preferences for life. Will they have preferences toward good or toward evil?

This unit is designed to help children understand and evaluate the influences around them. It will help them start to recognize the difference between good and evil. It will give them a foundation of goodness in their hearts by teaching them what God wants them to think about!

The New Testament teaching about goodness centers on the fact that goodness starts in the mind. Being good involves the heart before it involves actions. Certainly, anyone can go through the motions of being good. But only those who "think about such things" will grow up in every way to be like Christ.

Summary

Grow in the grace and knowledge of Jesus Christ by thinking about and practicing what is good.

- Know what is good.
- Put goodness on everyday, like clothes.
- Live in the Spirit, so you can do what is good.
- Keep thinking about and practicing goodness.

Lesson Aims

Scripture focus	Bible focus	Life focus
Lesson 1 Romans 12:9-21	Cling to what is good and overcome evil with good.	Grow in goodness by 1) identifying what goodness is and 2) telling the difference between good and evil.
Lesson 2 Colossians 3:12-17	Clothe yourself with good things.	Grow in goodness by choosing a way to "wear" it.
Lesson 3 Galatians 5:19-25	Goodness comes from being godly, being like God.	Grow in goodness by living in the Spirit.
Lesson 4 Ephesians 5:8-20	Think about and practice what is good.	Continue to grow in goodness by thinking about it and practicing it.

Memory Passage: Philippians 4:8, 9

"Finally, brothers, whatever is true, whatever is noble, whatever is right, whatever is pure, whatever is lovely, whatever is admirable—if anything is excellent or praiseworthy—think about such things. Whatever you have learned or received or heard from me, or seen in me—put into practice. And the God of peace will be with you."

Classroom Supplies
- corrugated cardboard
- small nails (about the size used in hanging pictures)
- marker
- glue
- penny

Curriculum Supplies
none

Memory Passage Review Activity

Size a rectangle piece of cardboard about 12 by 16 inches. Glue a 1-inch wide double layer strip of cardboard around the edges to create a frame. Push fifteen nails into the cardboard in six rows, alternating rows of three nails with rows of two nails. Be careful not to push the nail through the cardboard. Divide the memory passage into fifteen sections including the reference. Write each phrase beside a nail in order from left to right, row by row. Players shake and move the game board so the penny slides or hops around the nails in the correct order of the memory passage. Players say the phrases aloud as the penny slides by each one.

Lesson 1

Growing in Goodness

Idenfifying Goodness

Romans 12:9-21

Bible Focus

Cling to what is good and overcome evil with good.

Life Focus

Grow in goodness by identifying what goodness is and by telling the difference between good and evil.

Growing Up in the Word: Philippians 4:8, 9

Set up one or both of the following activities for students to do as they arrive. Greet the students by name, explain the activities, and invite them to join the fun.

Memory Activity 1

Classroom Supplies
- balloons
- permanent marker
- masking tape
- poster board

Curriculum Supplies
none

Before class, use the masking tape to outline an area about 3 feet square in a corner of the room. Inflate forty balloons and use the marker to mark five each with the following words: true, noble, right, pure, lovely, admirable, excellent, praiseworthy. Write the words of Philippians 4:8, 9 on the poster board and display it in the classroom.

To play, make a large playing area in the room. Push chairs and tables out of the way. Distribute the balloons randomly around the room. Shout out one of the eight words listed on the balloons. Students search the balloons in the room looking for a balloon with the chosen word. When a student finds the word, that student rubs the balloon to create static cling and places the balloon so it will stick to her head. The student then runs to the area marked with masking tape. When all five students have arrived in the taped area, the group reads the memory passage aloud in unison, pausing at the chosen word. At that time, the five students with balloons shout the word in unison. Then the group finishes the verse. Repeat using a different word. Adjust the activity for your group size and time. Use fewer balloons for a small group. Choose two or more words per round for a shorter game.

Say: **Our Scripture passage today tells us to cling to what is good. What good things have you been clinging to? Why are these things good? Why does the Bible tell us to think about these things? We stuck these balloons to our**

heads to remind us that we are to think about these good things, and we are to cling to what is good.

Memory Activity 2

Classroom Supplies
- poster board
- marker

Curriculum Supplies
none

Before class, write the words of Philippians 4:8, 9 on a sheet of poster board. Display it in the lesson area.

Gather the students in a circle. Read Philippians 4:8, 9 by short phrases, and have students repeat after you. Set the verses to your own rhythm. Say one short phrase at a time. Wait for the students to repeat. Then move to the next short phrase. Vary your voice to match what you are saying. For example, use a noble voice for the word noble. Use a lovely voice for the word lovely. After your demonstration, have students lead the class in repeating the verse. Go around the circle, each student leading a different short phrase from the passage.

Say: **We've used our voices today to make sounds that match what our memory passage is about. But our verse doesn't tell us to sound true, noble, right, pure, lovely, admirable, excellent, or praiseworthy. What does it tell us to do with things that are true, noble, right, pure, lovely, admirable, excellent, and praiseworthy?** Give kids time to respond. **Yes, we are to think about them and practice them. Why does God want us to think about these things that are good and worthy of praise?** (Things that are true, noble, right, pure, lovely, admirable, excellent, and praiseworthy are from God. Doing this thinking and practicing brings us peace.)

Why Grow Up?

Classroom Supplies
- two brownie mixes and the necessary ingredients
- napkins

Curriculum Supplies
none

Before class, make two batches of brownies. To one brownie mix, add 1 cup of salt. Keep the two batches separate, but make an appealing presentation of both batches.

Say: **Most of us know the difference between good tasting and bad tasting food. Let's name some foods that taste good.** Give kids time to respond. **What do we do when we taste something good?** Give kids time to respond. **Now let's name some foods that taste bad. What do we do when something tastes bad?** Give kids time to respond.

Bring out the brownies that were made with the salt. **Now look at these brownies. Are brownies a good tasting food or a bad tasting food?** Give kids time to respond. **Yes, we all agree—they taste good. Can we tell how these brownies will taste by looking at them? No, we can't be sure. We'd have to taste them to find out for sure.** Distribute the brownies and napkins and let the students take a bite. Wait for their reactions, then ask: **What's wrong?** Take a brownie and taste it yourself. Say: **This is awful. It smells good; it looks good, but it tastes awful. What does this mean?** Allow time for responses. **Can food look good but taste bad? Yes!**

Our goal this month is to grow in goodness. We grow up in Christ when we grow in his goodness. Growing in goodness takes knowing the difference between good and evil. We tell the difference between good and bad food by testing it with our taste buds. We tell the difference between good and evil by testing it against what God says. Sometimes things that are evil can look good, but they aren't good. We have to watch out. We have to be careful. We

have to know what God says is good. Then when we run into those evil things that look good, we can do just what we did with these awful brownies—spit them out!

Bring out the second plate of brownies. **Here's another plate of brownies. I'm sure these are good. I'm the cook. I made them. They are good.** Distribute brownies and napkins. **God is the cook of good. He is the one who can tell us what is good.**

How to Grow Up

Classroom Supplies
- Bibles
- chalk and chalk board or dry erase markers and white board

Curriculum Supplies
none

Divide the class into three groups. Assign one of the following passages to each group: Romans 12:9-13; Romans 12:14-16; and Romans 12:17-21. Instruct the groups to create a dramatic reading that will communicate the meaning of the Scripture passage. The reading should contain actions and a variety of voices. For example, some sentences may be presented by the entire group, by the girls, by a solo voice, or by duet voices.

Ask groups to present their dramatic readings. After the presentation, make two columns on the chalkboard. Use the headings: "Hate What Is Evil" and "Cling to What Is Good." Say: **From Romans 12:9-21, let's make two lists—things that are evil and things that are good.** The evil list would include cursing, pride, conceit, repaying evil for evil, revenge, being overcome with evil. The good list would include devotion to one another, honoring others above self, zeal and spiritual fervor, joyful hope, patience in affliction, prayer, sharing with those in need, hospitality, blessing those who persecute, rejoicing with those who rejoice, mourning with those who mourn, living in harmony, associating with people of low position, living at peace with everyone, leaving room for God's wrath, giving food and drink to enemies, overcoming evil with good.

Ask: **What is the difference between good things and evil things?** (Good things bring honor and glory to God. Evil things don't bring honor and glory to God.) **Look at this list of things that don't honor God. What other things could we add to the evil list?** Add the students' suggestions. **Look at this list of things that honor God. Do any of these good things surprise you? Why would God instruct Christians to do these good things? Are these good things easy to do? What other good things could we add to this list?** Keep both lists on the board to refer to during the challenge time.

This passage in Romans gives us a very important message. Let's look again at verse 21. The world is full of good things as well as evil things. We can choose the good, or we can choose the evil. What does verse 21 tell us to choose? (Good is stronger than evil!) **That's great news! Evil is all around us; it even seems to be stronger than good. But it isn't; goodness is stronger than evil. We can overcome evil by doing what is good and by choosing good things. Good things honor and glorify God.**

Ready to Grow Up!

Say: **We have a special mission for this week. In order to complete our mission, we'll need some help from a special wallet.** Distribute materials and

Classroom Supplies
- scissors
- pens or pencils
- markers

Curriculum Supplies
copies of Inspector Goodness wallet page 187 and encouragement cards page 190

direct the students to make their wallets. If time permits, they may color the wallets with markers. When the wallets are complete, discuss the cards. The cards fit into the section of the wallet with a flap.

Say: **Look at all the important features in this wallet. We have made these wallets to help us with our mission. But what is our mission? Look at your wallets and find the mission assignment.** Ask a student to read the mission statement: To grow in goodness in order to be like Jesus.

Say: **Look at the cards. When should we use these cards? What if a classmate makes a good grade on a test or receives a special award? What card will you give your classmate?** Allow students to respond. **When you do that, you will be doing what God says is good—you will be rejoicing with one who rejoices.**

What if a classmate needs your prayers? What card will you give your classmate? Allow students to respond. **When you do that, you will be doing what God says is good—you will be faithful in prayer.**

What if you see a classmate treat the teacher with kindness and respect? What card will you give your classmate? Allow students to respond. **When you do that, you will be doing what God says is good—honoring others above ourselves.**

What if a classmate hurts us, teases us, or is mean to us? What card will you give your classmate? Allow students to respond. **When you do that, you will be doing what God says is good—blessing those who curse you. You will be overcoming evil with good.**

Not only are we going to look for goodness this week, we are going to do good things as well.

How can we honor others above ourselves? (Treat the teacher with kindness and respect, let other students ahead of us in line, give others a turn on the playground equipment.) **When we do these things, we are doing what God says is good—honoring others above ourselves.**

Ask each student to write his last name on his badge. Say: **We are now agents of Inspector Goodness. Raise your right hand and let's say the Inspector Goodness pledge together.** Do so.

Let's pause right now and ask God to open our eyes to the goodness around us and to give us opportunities to overcome evil with good. Lead the students in a prayer time.

Growing Up Every Day

Classroom Supplies
none

Curriculum Supplies
none

Say: **Growing up in Christ means growing in his goodness. There is so much evil around us every day that it is easy to get mixed up with it and to be overcome by it. That is why God's Word tells us to cling to what is good. What does it means to cling? Balloons with static cling to people. Sand burrs cling to our pant legs. Small children cling to their parents. God tells us to cling to what is good.**

We all want goodness in our lives. In order to have goodness, we must choose to do good things and think good thoughts. Philippians 4:8, 9 tells us that if we think about good things, God's peace will be with us. Lead students in reciting the memory passage. Then close by leading students in reciting the Inspector Goodness pledge found on their wallets.

Lesson 2

Growing in Goodness

"Wearing" Goodness

Colossians 3:12-17

Bible Focus

Clothe yourself with good things.

Life Focus

Grow in goodness by choosing a way to "wear" it.

Growing Up in the Word: Philippians 4:8, 9

Set up one or both of the following activities for students to do as they arrive. Greet each student by name, explain the activities, and invite her to join the fun.

Memory Activity 1

Write the following phrases of the memory passage on separate index cards. Make two sets. Attach the index cards in order around the outside edges of the two tables, one set per table. Place the item listed with the phrase next to the index card with that phrase.

Philippians 4:8, 9—Finally, brothers (sunglasses); whatever is true (one ring); whatever is noble (one ring); whatever is right (one ring); whatever is pure (one ring); whatever is lovely (one ring); whatever is admirable (one ring); if anything is excellent or praiseworthy (one ring); think about such things (hat); Whatever you have learned or received or heard from me (socks); or seen in me (belt); put into practice (coat); and the God of peace will be with you (shoes).

Divide students into two teams. Assign each team a table. Choose a player from each team to start. At the signal, the two players are to dress themselves in the items on the table. They are to start at the beginning of the passage and proceed in order until they have put on all the items. As they go, they are to recite the verse. As they dress in each item, they are to say the phrase that accompanies it. For example, a player puts on sunglasses while saying, "Finally, brothers." Team members should encourage their players by reciting the phrases with them. The first player to finish receives a point for her team. After each race, return the items to their places and choose another pair to race. Play until all the students have had a turn "putting on goodness." When finished, have the group recite the memory passage together. If you have a large class, set up a third table

Classroom Supplies
- two tables
- index cards
- two pairs of sunglasses
- fourteen finger rings
- two hats
- two pairs of socks
- two belts
- two coats
- two pairs of shoes

Curriculum Supplies
none

and have the students race in groups of three.

Ask: **Would anyone like to guess what the point of this race was? Of course, it was fun, but does it have any meaning for us? What does dressing have to do with goodness? Today's lesson Scripture tells us to clothe ourselves with goodness. We can choose to wear goodness just as we choose our clothes and jewelry.**

Memory Activity 2

Classroom Supplies
- scissors
- markers
- one 6-foot strip of butcher paper for each group
- cellophane tape
- various colors of construction paper
- one thesaurus for each group
- Bibles

Curriculum Supplies
none

Divide the class into two or three small groups and distribute supplies. Instruct groups to draw a life-sized figure on the butcher paper. (Have a student lie on the paper to be traced.) Each group will dress its figure in goodness. After the groups have decided what their figures will wear (a dress, a sports uniform, scuba gear, school clothes), they are to make the clothing out of construction paper. Several pieces of paper will have to be joined together to make an article of clothing. Ask the students to label each piece of each article of clothing with one of the qualities from the memory passage that we are instructed to think about. Each word may be used only once. Students should consult the thesaurus to discover synonyms for each of the eight qualities from Philippians 4:8, 9. When finished, students should give their figure a name that fits with the teaching of Philippians 4:8, 9 (like Noble Norm, Terri Truth, or Robby Right) and attach it to the wall.

Say: **We dressed our figures in construction-paper clothes that are labeled with the good things we've been instructed to think about. Let's read some of the words you have written on your characters.** Have groups explain why they named their characters the way they did. **What does dressing have to do with thinking about good things? Today's lesson Scripture tells us to clothe ourselves with goodness. We can choose to wear goodness just as we choose our clothes and jewelry.**

Why Grow Up?

Classroom Supplies
- one student-sized girl's vest
- one adult-sized woman's vest
- one student-sized suit coat
- one adult-sized suit coat
- one student-sized hat
- one adult-sized hat
- six signs with the following words: truth, lies, forgiveness, unforgiveness, thankful, unthankful

Curriculum Supplies
none

Ask for three female and three male volunteers. Give one boy and one girl the hats. Give two girls the vests. Give two boys the suit jackets. Ask all six students to perform the following tasks: walking, sitting, running, jumping jacks, writing name on the chalkboard, wiping off the table, stacking chairs, bending over to pick up an item. As the students perform tasks, comment about the difficulty those wearing the oversized clothing are having. Also comment that those wearing the fitted clothing don't seem to be having trouble.

Say: **Thinking about and practicing God's goodness is like choosing what we wear every day. What kinds of clothes do you choose to wear? Would any of us choose to wear clothes that would fall off of us? No, we want clothes that fit, clothes that we don't have to worry about falling off, clothes that won't get caught in the car door or in a locker or on a desk, and clothes that allow us to see what's going on.**

Choosing to think about and practice what is good is like wearing clothes that fit. We don't have to worry about the trouble that comes with evil.

Let's say that this suit jacket that fits represents truth and this oversized suit jacket represents lies. Have the students hold the truth and lies signs. **When we practice God's goodness by speaking the truth, we don't have to worry about consequences; we don't have to worry about getting caught in a lie. Truth is a perfect fit. However, when we practice evil by speaking lies, we have to worry about consequences; we have to worry about getting caught. Speaking lies is like wearing clothes that are too big. We trip over them. They get caught in furniture and doors.** Show the excess material of the oversized coat that could get caught in a doorway, locker, or desk. **Speaking lies is a tangled mess.**

The same is true of forgiveness and unforgiveness. Have the students wearing the vests hold the signs. **If we forgive, then we don't have to worry about not being forgiven by God. We won't be hindered by this excess baggage.** Show the excess material in the oversized vest. **But if we don't forgive, then we'll have a heavy heart because God won't forgive us.**

Give the students wearing the hats the thankful and unthankful signs. Say: **Gratitude is also a perfect fit. It is always good to be grateful for what we have and for what God has done for us. But if we are ungrateful, then we might as well be wearing clothes that don't fit. Ungratefulness will eventually get us into a big mess. It will keep us from seeing and receiving the good things God has for us.** Pull the oversized hat down over the student's eyes.

The good news is that we can choose to put on the good things of God!

How to Grow Up

Classroom Supplies
- Bibles
- pencil
- paper
- dictionaries

Curriculum Supplies
none

Have the students find Colossians 3:12-17 in their Bibles. Read the passage aloud. Divide the class into two groups: boys and girls. If you have a large group, have two groups of boys and two of girls. Instruct each group to create a clothing store based on Colossians 3:12-17 and Philippians 4:8, 9. Suggest that the girls create a boutique and the boys a sporting goods store. Both groups are to create a line of clothing and accessories that will communicate what "goodness clothing" God's people should wear. Encourage the use of alliteration—same beginning sounds for names of products (see the samples below). Students should also define each product. Provide dictionaries for students to look up the definitions of words they don't understand.

Compassion Cold Cream—smooth out the wrinkles of insensitivity.

Humility Helmets—wear one for protection against pride.

Gentleness Guards—guard against roughness and harshness.

Patience Perfume—one spritz and you won't mind waiting.

Also encourage students to create a name and an advertising slogan for their store.

After a few minutes, gather the groups to give their sales pitches. Praise each group for their creativity.

Say: **Wouldn't it be great if these were real products? Wouldn't it be great to go to the store and buy patience to wear? It would make living for Jesus easier, wouldn't it?**

In today's Scripture passage, we are told to clothe ourselves with the good things of God. Our Scripture passage and our memory passage tell us what some of those good things are. But how are we to wear them like we wear

clothes? It isn't our bodies that wear God's goodness. It is our souls. We can dress our souls with God's goodness by using our minds to put the good things of God on our souls. We'll discuss how to do that at our meeting of the agents of Inspector Goodness.

Classroom Supplies
none

Curriculum Supplies
- Reproducible page 188
- Inspector Goodness pledge and mission written on a sheet of poster board

Ready to Grow Up!

Say: **It's time to call to order the meeting of the agents of Inspector Goodness. Agent** (name of child) **will lead us in the Inspector Goodness pledge. Now Agent** (name of child) **will lead us in reciting our mission.**

Now we will report on the activities of this past week. Give students a chance to tell of their experiences of looking for goodness. **What good things did you see? What good things did you do?** Encourage each student to report.

Say: **You've done a good job this week growing in goodness. Excellent. Now it is time to receive your assignments for this week. Each morning this week while you get dressed, you are to dress your souls in goodness as well. As agents of Inspector Goodness, we have certain good qualities that we must wear. Let's review the good qualities from our Scripture passage today. They are compassion, kindness, humility, gentleness, patience, thankfulness, and love. Now let's review the good qualities from our memory passage. We are to think about whatever is true, noble, right, pure, lovely, admirable, excellent, and praiseworthy.**

Distribute the reproducible from page 188. Say: **Here's Inspector Goodness. He's has clothed his soul with goodness. We're going to follow his example and clothe our souls with goodness. Each morning as you dress, say the Inspector's prayer. Now, let's practice clothing our souls with goodness.**

Lead the students to say the Inspector's prayer with you and pantomime the actions of dressing.

Lord, I put on my shirt and clothe my soul with compassion. Compassion helps comfort those who are having a bad day.

Lord, I put on my pants and clothe my soul with kindness. Kindness treats others the way I want to be treated.

Lord, I put on my socks and clothe my soul with humility and gentleness. Humility lets others take the first turn. Gentleness speaks softly to others and listens without arguing.

Lord, I put on my shoes and clothe my soul with patience and forgiveness. Patience waits willingly until others have taken a turn. Forgiveness gives up bad feelings I have toward those who hurt me.

Lord, I put on my belt and clothe my soul with thankfulness. Thankfulness is happy with what it has and doesn't keep asking for more.

Lord, I put on my coat and clothe my soul with love. Love treats people in ways that will win them to Jesus.

Lord, I put on my hat and promise to think about whatever is true, noble, right, pure, lovely, admirable, excellent, praiseworthy.

If a student doesn't normally wear one of the articles of clothing such as a belt, hat, or coat, encourage her to walk through the actions of putting them on and say the prayer.

Say: **When we clothe our souls with goodness, God's peace is with us. Goodness will help us in whatever we do, whether in word or deed, to do it all in the name of Jesus. When we do everything in the name of Jesus, we grow up to be like Jesus. Let's pause right now to dedicate the week ahead to growing up in Christ by clothing our souls with goodness every day.**

Growing Up Every Day

Ask volunteers to dress in the same articles of clothing they dressed in for "Why Grow Up?" Say: **Wearing God's goodness is much like wearing clothes—clothes for our souls. Each morning this week as you get dressed in goodness, remember that God's goodness fits perfectly. When we wear his goodness, we won't be hindered by excess baggage.** Show excess material on oversized vest. **We won't get tangled in a mess.** Show excess material on oversized coat. **And we will always be able to see where God is leading us.** Pull oversized hat down over volunteer's eyes.

Say: **Wearing God's goodness begins with thinking about God's goodness. Our memory passage tells us that God's peace and goodness begins with what we are thinking. Let's recite the memory passage together.**

Classroom Supplies
volunteers and clothing from "Why Grow Up?"

Curriculum Supplies
none

Lesson 3

Growing in Goodness

Living in Goodness

Galatians 5:19-25

Bible Focus
Goodness comes from being godly, being like God.

Life Focus
Grow in goodness by living in the Spirit.

Growing Up in the Word: Philippians 4:8, 9
Set up one or both of the following activities for students to do as they arrive. Greet each student by name, explain the activities, and invite him to join the fun.

Classroom Supplies
- tagboard
- poster board from previous lessons with Philippians 4:8, 9 written on it
- masking tape
- sauce pan
- wooden spoon

Curriculum Supplies
none

Memory Activity 1
Before class, make nine right footprints and nine left footprints from tagboard. Write the following key words on the footprints, alternating right and left prints: brothers, true, noble, right, pure, lovely, admirable, excellent, praiseworthy, things, learned, received, heard, me, practice, God, peace, you. If possible, cover the footprints with clear adhesive-backed paper.

Lay the footprints in order out on the floor of the classroom. Use a pattern of your choice for walking. For example, at one point, have the students make a scissors step or a waltz step. Students will walk the footprints while saying the memory passage. The words on the footprints are hints to help them with the passage. Have the students refer to the poster board if they need more help.

As the students walk the path, beat a sauce pan with a wooden spoon to keep beat. Each time the students walk through the path, increase the rate of the beat.

Ask: **Which was easier: saying the memory passage while keeping step to a slow beat or while keeping step to a fast beat?** (Keeping step to a slow beat gave us more time to think about the words to the memory passage. Keeping step to a fast beat made it more difficult to think about the words to the memory passage.) **We had to think hard just about making the right steps! Whether it was slow or fast, we kept in step with the beat by following the beat.**

Today's lesson instructs us to keep step with God's Spirit. What do you think it means to keep in step with God's Spirit? (We keep in step with God's Spirit when our spirit follows what God says is good.) **Our memory passage tells us several things that God says is good. What are they?** Give kids time to respond.

Memory Activity 2

Divide the class into pairs. Give each pair one copy of the reproducible page and twenty-four pennies. The students are to cover each of the twenty-four words on the page with a penny. The students play by taking turns flipping over three pennies at a time. If the three words are a set, that player keeps the three coins. Each set contains one of the eight words from Philippians 4:8, 9 and two synonyms that define it. Sets can be matched by sight—all three members of each set contain the same picture. The players should read the words of each set aloud so they can define the eight words of Philippians 4:8, 9.

Classroom Supplies
twelve pennies for each student

Curriculum Supplies
reproducible page 189

Talk through the list of eight things that Philippians 4:8, 9 tells us to think about, and ask the students to give an example of each one. If the students have trouble, use one of the synonyms from the activity to help define the term. Some descriptions may apply to more than one word. Some ideas follow:

1. **true**, a student is honest about what happened to the broken lamp;
2. **noble**, a student gives his time after school to help another student understand math;
3. **right**, a student follows the rules of the game;
4. **pure**, a student says no to watching a TV show with bad language;
5. **lovely**, a student thanks God for the beautiful weather;
6. **admirable**, a student congratulates another student for winning an award;
7. **excellent**, a student studies hard to make an A on a test;
8. **praiseworthy**, a student makes a list of things to praise God for.

Why Grow Up?

Before class, cut up several pieces of fruit and put a toothpick in each piece. Leave several pieces of fruit intact for the demonstration. Set out the fruit plate for the students to snack on while you have your discussion.

Classroom Supplies
- several pieces of edible fruit
- several pieces of realistic plastic or silk fruit
- a realistic silk plant
- a living plant
- napkins
- toothpicks

Curriculum Supplies
none

Show the class the plants. Say: **One of these plants is living. One is not living. Which do you think is which?**

Let's make a list of the ways we could discover which plant is which. Make the list and then walk through each suggestion to determine which is real and which is silk. The students could touch or smell the plants. They could look for which was planted in dirt. They could examine the leaves and stems.

Show the class the fruit. Say: **Some of this fruit is for eating and some is for decoration. Which is which? How can we test this fruit?** (Students could take a bite of the fruit.)

Say: **In order for us to discover which plant is living and which is not, we had to use our knowledge of the difference between living and not living. Could we have discovered which plant was living if we didn't know what a living plant is? How do we know what a living plant is? We live in a world that is full of living plants. Since we live among them, we know what they are.**

In order for us to discover which fruit is for eating and which is for decoration, we had to use our knowledge of the difference between food and decoration. Could we have discovered the difference between the fruit if we didn't know what food is? We need food every day. Since we need food to live, we know what food is.

In order for us to know the difference between good and evil, we must live in God's Spirit. We've already discovered that God is the source of goodness. He is the one who tells us what goodness is. When we live in his Spirit, we will know what goodness is. When we keep in step with the Spirit, we will learn what goodness is. We can know the difference between goodness and evil just as we know the difference between living and non-living plants as well as food and decorations. Our goal this month is to grow in goodness. We want to grow up in every way to be like Jesus Christ. When we grow in goodness, we grow up to be like Jesus.

Classroom Supplies
two sheets of poster board

Curriculum Supplies
none

How to Grow Up

On one poster board in bold letters, write the word "sin." On the other, write the word "Spirit." If possible, divide the class into nine groups. Each group should have at least two members. If your class is small, pair up students and leave some topics uncovered.

Assign each group one of the following "Spirit vs. Sin Actions" from Galatians 5:19-25:

1. love and hate;
2. joy and jealousy;
3. peace and discord;
4. patience and impatience;
5. kindness and anger;
6. goodness and making trouble;
7. faithfulness and unfaithfulness;
8. gentleness and harshness;
9. self-control and unrestraint.

Instruct each group to create a short skit or pantomime with two endings—one that demonstrates the action led by the Spirit and one that demonstrates the action led by sin. Groups should begin by naming actions that result from their assigned pair of words. They should also discuss times when they have seen others demonstrate both actions. From this they should choose or create a situation to use for the basis of their skit. Walk among the groups and help them with definitions and situations as needed.

When ready, have the groups present their skits. Have them present their skits with the sin ending first. Then have them present their skits with the Spirit ending. Introduce each sin skit by saying the following: **Sometimes we want to act like this.** Introduce each Spirit skit with the following: **Since we are keeping in step with the Spirit, we act like this.**

After each presentation, write the fruit of sin on the sin poster board and the fruit of the Spirit on the Spirit poster board.

Say: **Our goal is to grow in goodness. How do we know what is good and what is sin?** (God tells us in his Word.) **God is goodness. He tells us what is good and what is evil. Find Galatians 5:19-25 in your Bibles. Let's read what God says is good and what God says is bad.** Read the verses aloud. **Now look at our posters. Do they match what God says is good and what God says is bad?** Add any information from Scripture that is missing on the posters.

Say: **Keeping in step with the Spirit means that we know what God wants, and we follow it.**

Ready to Grow Up!

Before class, ask the students to bring the lyrics to some of their favorite secular and Christian music to class. This activity hinges on using the lyrics to songs that your students are listening to. Be prepared in case students forget their music. Bring lyrics to the songs you know your students are listening to.

Say: **Let's begin our meeting of the agents of Inspector Goodness with the Inspector Goodness pledge and motto.**

Now we will report on the activities of this past week. Give students a chance to tell about wearing goodness. **How did wearing goodness like clothes help you think about and practice goodness? Did you experience God's peace this week?**

Today, we are going to talk about how we can keep in step with God's Spirit. In order to keep in step with the Spirit, we must learn to evaluate the things in our lives according to what God says is good and what God says is evil. We've made a list of the fruit of sin and another list of the fruit of the Spirit on posters. We're going to look for this fruit in the lyrics of the music we listen to.

Choose the lyrics from a Christian song first. Read them aloud. Ask: **What is this song about? Is this subject something that helps you to think about whatever is true, noble, right, pure, lovely, admirable, excellent, or praiseworthy? Does the story of the song show the fruit of the Spirit—love, joy, peace, patience, kindness, goodness, faithfulness, or self-control? Does the story of the song show the fruit of sin—hate, jealousy, discord, impatience, anger, making trouble, unfaithfulness, harshness, or unrestraint? Is this a song that keeps in step with God's goodness or with evil? If we are going to grow in goodness, is this a song we should listen to?** Give kids time to respond.

Talk through the lyrics of several songs as time permits. Bleep out any inappropriate words, but point out that songs with words that have to be bleeped out do not keep in step with God's goodness. Gently help students evaluate what they listen to according to what God says is good. If time permits, discuss television shows and video games.

Say: **Your mission this week is to keep in step with the Spirit by checking to see if the music you listen to and the television shows you watch keep in step with God's Spirit. Let's ask God to help us with our mission this week.** Lead the students in a time of prayer.

Classroom Supplies
lyrics to students' favorite Christian and non-Christian songs

Curriculum Supplies
none

Growing Up Every Day

Say: **Since we are to keep in step with the Spirit, we are going to label these shoestrings with words that remind us of what God says is good. Here are the words that we are going to write on our shoestrings: true, noble, right, pure, lovely, admirable, excellent, praiseworthy, love, joy, peace, patience, kindness, goodness, faithfulness, self-control.** Write the words on chalkboard. Have the students use markers to write the words on their shoestrings.

Say: **This week tie your shoestring to your jacket, book bag, or wear it in your shoe. When you need to be reminded what God says is good, look at your shoestring and remember that these things will keep you in step with the Spirit.** Close by having students recite the memory passage Philippians 4:8, 9.

Classroom Supplies
- wide shoestrings
- permanent markers

Curriculum Supplies
none

Lesson 4

Growing in Goodness

Practicing Goodness

Ephesians 5:8-20

Bible Focus

Think about and practice what is good.

Life Focus

Continue to grow in goodness by thinking about it and practicing it.

Growing Up in the Word: Philippians 4:8, 9

Set up one or both of the following activities for students to do as they arrive. Greet each student by name, explain the activities, and invite her to join the fun.

Classroom Supplies
- index cards
- marker
- stopwatch
- snacks

Curriculum Supplies
none

Memory Activity 1

Before class, write the eight qualities from Philippians 4:8, 9 on separate index cards. Make two sets—one for each group. In class, divide the students into groups of eight and form pairs within each group. If you don't have enough students for two groups of eight, divide the class into two equal groups. Then form pairs. Adjust the group size so that everyone has a partner. This may make one group larger than the other. If one student doesn't have a partner, have a leader or helper join him.

Have the students draw a card from the card stack and keep the contents quiet. Pairs take turns, while others students watch, trying to get their partner to guess the word on their card. One partner gives clues to the word while the other partner guesses. Students may use words or motions as clues, but they may not use the word in their clues. Give students a set amount of time to guess the word. Use the stopwatch to time. For those who do so successfully, award a snack and a chance to say the memory passage from memory.

Ask: **According to our memory passage, what are we to put into practice?** (Everything we have received, seen, or heard from the writer—Paul.) **What might those things be?** (Things that are true, noble, right, pure, lovely, admirable, excellent, and praiseworthy.) **Name some ways to practice these things. What promise does this verse give us if we think about and practice these things?** (Peace.)

Memory Activity 2

Before class, write the letters of the word "peace" on separate slips of paper, tape one letter to the bottoms of five chairs. For a larger class, make two sets.

In class, distribute one sheet of paper to each student. Ask the students to number their papers from 1 to 10. As you read the following phrases of the memory verse (the order is scrambled), students will write them on their papers. Challenge the students to think about where each phrase fits into the passage. They should estimate where that phrase would fit on their papers if the entire passage was written out. Then they are to write the phrase in the place. Students try to produce the memory passage written in its correct order.

Finally, brothers, whatever is true/if anything is excellent or praiseworthy/whatever is noble, whatever is right/Whatever you have learned or received/whatever is pure, whatever is lovely/or heard from me, or seen in me/whatever is admirable/put into practice/And the God of peace will be with you./Philippians 4:8, 9

After all the phrases have been read and students have written them in "order" on their papers, read the passage to check how well they did. When finished, have students look under their chairs for a letter. When all the letters are found, unscramble them to reveal the word peace.

Say: **Our memory passage gives us a promise. What is the promise?** (Peace.) **If we follow the instructions of this verse, the God of peace will be with us. Let's think of reasons why peace would be the result of thinking about and practicing the instructions of this verse. Why would we have peace if we tell the truth? Why would we have peace if we do what is right? Why would we have peace if we keep ourselves pure? Why would we have peace for doing noble things like being generous? Why would we have peace for thinking about what is lovely? Why would we have peace for doing things that are admirable? Why would we have peace for doing excellent work? Why would we have peace for praising God?** (All of these things bring peace because we won't have the worry of hurting another person, keeping our story straight, or suffering the consequences of wrong actions. When we think about and practice goodness, we don't have to worry about the trouble that comes with thinking about and practicing evil.)

Classroom Supplies
- pencils
- paper
- cellophane tape

Curriculum Supplies
none

Why Grow Up?

Say: **Here are the balls from some popular sports. Do any of you like to play one or more of these sports? I'd like to see a demonstration of how these balls are used.** Divide the class into pairs. Give each pair one ball and the extra equipment if needed. Ask each pair to demonstrate how to use their assigned ball. Give them a few minutes to plan their demonstration. Then have students present their demonstrations.

Say: **Wow! Those were great demonstrations! How many of you are good basketball players? football? baseball? golf? tennis? soccer? What makes a person good at any sport? Yes, some have natural talent. But everyone has to practice to become good at any sport. Practice is what makes a person good at any skill.**

Classroom Supplies
various sports balls and basic equipment such as basketball, football, soccer ball, baseball and bat, volleyball, tennis ball and racquet—one for every two students

Curriculum Supplies
none

Imagine this. You are playing in a close basketball game. The score is tied. Ten seconds remain on the clock. You have the ball under your basket. You shoot! What happens? If you've practiced shooting, you have a good chance of making the points. If you haven't been practicing, you might make the shot by chance, not skill. If your team is in that situation, you want the best shooter on the team to have the ball. That person will probably be the player who practices the most. Practice not only makes us better at the game, it also makes the game easier and more exciting to play.

How do you practice? Yes, you repeatedly perform the moves needed to play the game. In basketball, you dribble and shoot. In football, you block and pass. Each sport has its own set of skills that must be mastered to be good at the game.

Our memory passage and our lesson Scripture both tell us to practice what is good. How do we practice goodness? Come to practice and find out!

Classroom Supplies
Bibles

Curriculum Supplies
none

How to Grow Up

Say: **Let's begin our practice by quoting the memory passage, Philippians 4:8, 9.** Have the students quote the passage together in unison.

Say: **The first step in learning to play a game is learning the rules. We learn the rules about growing in goodness by looking at what God says is good. We read the rule book—the Bible. We learn the difference between good and evil, and we decide to cling to what is good.**

Open your rule books (Bibles) to Ephesians 5:8-14. Read the passage or have a volunteer do so. **These verses have a key phrase that tells us to learn the rules about goodness. What is it?** (Find out what pleases the Lord.)

What do we learn in these verses that pleases the Lord? (Live as children of the light. Be good, righteous, and truthful. Have nothing to do with the fruitless deeds of darkness, but instead, expose them.)

Let's continue by reading Ephesians 5:14-20. What is the key phrase in this passage that tells us to learn what goodness is? (Understand what the Lord's will is.)

What do we learn in these verses that the will of the Lord is? (Live as wise not unwise. Make the most of every opportunity. Don't be drunk. Be filled with the Spirit. Speak songs, hymns, and spiritual songs to one another. Sing to the Lord. Give thanks for everything.)

When we learn the difference between good and evil, we have a choice. That choice is between being children of the light and being children of the darkness. Children of the light decide to grow in God's goodness—they decide to cling to what is good. When we decided to cling to what is good, we found that a good way to cling to what is good was to wear goodness like clothes. Wearing goodness like clothes helps us to keep in step with the Spirit. When we keep in step with the Spirit, we choose things that match what God says is good. When our actions and speech match what God says is good, then we are practicing goodness.

The last two verses of our passage tell us two more ways we can practice goodness. Let's look at those verses again. What do they tell us to do to practice goodness? (Speak to one another with psalms, hymns, and spiritual songs—

this means we are to encourage one another. We are also to give thanks for everything.) **Two ways we can practice goodness are by encouraging one another and giving thanks.**

Ready to Grow Up!

Say: **Practice not only includes learning the rules of the game, it also includes performing the skills of the game. Let's do that now.**

Let's call to order the agents of Inspector Goodness by saying the Inspector Goodness pledge and the motto.

Now we will report on the activities of this past week. Give the students a chance to tell about the songs, movies, and TV shows that they evaluated according to God's goodness. **Did you discover any songs or movies that didn't keep in step with God's Spirit? What did you do about them?**

Today, we are going to practice two more ways to practice goodness. Depending on your group size, form one or more groups for the following activity. Have groups stand in a circle. Give each group a different ball. **When we play a team sport, we like to encourage our teammates when they play well. We also like to encourage them when they are having a bad day and perhaps feeling a little awkward. We're going to pass this ball around. When you receive the ball, say one phrase you could use to encourage a teammate.** Ask the groups to pass the ball as they would for that sport. For example, the basketball can be passed with a bounce. The volleyball can be volleyed around the circle. The football can be hiked. Examples of encouraging words for teammates follow: Good job! Way to go! You're hot! Good shot! Excellent! Awesome! What a move! You're getting it! We like it! You work hard! Your hard work is paying off! I'm glad we're on the same team! and so on.

Say: **Remember, practicing what is good means saying good things to each other. When we encourage each other, we are practicing good. The words we use to encourage each other in sports are the same words we can use to encourage each other in life. Encouraging each other is a excellent way for us to practice goodness.**

Expressing thanks is another excellent way for us to practice goodness. Have groups change balls. If you just have one group, give them a different ball. **This time as we pass the ball, we are going to give thanks to God. Think of something you are thankful for. When the ball comes to you say, "Thank you, Lord for" and name the item.** Take time for each student to have a turn.

When we are busy looking for things to thank God for, then we are busy thinking about and practicing what is good. When we are busy complaining about what we don't have, then we can't practice what is good.

As agents of Inspector Goodness, your assignment this week is to practice goodness. You are to encourage and thank. Thank God for everything. You can also thank your family, friends, and teachers. You have a lot to thank them for. We're going to add some new cards to our Inspector Goodness wallets that will help us encourage and thank. Distribute cards for the students to prepare and place in the pocket of their wallets. If they have misplaced their wallets from lesson 1, they may make new ones at this time.

Classroom Supplies
- balls from "Why Grow Up?"
- scissors

Curriculum Supplies
reproducible page 190

Classroom Supplies
none

Curriculum Supplies
none

Growing Up Every Day

Lead the students to recite the memory passage, Philippians 4:8, 9. Then lead them in prayer, asking for God's help to grow in goodness by using encouraging and thankful words.

Say: **Grow in goodness this week. We must learn to think about the good things God has done before we can practice the goodness of God. Our actions come from what is in our hearts so we must be thinking goodness before we will practice goodness. Let's grow up in every way to be like Jesus.** Close by asking students to say the Inspector Goodness pledge.

Inspector Goodness Wallet

1. Cut out the wallet along the solid lines.
2. Fold it in half lengthwise so the pictures show on the outside.
3. Fold the gadget flap over the gadget section.
4. Start at the I.D. card and fold the wallet up along the dotted lines until the cell phone sections are together.
5. Fold the top section of the cell phone down over the bottom section of the phone.
6. Paste your photograph in the I.D. section or use one that is provided on this page.

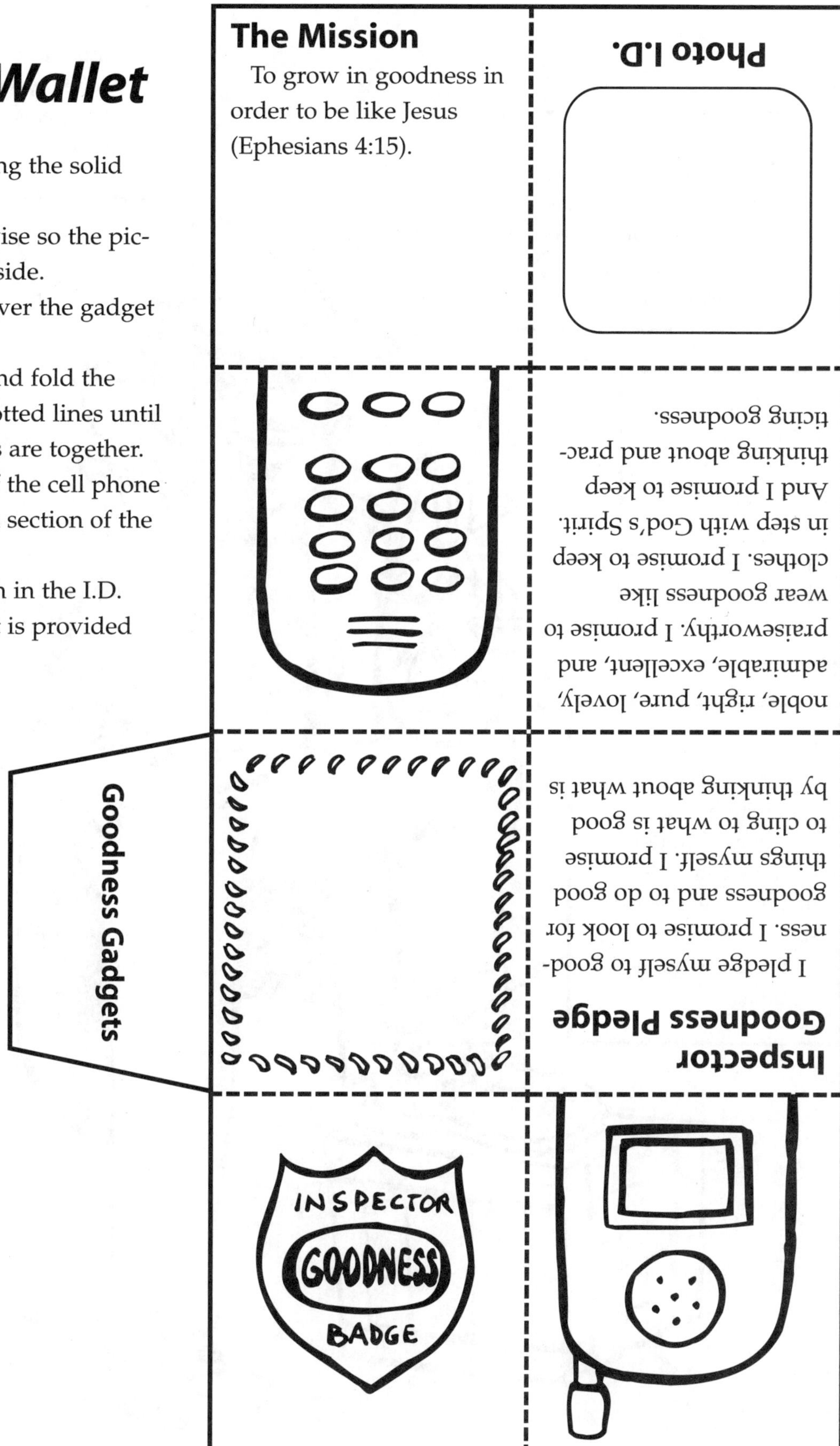

Lord, I put on my coat and clothe my soul with love. Love treats people in ways that will win them to Jesus.
Lord, I put on my hat and promise to think about whatever is true, noble, right, pure, lovely, admirable, excellent, praiseworthy.
Lord, I put on my belt and clothe my soul with thankfulness. Thankfulness is happy with what it has and doesn't keep asking for more.
Lord, I put on my shirt and clothe my soul with compassion. Compassion helps comfort those who are having a bad day.
Lord, I put on my socks and clothe my soul with humility and gentleness. Humility lets others take the first turn. Gentleness speaks softly to others and listens without arguing.
Lord, I put on my pants and clothe my soul with kindness. Kindness treats others the way I want to be treated.
Lord, I put on my shoes and clothe my soul with patience and forgiveness. Patience waits willingly until others have taken a turn. Forgiveness gives up bad feelings I have toward those who hurt me.

Triple Concentration

Place a penny over each word. Flip over three pennies for each turn. When you find a set of three matching words, keep the three pennies. The player with the most pennies at the end of the game wins.

Truth!	Truth!
Noble!	Noble!
Right!	Right!
Pure!	Pure!
Excellent!	Excellent!
Lovely!	Lovely!
Praiseworthy!	Praiseworthy!
Admirable!	Admirable!
Goodness Rules!	Goodness Rules!
Bless You!	Bless You!

Thank you!	Thank you!
Thank you!	Thank you!
Thank you!	Thank you!
Thank you!	Thank you!
Thank you!	Thank you!
Good job!	Good job!
You're a good friend!	You're a good friend!
Way to study!	Way to study!
You're doing great!	You're doing great!
Wow!	Wow!

UNIT 8

Growing in Love for Christ

Unit Aims

Know:	Evaluate Peter's responses to Jesus' death and resurrection.
Feel:	Feel willing to do whatever Jesus asks: believe, follow, or serve.
Do:	Make a change that shows how much you love Jesus.
Memorize:	John 14:23, 24

Why Grow in Love for Christ?

This unit focuses on Peter's life and how he grew in his love for Jesus. The memory passage, John 14:23, 24, emphasizes the fact that love for Jesus is shown by obedience. Peter didn't always make the right choices, but Jesus still called him to serve. Jesus calls us to serve him as well. This month as your students follow Peter through the last week of Jesus' life, they will grow in their love for Christ.

Through Peter's eyes, your students will explore serving others, resisting temptation, following and believing Jesus. They will be asked to love Jesus by serving their families, friends, neighbors, and community. They will discover that leading a life of service to others shows how much they love, believe, and follow Jesus. They will also discover that serving others can help them resist temptation.

Summary

Grow in the grace and knowledge of Jesus Christ by following the example of how Peter learned to love Jesus.

• Learn to believe, follow, or serve Jesus—like Peter.

Lesson Aims

Scripture focus	Bible focus	Life focus
Lesson 1 John 13:1-17, 31-38	I will learn to serve others.	Love Jesus by serving others.
Lesson 2 John 18:15-18, 25-27	I will learn to resist temptation.	Love Jesus by following him no matter what.
Lesson 3 John 20:1-9, 19, 20	I will believe.	Love Jesus by believing what he said.
Lesson 4 John 21:3-17	I will learn to follow.	Love Jesus by believing him, following him, or serving him.

Memory Passage: John 14:23, 24

"Jesus replied, 'If anyone loves me, he will obey my teaching. My Father will love him, and we will come to him and make our home with him. He who does not love me will not obey my teaching. These words you hear are not my own; they belong to the Father who sent me.'"

Classroom Supplies

- Two dowel rods
- two magnets
- two lengths of string
- paper clips
- marker

Curriculum Supplies

Reproducible page 210 (fish)

Memory Passage Review Activity

Reduce fish by fifty percent. Make 12 copies in one color and 12 in an additional color. Divide the memory passage into twelve sections including the reference, one for each fish. (See lesson 1.) Make two sets of fish. Put a paper clip in the mouth area of each fish.

Prepare the fishing poles by attaching a length of string to end of each dowel rod. Attach a magnet that will attract the paper clip to the end of each string.

Place both sets of fish in a large basket or box. Two players race to get their color of fish out of the box and in order on the floor. If a player hooks a fish that belongs to his opponent, he must throw the fish back. Determine a fair distance for students to stand from the box.

Lesson 1

Growing in Love for Christ

Love Jesus? Serve Others

John 13:1-17, 31-38

Bible Focus

I will learn to serve others.

Life Focus

Love Jesus by serving others.

Growing Up in the Word: John 14:23, 24

Set up one or both of the following activities to do as students arrive. Greet the students, explain the activities, and invite them to participate.

Classroom Supplies
- poster board
- marker
- cellophane tape
- two colors of paper

Curriculum Supplies
reproducible page 211 (hearts)

Memory Activity 1

Before class, write the words of John 14:23, 24 on the poster board and post it in the room. Make two sets of memory passage hearts. Cut the hearts apart and write the following twelve phrases of the memory passage on separate hearts: Jesus replied,/ "If anyone loves me,/ he will obey my teaching./ My father will love him/ and we will come to him/ and make our home with him./ He who does not love me/ will not obey my teaching./ These words you hear/ are not my own;/ they belong to the father who sent me"/ John 14:23, 24.

Begin to memorize the Scripture by reading short passages and having students repeat after you. Tell the class that they are to play a game of tag, but give them no further instructions. Move all the furniture out of the way. Give the signal to begin play. Start taping a heart to each student. After an initial moment of craziness or no activity, the class will want to know what you are doing. Tell them you are playing tag. If they don't ask you to tell them the rules, volunteer them.

Divide students into two teams. Give each team a set of the memory passage hearts. Students will divide the hearts among the team. At the signal, each team tries to freeze members of the other team by taping a heart to them. A person is frozen when a memory passage heart is taped to him. (It counts as a tag even if the heart falls off.) To get unfrozen, the player must repeat the first phrase of the memory passage (Jesus replied, "If anyone loves me, he will obey my teachings.") over and over until a teammate removes the heart and tapes it to the wall. The first team to collect all the hearts from the other team and put them in order wins.

Ask: **Is tag more fun with rules or without rules? Why is it more fun with rules?** Give kids time to respond. **It was probably more fun with the rules because you knew what you were to do and no one got hurt. We show love to others when we follow the rules. Our memory passage tells us that we show Jesus our love by following his rules—by obeying his teaching. Find the words of the passage that tell us how Jesus knows we love him.** ("If anyone loves me, he will obey my teaching.") **Find the words of the passage that tell us Jesus knows we don't love him.** ("He who does not love me will not obey my teaching.")

Classroom Supplies
- red construction paper
- four serving trays
- poster board
- markers

Curriculum Supplies
reproducible page 211 (hearts)

Memory Activity 2

Before class, write the words of John 14:23, 24 on the poster board. Make two copies of the reproducible page on red paper. Cut the hearts apart and write the following twelve phrases of the memory passage on separate hearts: Jesus replied,/ "If anyone loves me,/ he will obey my teaching./ My father will love him/ and we will come to him/ and make our home with him./ He who does not love me/ will not obey my teaching./ These words you hear/ are not my own;/ they belong to the father who sent me."/ John 14:23, 24. /Separate the hearts according to design. Put each design set on a separate tray so that the design side shows.

Divide the class into two groups. Sit groups together around separate tables. Assign a number to each group member. One member from each team will serve hearts to the members of the other team. As hearts are served, teams will work to place them in order. Begin by asking students assigned the number one to serve four hearts. Teams work with those four hearts. If they have two hearts with the same information, they will return one of them to a serving tray when the second set of hearts is served. After a short time, have students assigned the number two to serve four hearts and pick up any extra hearts. Continue this process until both groups have a complete set of hearts in the correct order. Students may refer to the memory passage written on the poster board for help. After the groups have put the Scripture together, have them practice reading it to each other.

Say: **In order to complete our memory passage, we had to serve and be served. Let's name some times that we serve or someone serves us.** Discuss and give suggestions as needed. **Is serving something that happens everyday?**

In today's lesson we will see how Jesus taught Peter and the other disciples to serve others. Jesus teaches us to serve others too. If we love Jesus, we will obey Jesus by serving others.

Why Grow Up?

Say: **We all have people who love us; we all have people who we love. How do we know someone loves us? How do we know that we love someone?** (Spending time, giving gifts, saying words of praise and love, and doing kind things.) Guide students to recognize that serving is an act of love. **Let's name ways that others have shown their love to us through acts of service.** (Mom made me cookies, Dad fixed my bike. My sister washed my clothes.) **Now let's**

name ways that we have shown our love to others through acts of service. Allow time for all students to share. **We can always grow in doing more acts of service for the people we love.**

Has anyone ever washed your feet to show you that they love you? Have you ever washed anyone's feet to show him that you love him? In Jesus' day, washing someone's feet was the job of a servant. Walking in sandals on dusty roads easily made everyone's feet dirty. It was expected that a servant would wash the feet of his master and guests. So the disciples were really surprised when Jesus—their master—washed their feet. Let's find out what happened.

Classroom Supplies
- paper
- pencil

Curriculum Supplies
none

How to Grow Up

Gather students around a blanket. Have students find and silently read John 13:1-17.

Choose the following actors: Jesus, Peter, disciples. Choose the following readers: narrator, Jesus, Peter. Explain that the actors will be acting out the story while the readers read the story. Instruct readers to read their parts so that the actors can act out what they are reading.

As the narrator is reading John 13:1-5, the Jesus actor should wash two or three students' feet. When Jesus approaches Peter, the Peter reader should read verse 6b. Continue until the passage has been read and acted. Prompt players as needed. If a student won't play the part of Jesus, play it yourself.

Divide the class into groups of four or five and seat them in small groups around the room. Supply each group with a bowl of water, a washcloth, and a towel. Instruct students to wash the feet of the person on their left. Choose a student to begin. Continue until everyone has had their feet washed and has washed someone's feet. Try to keep this a serious activity like the example in the Bible. When they have all had the chance to have their feet washed return to the blanket.

Ask: **Why do you think Jesus washed the disciple's feet?** (To show his love for them. To show them how to treat others.) **Why do you think Peter didn't want Jesus to wash his feet?** (Washing someone's feet was a job of a servant or a slave, so Peter did not want to see Jesus in that position.) **How do you think Judas was feeling at this time?** (He probably felt guilty and he probably did not want Jesus to show him love.) **How did you feel when you were getting your feet washed? How did you feel when you were washing another person's feet? John 13:15 says that Jesus washed the disciple's feet as an example of how we should serve others.**

Classroom Supplies
- Bibles
- bowl of warm water
- towels
- index cards
- blanket

Curriculum Supplies
none

Let's read more of this story. I will read John 13:31-38, and you can follow in your Bible. After reading the passage, ask: **What does Jesus predict Peter will do when Jesus is no longer with him?** (Deny knowing Jesus three times before the rooster crows.) **How do you think Peter feels when he hears these words from Jesus?** Discuss. **Next week we will find out what happens to Peter and whether or not he denied Jesus.**

What was the new command that Jesus gave the disciples? (To love one another.) **Let's look back at John 13:34 to find out what Jesus is calling us to do. Let's read that verse together. If we love one another as Jesus loves us, then we will serve others as Jesus served us.**

Classroom Supplies
- chalkboard
- chalk
- pencils
- colored paper

Curriculum Supplies
reproducible page 210 (fish)

Ready to Grow Up!

Before class, make one copy the reproducible for each student. Use a variety of colors of paper.

Say: **Jesus loved his disciples. How do we know that Jesus loved his disciples?** (He washed their feet.) **Jesus' actions tell us that he loved his disciples. Jesus told us to love one another as he loved us. This means that we can love others by serving them. How does serving others show that we love them?** (Acts of service are acts of love because they show kindness and because they show that we care about the comfort of another person.)

Each week we will be talking about ways that we can show others that we love them. When we do this we will also be showing Jesus that we love him. Let's review our memory passage. Have students read the passage from the poster board.

This week will be serving our families. Let's list ways we can show our families that we love them. Let's think of acts of service that will cause our moms and dad, brothers and sisters to think, "Wow! My (son, daughter, brother, sister) loves me." I will write the ideas on the board. Give the students time to come up with their own ideas. Prompt them with these questions: How would your mom feel if you did the supper dishes without being asked? How would a younger sibling feel if you read him a story? How would your grandparents feel if you paid them a surprise visit?

Distribute fish. Tell the students to decide on an idea from the board or come up with their own idea and write it on their fish.

Say: **Jesus calls us to show others we love them by serving them. The idea you've chosen will give you the opportunity to serve others and show them your love and Jesus' love. When we serve others, we also show that we love Jesus. Bring your fish back with you next week, and be prepared to tell us how you did in your goal to serve your family.**

Classroom Supplies
- black butcher paper
- colored chalk

Curriculum Supplies
none

Growing Up Every Day

Before class, cover a large area of the classroom wall with black paper. Use colored chalk to draw several fish on the black paper. Make the fish by drawing a frown arc over a smile arc.

Have students bring their fish and gather at the black paper. Say: **Growing up in Christ means growing in love for Jesus. We show Jesus our love by doing what he has asked us to do. The lesson today taught us that Jesus wants us to serve other people. We have all chosen a way to serve our families this week. When we serve them, we will be growing in our love for Jesus.**

Let's commit to completing our chosen act of service. First choose a partner. When we've finished our prayer, each pair will draw the Christian sign of the fish on the black paper. One will draw the smile half and the other will draw the frown half. Then you will sign your names by your fish. The early Christians used a fish symbol to let others know of their love for Jesus. We are using it for the same reason. Gather students in a circle. Ask them to hold their fish in the center of the circle. Pray for students to show their love for Jesus and others. Then let pairs use chalk to draw their fish on the butcher paper.

Say: **Please bring your fish back next week so that we can put them up on the wall. By the end of the month, we will see all the acts of service that our class has done.**

Lesson 2

Growing in Love for Christ

Love Jesus? Resist Temptation

John 18:15-18, 25-27

Bible Focus
I will learn to resist temptation.

Life Focus
Love Jesus by following him no matter what.

Growing Up in the Word: John 14:23, 24
Set up one or both of the following activities to do as students arrive. Greet students, explain the activities, and invite them to participate.

Classroom Supplies
- M&M's brand candy-coated chocolates
- self-sealing bags
- poster board with memory passage written on it
- paper plates
- pens
- paper

Curriculum Supplies
none

Memory Activity 1
Before class, assemble one self-sealing bag of 55 M&M's brand chocolate candies for every four or five students. Display the memory passage in the back of the teaching area. Do not point it out to the students, but you do want them to become aware that it is there.

Divide students into groups of four or five. Give each team a paper, pen, plate and a bag of candies. Have students pour the candies onto their plate. Tell them to write as much of the memory passage as they can using only the help of the people in their group. Instruct them not to get help from anywhere else. They will get to keep the entire plate of candies to share with their group if they get the passage correct, but you will take away one piece for each word that is missing or wrong. Tell them not to touch the candies.

Observe the class. Have students noticed the poster board? Are they peeking at it? If they have not noticed it, walk by it a few times or stand by it while you are giving directions. Discretely take notes of what you see so you can share with your class later. If a student tells you about the poster board, just tell him not to look at it. When students finish, ask them to join you in another area of the room.

Say: **I placed two temptations before you as you were working to write the memory passage. What were you tempted to do?** (Look at the poster of the memory passage and eat the candies before they were earned.)

Let's review our memory passage. Do so. **These verses tell us to love Jesus**

by obeying his teachings. What does this say about how we should handle temptation? We are tempted to disobey every day. When we are tempted, we should do the right thing based on his teachings. We show Jesus that we love him when we resist temptation. In our lesson today, Peter is tempted. We will find out if he makes the right choice. Allow students time to eat their candy; they should each get about ten.

Memory Activity 2

Classroom Supplies
- magazines (used)
- scissors
- black markers
- construction paper
- glue

Curriculum Supplies
none

Instruct students to search the magazines for pictures of different kinds of houses. Students should cut out the houses and paste them onto separate sheets of construction paper. Divide the memory passage into phrases so that each house will have one phrase. Write the phrases under the houses. Mix the sheets and have students put them in order.

Say: **We found many types of houses. Every animal has some type of home—a tree, a cave, a tunnel. People live in different types of houses too. We all need a place to live. What do these houses have to do with our memory passage?** (Jesus said that if we follow his teachings, he and his father would make a home with us.) **Does this mean that Jesus will come to live with us at our house? What kind of home is Jesus talking about?** (Jesus is telling us that the Holy Spirit will make a home in our hearts.) **When we love Jesus, we obey him and his Spirit lives in our hearts.**

Why Grow Up?

Classroom Supplies
none

Curriculum Supplies
copies of the situations listed here

Divide the class into pairs. Give each pair one of the following situations. Ask students to answer the following questions about their situations: What is the temptation? What would be the right thing to do in this situation? Why would it be hard to make the right choice in your situation?

1. Your dad asked you to clean out the garage. Your friends ride by on their bikes, and they ask you to join them.
2. You are at a friend's house for dinner. When dinner is served, your friend's family does not thank God for their meal.
3. Your friend has a journal that she writes in every night. She says she has written about you. When at her house, you see her journal. She leaves you alone in the room while she goes to get a snack.
4. A friend invites you to her house to do homework. When you get there she meets you outside. She tells you that she told her parents she was coming to your house. She suggests that you go to the park for a while.
5. You are spending the night at a friend's house. He wants to watch a television program that your parents do not approve of.
6. A popular girl in class invites you to sit with her at lunch. She makes it clear that your best friend is not invited. In fact, she said that she doesn't like your best friend. You really want to be a part on the "in" crowd.
7. While studying at the public library, you see a group of your friends crowded around a computer. They are looking at a website you know you should not be looking at, but they invite you to join them.
8. You are walking home from school with your friends when they begin mak-

ing fun and yelling names at a kid from your class. You don't know this kid very well.

When everyone is ready, ask each pair to read the situation, share the temptation, and name the right action to take. Ask: **Have you ever been tempted in one of these ways? Everyone is tempted. Jesus was tempted and so were his disciples. In today's lesson, we will find out how Peter was tempted.**

How to Grow Up

Classroom Supplies
- chalkboard
- chalk

Curriculum Supplies
none

Say: **Last week we learned that Jesus served his disciples by washing their feet. When Jesus was finished, he predicted something about Peter. What did Jesus say Peter would do? Let's review John 13:38.** (Jesus told Peter that he would deny Jesus three times before the rooster crows.) **Let's find out what happened.**

Divide the chalkboard into three columns and six rows. Place the following references at the top of the columns: John 18:15-17; John 18:18, 25; John 18:26, 27. Label the rows as follows: Who? What? When? Where? Why? How?

Direct students to read John 18:15-17 silently. Then choose readers to be the narrator, Peter, and the girl. Have the trio read the passage as if Peter and the girl were speaking. Then ask the six questions and record the answers on the chalkboard. **Who?** (Peter.) **What?** (First denial.) **When?** (During Jesus' appearance before the high priest.) **Where?** (At the door to the high priest's courtyard.) **How?** (Peter was tempted.) **Why?** (Peter was afraid to be associated with Jesus.)

Do the same with John 18:18, 25. This passage needs a narrator, Peter, and an unidentified questioner. **Who?** (Peter.) **What?** (Second denial.) **When?** (During Jesus' appearance before the high priest.) **Where?** (Around the fire in the high priest's courtyard.) **How?** (Peter was tempted.) **Why?** (Peter was afraid to be associated with Jesus.)

Again, follow the same procedure with John 18:26, 27. This passage needs a narrator, the relative, and a crowing rooster. **Who?** (Peter.) **What?** (Third denial.) **When?** (During Jesus' appearance before the high priest.) **Where?** (Around the fire in the high priest's courtyard.) **How?** (Peter was tempted.) **Why?** (Peter was afraid to be associated with Jesus.)

When the lists are complete, ask students to point out items that are the same on all three lists. Help students to discover that all three denials happened in a short amount of time.

Ask: **How do you think Peter felt when he heard the rooster crow?** Allow time for student responses and discuss them. **Peter failed to do the right thing, and when the rooster crowed, Peter must have remembered Jesus' words. Peter must have felt sick because he denied Jesus. He must have felt sad and lonely to have disappointed Jesus.**

Ready to Grow Up!

Before class, copy one fish for each student. Use a variety of colors.

Say: **Most of us probably feel sick or sad and lonely too when we give into temptation and disobey Jesus' teachings. When this happens we might wish with all our might that we had not done what we did. But we can never undo what we have done. It would be better if we never give into the temptation in**

the first place. Prayer will always strengthen us when we are tempted.

Another important way to ward off temptation is to actively love Jesus. We actively love Jesus when we serve others. Serving others is a good way to show that we love and follow Jesus. It is also a good way to resist temptation.

Last week we agreed together to serve our families. You were to bring back your fish with a message about what you did. Have students share what they did to serve their families as you tape the fish to the wall. Begin one wavy row of fish that extends out from the black butcher-papered wall. Tell students that you hope to have a row of fish that makes a circle around the room.

Say: **This week we have been talking about temptation. Serving others can help us resist temptation. It is a good way to get ourselves busy and to get away from what is tempting us.**

This week we will be serving our friends and neighbors. Let's write down some ideas of what we could do to serve our friends and neighbors. (Sweep a neighbor's sidewalk, make cookies for a neighbor, play with someone who looks lonely.)

Sometimes we do things for people and our service to them may go unnoticed. Remember we aren't serving to get thanked. We are serving to show that we love Jesus and that we love others. Let's read our memory passage. Do so.

Distribute new fish. Say: **This week your assignment is to show love to a friend or neighbor. You can pick an idea from the board or come up with your own idea. Write what you've selected to do on your fish.**

Classroom Supplies
- chalkboard
- chalk
- colored paper
- markers
- tape

Curriculum Supplies
reproducible page 210 (fish)

Growing Up Every Day

Instruct students to bring their fish and gather at the black wall. Say: **It is wonderful to know that when we make the wrong choice to give into temptation that God will forgive us. It is better, though, to resist the temptation rather then to suffer the pain that we feel when we make the wrong choice.**

What temptations are you struggling with? I want you to think about them right now. Remember, God gives us just what we need to resist temptation. One of the ways we can resist temptation is to keep ourselves busy serving others. When we are busy serving others, we show that we love them and that we love Jesus. Jesus said, "If anyone loves me he will obey my teaching." Our memory passage also tells us that if we love Jesus, he will love us, and the Holy Spirit will live in our hearts. The Holy Spirit will direct us in the decisions we make. He will help us resist temptation.

Before we pray and commit our acts of service to the Lord, pick a partner. Let's gather in a circle. Put your fish in the center. We will each pray silently. I will suggest to you what to pray about. Give students the following ideas for their prayer time: Thank the Lord for this learning time; ask his help to grow in love for him; admit to God that you are tempted; tell him how you are tempted; ask his help to make the right choices that honor him when you are tempted; ask for the desire to serve others instead of the desire to give into temptation.

Say: **Now you and your partner may draw the sign of the fish and sign your names. Remember that the fish is a symbol that means you love Jesus. Please bring back your fish next week, so we can put them on our wall.**

Classroom Supplies
colored chalk

Curriculum Supplies
none

Lesson 3

Growing in Love for Christ

Love Jesus? Believe Him

John 20:1-9, 19, 20

Bible Focus

I will believe.

Life Focus

Love Jesus by believing what he said.

Growing Up in the Word: John 14:23, 24

Set up one or both of the following activities to do as students arrive. Greet the students, explain the activities, and invite them to participate.

Classroom Supplies

- Paper
- pencil
- scissors
- chalkboard
- chalk
- paper bag

Curriculum Supplies

none

Memory Activity 1

Before class, write John 14:23, 24 on four slips of paper, one sentence per slip. Cut out 30-35 more slips of paper and leave them blank. Put all the slips in a small paper bag. Divide the chalkboard into four sections.

Tell the class you have put them memory passage on four slips of paper, and they are in the bag. Tell them that when a part of the memory passage is selected, they will write it on the board in the section it belongs. The first section is for the first sentence and so on.

Call a student up to select a slip. Kids should be drawing more blanks than verses. Keep shuffling up the slips. After about ten slips have been drawn, ask the students if they believe the verse is in the paper bag. Assure them that all four slips are in there. Continue drawing slips until the passage is completely written on the board.

Say the verse as a class after it is written on the board. Erase the first sentence and say the verse again. Continue doing this until the whole verse is erased.

Say: **Did you have trouble believing that the memory passage was in this bag? Did you think I had forgotten to put the passage in the bag? Did any of you believe the entire time that the passage was in the bag? Sometimes it is hard to believe what we cannot see. We will learn in our story today that we can believe everything Jesus says. Peter and the other disciples learn that they can believe everything Jesus has taught them.**

Memory Activity 2

Have the students sit in a circle. Pick one person to be it. He will sit in a chair in the middle of the circle blindfolded. Pick another person to stand behind him. He will disguise his voice as he speaks to the person who is wearing the blindfold. First, he will say his name or pretend to be someone else by saying another name. He will then recite the memory passage. When he is finished, he will ask, "Do you believe I am who I say I am?" The blindfolded person has to guess if the person talking is really who he says he is. Continue the game until everyone has a chance to be blindfolded and to say the memory passage. Have the memory passage available for those who have not quite memorized it.

Say: **Sometimes it is hard to believe what we cannot see. When we are told that something is going to happen, we have to choose to believe that it will. If a friend has told you for three months that he is going to have you over to his house but he never invites you, does it begin to be hard to believe him? We will learn in our story today that we can believe everything Jesus says. Jesus teaches his disciples and Peter that they can believe everything he has taught them.**

Classroom Supplies
- Chair
- blindfold

Curriculum Supplies
none

Why Grow Up?

Do one of the following experiments.

Experiment one: **How many of you believe that I can get this egg into this bottle?** Put the boiling water into the bottle. Swish it around for a minute. Pour the water out and place egg on the opening of the bottle. The egg will slip into the bottle. The steam causes the egg to fall into the bottle. **Do you believe that I can get the egg out without breaking the bottle?** Turn the bottle upside down with the opening in your mouth. Blow into the bottle for 30 seconds. The egg will fall out.

Experiment two: **Do you believe that I can make an egg float?** Put the egg into the cup of hot water. The egg will sink to the bottom. Add at least three tablespoons of salt to the cup. Stir to dissolve the salt. The salt makes the water more dense and the egg will float.

Many of you didn't believe I could make the egg go in the bottle or float until you saw me do it. Often we are told something will happen but we don't truly believe it until we see it with our own eyes. Or maybe we don't understand any way that something could happen. Jesus told his disciples that he would come back to life after being dead for three days. Many of them did not understand what he meant—people just don't come back to life after being dead. When Jesus was raised from the dead, Peter learned to believe everything Jesus had taught him even if he didn't see it or understand it.

Classroom Supplies
Experiment One
- egg (boiled and peeled)
- small necked jar (ketchup bottle)
- boiling water

Experiment Two
- one clear, plastic or glass cup
- hot tap water
- 3 tablespoons of salt
- one small egg

Curriculum Supplies
none

How to Grow Up

Divide the class into eight groups. Assign each group one or two verses of John 20:1-9, 19, 20: Group 1 verse 1, group 2 verse 2, group 3 verses 3 and 4, group 4 verse 5, group 5 verses 6 and 7, group 6 verses 8 and 9, group 7 verse 19, and group 8 verse 20. Instruct students to write out the words to each verse. However, they are to replace some words with pictures that are either drawn by

Classroom Supplies
- magazines (used)
- scissors
- butcher paper
- pencils
- markers
- crayons
- glue

Curriculum Supplies
none

them or cut from a magazine to go with the verse. Help them begin by telling them to choose words from the verse to illustrate. These words should be words that can easily be drawn or easily found in a magazine.

When they are finished, have them tape their rebus pictures in time sequence on a wall around the room. Have each group select a speaker to read their verse aloud from their rebus illustrations.

Say: **Who is the other disciple talked about in the story?** (John) **When did John believe that Jesus was alive?** (When he saw the empty tomb.) **What do you think Peter thought happened to Jesus when he saw the empty tomb and the clothes?** (Peter was probably confused. He might have thought that someone had taken Jesus body.) **When do you think Peter believed Jesus was alive?** (When he saw him in verses 19 and 20.) **Jesus taught Peter to believe his teaching even though he might not understand it or even be able to see it. Jesus' resurrection taught us that we can believe God's Word even when we might not understand it.**

Ready to Grow Up!

Classroom Supplies
- chalkboard
- chalk
- colored paper
- markers
- tape

Curriculum Supplies
reproducible page 210 (fish)

Before class, copy one fish for each student. Use a variety of colors of paper.

Say: **We can believe every word of the Bible. There are many parts of God's Word that we don't understand, but we can believe what we read. We can believe that Jesus exists even though we can't see him here with us. Belief is a sign that we love Jesus. It is this belief and love that motivates us to what Jesus teaches. Let's read our memory passage.** Do so.

Say: **For the past few weeks, we've been following Jesus' teaching about serving others. Last week you were to serve your neighbors and friends. What did you do?** Have students report. As they do so, tape their fish from last week to the wall with the row of fish started last week. **When we serve others, we show that we love Jesus.**

This week we will be serving our community. Let's list some ideas of what we can do for our community. (Pick up litter in a park. Help at a neighborhood shelter. Take canned foods to a food bank. Visit or send cards to the residents of a nursing home.) **Helping people in your community is a way to grow in your love for Christ. By showing them kindness we are sharing God's love for them. We also show that we believe Jesus.**

Distribute new fish. Say: **This week your assignment is to show love for our community. You can pick an idea from the board or come up with your own idea. Write what you've selected to do on your fish.**

Growing Up Every Day

Instruct students to bring their fish and gather at the black paper. Say: **Growing in Christ means believing him. Everything written in the Bible is true, and we can trust it. Do your actions show that you believe Jesus? Our actions show what we think about Jesus. Do they show that we love him? If we are busy serving others, then our actions show that we love and believe Jesus.**

We've all chosen an act of service for our communities. Let's commit our

service to God. First, choose a partner. Now let's gather in a circle. Put your fish in the center. Let's pray: "God, thank you for our lesson today. We learned how important it is to believe in you even when we can't see or understand. We want to grow in Christ's love. Give us the opportunity to share our love time with our community. Thank you Lord for this special time together. Amen."

Now you and your partner may draw the sign of the fish and sign your names. The fish is a sign early Christians used to tell other Christians that they loved Jesus. Please bring your fish back next week so we may add it to our wall.

Classroom Supplies
colored chalk

Curriculum Supplies
none

Lesson 4

Growing in Love for Christ

Love Jesus? Follow Him

John 21:3-17

Bible Focus

I will learn to follow.

Life Focus

Love Jesus by believing him, following him, or serving him.

Growing Up in the Word: John 14:23, 24

Set up one or both of the following activities to do as students arrive. Greet the students, explain the activities, and invite them to participate.

Classroom Supplies
none

Curriculum Supplies
one set of hearts with the memory passage from lesson 1

Memory Activity 1

Have students sit in a circle. Shuffle the hearts and give one to each student. The student with the heart that reads, "Jesus replied," will stand up. He finds the person that has the next part of the verse. He asks that person to follow him. Then that person does the same thing. This continues until all students are following the leader around the room. Then have the students stand in a row and hold up their fish in order. Have the kids take turns saying the memory passage turning the fish over so only some of the phrases are showing.

Say: **Playing follow the leader is fun, and it is just a game. Jesus calls us to follow him, and it is important that we do. We can't follow Jesus around the room in the same way that we followed our leader today. How do we follow Jesus?** (We follow him by obeying him.) **What does our memory passage say about people who do what Jesus teaches?** (Those are the people who love Jesus.) **Are you following Jesus in a way that shows your love for him?**

Classroom Supplies
- newspapers
- scissors
- butcher paper
- glue

Curriculum Supplies
none

Memory Activity 2

Divide the class into groups of three or four. Give each group a piece of butcher paper, a stack of newspapers, scissors, and glue. Instruct students to write the memory passage using letters and words from the newspaper. They will be able to find some words intact and other words will have to be pieced together.

Say: **Newspapers are a source of knowledge; they tell us what is happening in the world. The Bible is a source of knowledge; it tells us how to follow**

Jesus. Our memory passage tells us obey the teachings of the Bible. Many people read the newspaper everyday to learn about the world; those who love Jesus need to read the Bible everyday to learn Jesus' teachings.

Why Grow Up?

Classroom Supplies
- index cards
- paper
- pencils

Curriculum Supplies
none

Before class, write each of the following words on index cards: dog, television set, cat, clock, candle, bed, sunflower, bear, Christmas tree, flag, baseball, snowman, egg.

Divide the class into pairs. Have one student from each pair draw from the set of cards. That student is to tell his partner how to draw the object without naming the object. For example if the card had "car" written on it, the student might tell his partner to draw a rectangle and then draw a circle on the front bottom corner and on the back bottom corner. After the student guesses what they were asked to draw, have pairs switch places. You may want to come up with harder things to draw based on the age of your students. If time permits, shuffle the cards and give the students another chance to give directions and to draw.

Ask: **How easy was it for you to draw your object just from the directions your partner gave?** Discuss. **It might not have been too hard, but it would've been easier if you had known what the object was that you were to draw. Following directions was an important part of this activity. What could have happened if you didn't follow your partner's directions?** Discuss. **Our memory passage says that if we love Jesus, we will follow Jesus' instructions. Following Jesus' directions is an important part of being a Christian.**

How to Grow Up

Classroom Supplies
- fishing net
- fireplace logs
- Bibles
- scissors

Curriculum Supplies
reproducible page 212 (knots)

Before class, prepare fourteen knots. Write the following answers in separate knots: "I'm going out to fish."/ No fish./ Sea of Tiberias./ "Friends, haven't you any fish?"/ Zero fish./ 153 fish./ Right side of the boat./ "It is the Lord?"/ A hundred yards./ "Come and have breakfast."/ Third time./"Do you love me?"/ "Yes, Lord."/ "Feed my sheep."/ Put the knots in the fishing net.

Set up the logs to look like a campfire. Gather the students around the logs. Say: **If we were outside today, we might use these logs to make a campfire. How many of you have been around a campfire? What are some of the things that you do around a campfire?** Discuss. **After Jesus' resurrection, he appeared to his disciples at a campfire. What do you suppose happened?** Discuss. **Also during this morning visit, the disciples used a fishing net.** Show net. **How many fish will this net hold? How big would the net need to be to hold 153 fish? I'm sure the net the disciples used was much bigger than this one, because they caught 153 fish!**

Have students silently read John 21:3-6. Say: **How do you think Peter and the other disciples felt after fishing all night without catching any fish?** (They were probably very tired and discouraged.) **What do you think they thought when a man they did not recognize told them to try fishing on the other side of the boat?** (They probably weren't sure if they should believe him.)

Have students silently read John 21:7-14. Say: **How was John able to recognize Jesus?** (He must have remembered another time that Jesus told the disciples where to catch fish after they had fished all night without any success.) **Why do you think Peter ran through the water to get to Jesus?** (He was too excited to wait for the boat to get to shore. He was very happy to see Jesus.) **How did Jesus serve the disciples?** (He built a fire and cooked them some fish. He invited them to eat with him.) **How many times had Jesus appeared to the disciples after his resurrection?** (Three.)

Have students silently read John 21:15-17. Say: **What did Jesus ask Peter to do?** (Feed and take care of his sheep.) **What does that mean?** (Jesus is asking Peter to take care of his followers by teaching them about Jesus.) **How many times does Jesus ask Peter to feed his sheep?** (Three.) **Think back to the lesson about Peter denying Jesus. How many times did Peter deny Jesus?** (Three.) **Why do you think Jesus asked Peter the same question three times?** (Jesus was helping Peter understand that he was forgiven. He was also telling Peter how he could show his love for Jesus.) **Did Peter follow Jesus' instructions to feed his sheep? Yes. After this breakfast by the sea, Peter became one of the early church's greatest leaders. Peter spent the rest of his life loving Jesus by following Jesus' instructions to teach others to follow Jesus.**

Have students take turns selecting a knot from the net and asking a question from the lesson that can be answered with the answer that is written on the knot.

Classroom Supplies
- markers
- colored paper
- scissors

Curriculum Supplies
reproducible page 212 (knots)

Ready to Grow Up!

Before class, copy the reproducible knots for each student. Use a variety of colors.

Say: **Jesus asked Peter to feed his sheep. We know Jesus was instructing Peter to follow him and tell other people about him. When we follow Jesus' instructions, we show Jesus that we love him.** Have students review memory passage.

Say: **We have been busy serving others this month. Last week you spent some time serving the community. What did you do?** As students report, tape their fish from last week to the wall, continuing the wavy row that was begun two weeks ago. **By serving others we were following Jesus' example. Jesus showed love and kindness for everyone.**

This week we will be serving others in a slightly different way. We are going to write note of kindness and encouragement to some of the people we have served this month. We're going to begin by listing encouraging words on the board. What might we say to someone to encourage them? Remind them that Jesus loves them. Tell them that they can believe every thing that Jesus teaches. Invite them to follow Jesus.

Distribute reproducible page. Say: **This week your assignment is to show love to two people by writing a note of encouragement. It would be great if you chose people that you have served this past month. You can use some words from the board in your note.** When students are finished with their notes, help them as needed to fold the notes into knots and to write the recipient's name on the outside.

Growing Up Every Day

Have the students bring their knots and gather at the black paper wall. Say: **We have watched this month as Peter grew in his love for Christ. Jesus taught him to serve others, to look away from temptation, to believe in him, and to follow him. Peter loved Jesus. Loving Jesus means doing what he has asked us to do. Let's recite the memory passage, John 14:23, 24.**

We have watched ourselves grow in our love for Jesus this month too. We've done many things that Jesus has asked us to do. We have a wall full of fish that tell what those things have been.

We're going to close this month's lessons by asking God to bless the words of encouragement and kindness that we've written. First, choose a partner. Gather students in a circle and have students place their knots in the circle. Lead them in prayer, asking God's blessing on the recipients of the notes.

Say: **Now you and your partner may draw the sign of the fish and sign your name. Remember the fish is a sign that you love Jesus.**

Classroom Supplies
colored chalk

Curriculum Supplies
none

I love you!
I love you!
I love you!

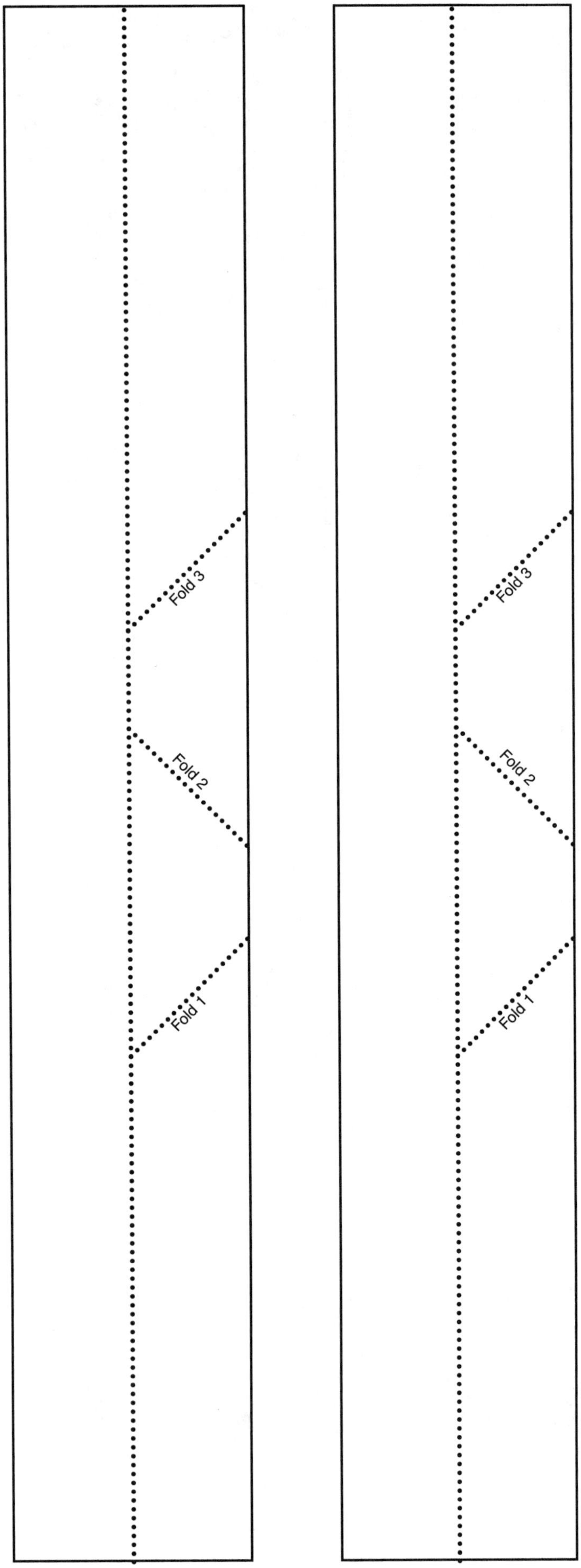

Knots

1.

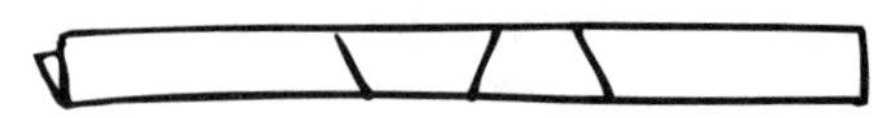

2.

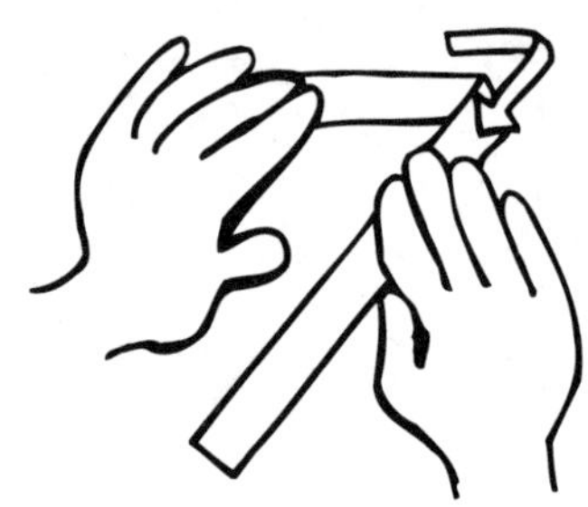

3.

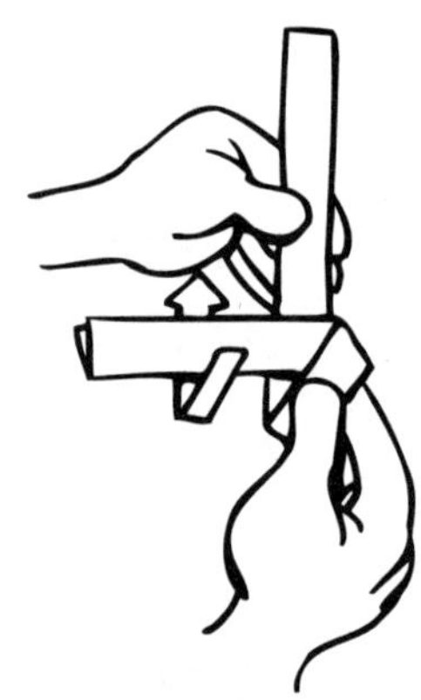

4.

5.

UNIT 9

Growing in Devotion to the Church

Unit Aims

Know:	Describe what the church did that showed it is from God.
Feel:	Feel a desire to be a part of the church; feel joy in being a part of the church.
Do:	Be devoted to the apostles' teaching, fellowship, breaking of bread, and prayer.
Memorize:	Acts 2:42, 46, 47

Why Grow in Devotion to the Church?

Students will be challenged to actively participate in the church as they discover the devotion, the joys, and the hardships of the apostles and believers in the early church. In Acts 2-6, students will learn about the beginning of the church on Pentecost and the growth of the church in the earliest days. They will explore the four aspects of the church as they learn the memory passage, Acts 2:42, 46, 47. Through the study of this passage and the other lesson Scriptures, students will learn how the early believers lived a life of devotion to the church.

This unit will help students grow in their own devotion to the church in their day-to-day lives as they learn practical ways to follow the pattern of the early church. Developing a devotion to the church now is important for eight- to twelve-year-olds so that they can carry a desire for and devotion to the church throughout their lives.

Summary

Grow in the grace and knowledge of Jesus Christ by being devoted to the four-part pattern of the church.

- Follow the example of the believers in the early church.
- Listen and respond to God's Word.
- Remember Jesus in the Lord's Supper.
- Fellowship and share at a personal level (spiritual needs, physical needs).

Memory Passage: Acts 2:42, 46, 47

"They devoted themselves to the apostles' teaching and to the fellowship, to the breaking of bread and to prayer.... Every day they continued to meet together in the temple courts. They broke bread in their homes and ate together with glad and sincere hearts, praising God and enjoying the favor of all the people. And the Lord added to their number daily those who were being saved."

Lesson Aims

Scripture focus	Bible focus	Life focus
Lesson 1 Acts 2:42-47	The early church did four things.	Identify four ways to be a part of the church.
Lesson 2 Acts 2:1-4, 14, 22-24, 32, 33, 36-41	Peter preached and the crowd responded to God's Word.	Actively listen to preaching and respond to God's Word.
Lesson 3 Acts 3, 4	The church prayed for courage to speak about Jesus.	Participate in prayer for the church and for opportunities to speak about Jesus.
Lesson 4 Acts 4:32-37; 6:1-6	The church cared for believers in need.	Participate in fellowship of the church and share on personal level.
Lesson 5 Acts 4:1-31; 5:12-14; 5:17-42	Peter, John, and other apostles stood up for their faith.	Continue to be devoted to four aspects of the church when facing difficult situations.

Classroom Supplies
- index cards
- manila clasp envelope

Curriculum Supplies
reproducible page 240 (flip book)

Memory Passage Review Activity

Paste each picture from the reproducible page on the right side of separate index cards. Paste them in the same location on each card. Then write one phrase of the memory passage on the left side of index card. Be sure to keep the pictures and words in order. The memory passage may be divided into these nineteen phrases: They devoted themselves/ to the apostles' teaching/ and to the fellowship,/ to the breaking of bread/ and to prayer./ Every day they continued/ to meet together/ in the temple courts./ They broke bread/ in their homes/ and ate together/ with glad and sincere hearts,/ praising God/ and enjoying the favor/ of all the people./ And the Lord added/ to their number daily /those who were being saved./ Acts 2:42, 46, 47/

Students will make a flip book from the cards after they put the cards in order. Shuffle the cards and store them in the manila envelope. Label the envelope, Growing in Devotion to the Church—Acts 2:42, 46, 47.

Lesson 1

Growing in Devotion to the Church

Devoted to the Church

Acts 2:42-47

Bible Focus

The early church did four things.

Life Focus

Identify four ways to be a part of the church.

Growing Up in the Word: Acts 2:42, 46, 47

Set up one or both of the following activities to do as students arrive. Greet the students, explain the activities, and invite them to participate.

Memory Activity 1

Ask students to locate Acts 2:42, 46, 47 in their Bibles. Give them a few minutes to study and to begin to memorize the passage. Students may use their Bibles if needed to help them as they play the game.

Divide students into two teams. Set a trash can or box at one end of the room. Tell each team to form a line several feet away from the trash can. Read the first phrase of the memory passage to the first team, leaving out a key word. The first team member will repeat the phrase, filling in the key word. After he answers, he will try to make a basket by throwing the ball into the trash can or box. Award four points for a correct answer and another four points for a basket. Keep score on the chalkboard so that students will see the fours as they add up. Continue with each phrase of the memory passage. Alternate teams until the memory passage is completed. Repeat the passage until all have a chance to play.

Say: **Four is an important number for us today. You scored four points for your answers. When your individual scores of four were added together, your team's total score grew.**

The early church devoted themselves to four things. Think about the memory passage. What are the four things? (Apostles' teaching, fellowship, breaking of bread, prayer.) **When the early church did these four things, they grew as a church and as believers. As we do these four things, we can grow too. Just as each team's total score grew every time someone scored four points, we will grow up in Christ as we devote ourselves to the apostles' teaching, fellowship, breaking of bread, and prayer.**

Classroom Supplies
- Bibles
- empty trash can or large box
- a soft ball about the size of a baseball
- chalkboard
- chalk

Curriculum Supplies
none

Classroom Supplies
- construction paper
- markers
- Plasti-Tak
- Bibles
- scissors

Curriculum Supplies
none

Memory Activity 2

Before class, prepare six sheets of construction paper. Turn the paper horizontally. Write one letter from the word "devote" on the left third of each sheet. Make the letters as large as possible. Divide the memory passage into six phrases, and write one phrase on the right two-thirds of each sheet. Write the first phrase on the sheet with the letter "D"; the second phrase on the sheet with the letter "E"; and so on. Separate the letters from the passage by cutting a wavy or angular line. Make the separation pattern on each sheet different.

Turn the letter sections over, and write the same letters on the back. Turn the memory passage sections over, and write one of the following words on the back side of each sheet: section 1 (D)—Love; section 2 (E)—Money and Possessions; section 3 (V)—Attention; section 4 (O)—Loyalty; section 5 (T)—Energy; section 6 (E)—Time. Hide the twelve sections of paper around the classroom and have students find them and work together to put the memory passage in order. When completed, have students find and read Acts 2:42, 46, 47 from their Bibles to check the answer. Then have students match the letters from the word devote with the memory passage sections. They will do this by matching the cutting lines. Have students Plasti-Tak the passage to the wall in a vertical column. If you have a large class, make two sets of the puzzle using a different color of paper for each set. Divide the group into two teams and have them race to put the passage in order and match it with the letters from the word devote.

Say: **When we put the memory passage in order, we also unscrambled a word. What is that word? What does the word "devote" have to do with our memory passage? Our memory passage tells us that the early church devoted themselves to four things. Name them.** (Apostles' teaching, fellowship, breaking of bread, and prayer.)

What does the word "devote" mean? How does a person act if he is devoted to something? (Help students include concepts such as being loyal to something, loving something, faithfully sticking with something, giving of yourself to something.) **What are some things that you are devoted to? Today we showed some devotion to a task when we completed this puzzle.**

Ask volunteers to turn over the construction paper signs. Say: **When we are devoted to something, we give our time, our attention, our loyalty, our energy, our money and possessions, and our love. We can be devoted to many kinds of things or people. Some people are devoted to learning something or to making themselves better at something. What are you devoted to?** (Sports, music, friends, family, Jesus.) **How do you show your devotion—how do you spend your time, energy, attention, money, love, and loyalty?**

The early church grew as they devoted themselves to the four things in Acts 2:42. We need to grow in devotion to the church too. As we grow in devotion to the church, we will grow up in Christ.

Why Grow Up?

Display the potted plant, watering can, and fertilizer. Say: **What four things does this plant need to grow?** Give students time to express their ideas. Accept their answers and emphasize soil, water, food, and light. **Four things that plants**

need to grow are soil, water, food, and light. In the church, we need four things to grow. Let's name those four things. (Apostles' teaching, fellowship, breaking of bread, prayer.)

The apostles' teaching is like the soil. We are grounded in our knowledge of Jesus. (Point to the soil.) **We grow as we learn more about Jesus.**

Pick up the watering can and water the plant. Say: **The water that the plant needs can represent fellowship. The water goes through the plant to make it grow stronger. We grow stronger as we share with each other and work together.**

Breaking of bread is the food. The plant needs food to grow. Sprinkle fertilizer around the plant. **We grow as we take part in the Lord's Supper and remember what Jesus has done for us by dying on the cross.**

Hold plant up the sunlight or the light source in the room. Say: **Just as the plant needs light, we need to pray to God. He is the light of our lives.**

What do you think might happen to the plant if it did not get one of the four things it needs to grow? Discuss. **The plant would not be healthy and would not grow if it did not receive the four things it needs. The four things we need—apostles' teaching, fellowship, breaking of bread, and prayer—will help us grow up in Christ. Let's take time now to ask God to help us grow in devotion to the church by making these four things a part of our lives.** Lead the students in prayer.

Classroom Supplies
- potted house plant
- watering can with a small amount of water
- fertilizer

Curriculum Supplies
none

How to Grow Up

Have students locate Acts 2:42-47 in their Bibles. Ask for volunteers to read the verses. Point out that the memory passage is a part of today's Scripture passage.

Divide the chalkboard into two columns. Title one column "Early Church." Title the other column "Church Today." Number from one to four in each column, leaving space for answers. Choose two students to record answers in the columns. Distribute bulletins or printed orders of worship. Say: **The Bible tells us that the early church met together and devoted themselves to four things. We are going to look at how we devote ourselves to the same four things when we meet together.**

Acts 2:42 lists the four things. What is the first one? (The apostles' teaching.) Have student record this in the "Early Church" column. **What is the apostles' teaching?** Discuss. **The apostles taught the people about Jesus' life, death, and resurrection. They taught the people how Jesus saves everyone who comes to him from their sins. Look at your bulletin. In the church today, what do we do to devote ourselves to the apostles' teaching?** (This could be the sermon or the Bible lesson. It could also include reading Scripture and the devotional time before the Lord's Supper and before the offering.) Have students record these ideas in the "Church Today" column.

Say: **What is the second thing the early church did?** (Fellowship.) Have student record this in the "Early Church" column. **Define fellowship.** Discuss the students' responses. **The early church enjoyed fellowship by sharing with others. What kinds of things does the Bible say that they shared? Look in Acts 2:44-47.** (They had everything in common so they literally shared everything

Classroom Supplies
- copies of church bulletin or other printed order of worship
- Bibles
- chalkboard
- chalk
- paper
- pencils

Curriculum Supplies
none

they owned. They sold what they had to give to those in need. They ate together in their homes. They shared spiritually by praising God together.) **What do we do when we meet together to share with others?** (Help others who have needs; share meals; have fun times together. This could include taking an offering and praising God through singing together. It would also include testimony time.) Have students record these ideas in the "Church Today" column.

Say: **What is the third thing?** (Breaking of bread.) Have students record this in the "Early Church" column. **What do we do today? Look in your bulletin.** (The Lord's Supper or communion.) Have students record this in the "Church Today" column. Say: **The Lord's Supper is a special time to remember that Jesus died on the cross for us. It is also a time to admit our sins and to ask for forgiveness. It is a time to celebrate that Jesus has saved us. It is a time to remember all that Jesus has done for us.**

What is the fourth thing? (Prayer.) Have student record this in the "Early Church" column. **Prayer was important to the early church and it is important to us. How is prayer a part of our church today when we meet together? Look in your bulletin.** (This could include prayer at the offering and Lord's Supper time. It could include prayer for those in need, and so on.) Have students record these ideas in the "Church Today" column.

When the chart is complete, divide the class into four groups. Assign each group one of the four activities—teaching, fellowship, breaking of bread, and prayer. Say: **Acts 2:46 says, "Every day they continued to meet together." The early Christians showed their devotion by doing these things every day. We do not meet together every day, but there are many ways we can be devoted to the four things every day.**

Instruct groups to make a list of things that they could do during the week to be devoted to their assigned topic. When lists are complete, have students share their lists with the class. Because the biblical precedent for the breaking of bread is that it is done on Sunday, ask that group to think of ways they can remember Jesus during the week and prepare for the weekly remembrance and of ways they can celebrate their salvation through Jesus.

Say: **We have talked about many ways to be devoted to the church. We can all grow in our devotion to the church by following the example of the believers in the early church.**

Classroom Supplies
- pencils
- cellophane tape
- scissors

Curriculum Supplies
one copy of reproducible page 241 (Score Four Folder) and 242 (numeral four diary sheets) for each student

Ready to Grow Up!

Distribute the reproducible pages. Instruct students to fold the Score Four Folder in half along the solid line and to cut along the dotted lines. Have students secure the folders by folding a piece of tape around each side. Students may write their names in the tab area of the folder. Also instruct students to cut along the solid lines around the numeral four.

Explain that this folder is to keep a record of their personal score as they grow in devotion to the church. Each week they will add one of the four areas to their card.

Say: **This week we are learning that the early church grew and that God added to their number as they devoted themselves to four things.**

We will grow in Christ as we devote ourselves to the same four things. As you watch your score grow larger on your Score Four Folder, you will know that you are growing up in Christ.

Have students locate row one in the first column of the Score Four Folder. It reads as follows: "Recite Memory Passage." Students can earn four points each day they can quote the entire memory passage. Instruct them to recite the memory passage to someone who can date and initial their numeral four diary sheet. For each time, they may give themselves four points on their score card. Show them how to record the fours in the grid and then add the fours and record their total score in the box for week one.

Say: **This week we are only scoring four for item number one. Bring your Score Four Folder back with you each week so that we can see how much you've grown. Each week we will add another way to score even more points. Think about how many points you can add to your score card. As you add points, you will be growing in devotion to the church.**

Growing Up Every Day

Have students make a design on the front of their Score Four Folders using the numeral four. They may create and color it any way they want as long as the numeral four is the center of their design.

Say: **Growing in Christ is exciting! Growing in devotion to the church is exciting! Learning, sharing in fellowship, remembering Jesus, and praying are four great ways to grow. Not only will devotion to these four things help us grow spiritually, it will also help add people to the church. It will help to increase the number of people who are a part of the church. The early church has given us a wonderful example to follow to help us grow in Christ and in devotion to his church. Are you excited about being devoted to these four ways to help you grow?**

Have students stand in a circle with their folders. Tell them to answer the following questions by holding up their design and shouting four. Ask the questions as if you are leading a cheer.

Plants need how many things to grow? (Four!) **The early church grew as they devoted themselves to how many things?** (Four!) **We can grow in Christ as we devote ourselves to how many things in the church?** (Four!) **Right! Let's all say the four things together!** Lead them enthusiastically in saying the following: "The apostles' teaching! Fellowship! Breaking of bread! Prayer!"

Say: **Every time you score four points this week, think of these four things. Let's say them together one more time before we go out to score four and grow in Christ.** Close with prayer.

Classroom Supplies
- crayons
- markers
- colored pencils
- score four folders

Curriculum Supplies
none

Lesson 2

Growing in Devotion to the Church

Devoted to the Apostles' Teaching

Acts 2:1-4, 14, 22-24, 32, 33, 36-41

Bible Focus
Peter preached and the crowd responded to God's Word.

Life Focus
Actively listen to preaching and respond to God's Word.

Growing Up in the Word: Acts 2:42, 46, 47
Set up one or both of the following activities to do as students arrive. Greet the students, explain the activities, and invite them to participate.

Classroom Supplies
- small pieces of paper
- envelopes

Curriculum Supplies
none

Memory Activity 1
Before class, prepare a numbered slip of paper for each student. Number four papers with the numeral four, four papers with the numeral three, eight papers with the numeral two, and number the remaining papers with the numeral one. Place each paper in an envelope so that students will not know their number until they open the envelope.

Place the envelopes on a table. Have each student select an envelope and hold it until you tell them to look inside. Divide the class into four teams. On your signal, students will open their envelopes to see if their team has at least one of each number among them. If not, they may send one member of their team back to the table to trade his envelope for another, take it back to the team, open it, and see if it supplies the number his team needs. Each team continues with process until they have all four numbers. In order to win, a team must have all four numbers and then recite the memory passage together. If time allows, keep the activity going until all four teams recite the memory passage.

Say: **Think about our memory passage. What do you think your four numbers represent?** (They represent the apostles' teaching, fellowship, breaking of bread, and prayer.) **How difficult was it to get all four numerals for your team? You kept going, though, until your team had all four numerals. Your goal was to obtain all four numerals, and you devoted yourselves to that goal.**

In order for your team to reach its goal, you had to listen to the coaching of your teammates and then respond by switching envelopes. When we devote ourselves to listening to the apostles' teaching and to responding to what we hear, then we will reach our goal of growing up in Christ. It is important that we stay devoted to our goal of growing in devotion to the church.

Memory Activity 2

Before class, write the memory passage on the board. Divide it into eighteen phrases.

Ask students to read the memory passage in unison, then have students sit in groups of two or three. Give each student one empty cup and one cup that has eighteen food pieces in it. In their groups, students will take turns sitting with their backs to the board so that they cannot see the memory passage. They will then try to recite the passage. The other students in their group who are looking at the verse may offer help if needed and tell the student who is reciting when he is correct. For each correct phrase, the student takes a piece of food from the full cup and adds it to the empty cup. When everyone has had a turn, allow students to eat what they have added to their cup as you discuss the passage.

Say: **Every time you said a part of the memory passage, you added food to your cup. What does the memory passage tell us that the Lord did to the early church?** (The Lord added to their number daily those who were being saved.) **Why do you think people were being saved and added to their number?** Give students time to look back at the passage. Guide them to see that people were responding to what they heard and saw in the early church and were being saved and added to the church as a result.

Say: **The early church was devoted to the apostles' teaching. They listened and responded, and they were being saved. The Lord added to their number and the church was growing. Every time you added food to your cup, the number of food items grew. As you add Scripture to your memory, you are growing in Christ.**

Classroom Supplies
- chalkboard
- chalk
- disposable cups
- small food item such as pretzels
- snack crackers or M&M's brand chocolate candies

Curriculum Supplies
none

Why Grow Up?

Ask: **What does it mean to respond?** Let students give their definition. If they have trouble defining the word, tell them that the dictionary says that to respond means to answer or to react. **If we respond to something we hear, we do something because of what we heard.**

I am going to give you some directions. Listen carefully and then respond to the directions. You may not ask any questions, and I cannot repeat any directions. The directions are purposely confusing so that the activity can be used later to help illustrate active listening. Speak at a normal rate and give the directions without pausing between sentences. After you read the directions, give each student a paper and pencil. Tell them to respond to what they heard.

Directions follow:

Draw a large circle in the center of your paper.

In the upper left corner of your paper, write your surname.

In the lower right corner of your paper, draw nothing.

Classroom Supplies
- paper
- pencils

Curriculum Supplies
none

In the lower left corner of your paper, draw a minuscule letter "x."

In the circle, write your first name backwards.

When you finish, turn your paper over, put your pencil on top of your paper, and put your right hand on your head.

After drawings are complete, ask students these questions and give them time to discuss their opinions. Say: **Did you listen carefully so that you could respond in the right way? Did you understand all the directions? Did you remember everything you were asked to do?**

Repeat the directions slowly as students check their response and make changes to their drawings. This time, allow students to ask questions about the directions. Explain words they do not understand. Say: **Sometimes it is hard to listen carefully. Is it easier for you to listen carefully when something is important to you? Why?**

The people of the early church thought that listening to the apostles' teaching was important. They listened carefully and responded to what they heard. The Lord added to the church those who responded and were being saved. Our Scripture lesson today tells about people listening to teaching and responding to God's Word.

Listening and responding to the directions you just heard was not important, but listening and responding to teaching about God is very important for us, just as it was for the people in the early church. We grow by listening and responding to what God wants for us.

Classroom Supplies
- Bibles
- chalkboard
- chalk

Curriculum Supplies
none

How to Grow Up

Have students locate Acts 2:1-4, 14, 22-24, 32, 36-41 in their Bibles and read the entire passage silently. Then guide the following discussion.

Say: **The people were listening to the apostles' teaching. Who was teaching that day?** (Peter.) **What was Peter teaching?** (Jesus was a man accredited by God. Jesus was put to death, and God raised him from the dead.) **What does "accredited" mean?** Explain that it means that God has proved that Jesus is his Son through the miracles Jesus did. **Verse 36 tells us that God made Jesus both Lord and Christ.**

How many people heard Peter teach about Jesus? Let students speculate. **How did the people respond to Peter's teaching?** (They were cut to the heart and asked what they should do.) **Find the people's words in verse 37. How did the people feel? How do you think the people said those words?** Have student volunteers read the words of the people in the way they might have said them.

Ask: **What were Peter's instructions?** (Repent and be baptized.) **Find Peter's instructions in verse 38. How do you think Peter said those words? Were these instructions important? Let's read the instructions the way Peter might have said them.** Have volunteers do so.

Say: **Peter also gave the people another instruction. Find it in verse 40.** (Save yourselves from this corrupt generation.) **This verse tells us how Peter said these words. Look again at verse 40. How did Peter say these words?** (In a warning and pleading way.) **Let's read Peter's words in a warning and pleading way.** Have student volunteers do so.

Say: **How do you know the people listened to Peter's teaching?** (They followed Peter's instructions by repenting and being baptized.) **The people listened to Peter's teaching, and they responded by obeying his instructions. They knew that the church was from God because of the miraculous way the apostles could speak to them in their own languages and because of the truth in the apostles' teaching. Three thousand people responded and were added to the church's number. How many people is three thousand?** Give students an idea by comparing three thousand to the size of your city or school system.

Following the discussion, direct students to perform a dramatic reading of the Scripture. Choose one student to read the words of Peter, one to read selected narration, and the rest of the class to read the remaining verses in unison. Write the following list on the board so that students can remember which verses they will be reading.

All: Acts 2:1, 4, 37b, 41
Narrator: Acts 2:2, 3, 14a, 37a, 38a, 40a
Peter: Acts 2:14b, 22-24, 32-33, 36, 38b-39, 40b

Explain to students how to find their parts. Then have them read aloud. As they do so, students should read in a dramatic way. They should read their verses the way the people and Peter might have said them.

Ready to Grow Up!

Before class, cut one reproducible page into the five picture sections. Make one copy of the page and of the diary sheet for each student.

Say: **The early church devoted themselves to four things. What were these four things? Let's look at your Score Four Folders and find out how your scored this week. Did you and your score grow this week as you memorized the memory passage? Let's say the memory passage together right now.** Allow students to use their Bibles if they are still unsure of the verse.

Say: **Which one of these four things have we been talking about today?** (The apostles' teaching.) **People listened to the apostles' teaching, responded, were saved, and the Lord added them to the church. They listened carefully, just as Peter asked them to do.**

Sometimes, even when we try to listen carefully, we do not understand or remember what we are being told. At the beginning of class when you listened to the directions to make a drawing, did you listen carefully? What did you do the second time you listened to the directions to make it easier to remember what you heard? What other things might you do to help you listen more carefully? Students may have ideas such as asking questions about what they did not understand, writing down the directions, seeing the directions. Allow them to discuss the things that help them listen.

Choose five students to act out the five ways to listen that are listed on the reproducible sheet. Assign them parts by handing them one of the cut apart sections of the reproducible. Set up an area where the five will sit together and pretend to listen to a speaker. Provide simple props such as paper and pencils and Bibles. They are to act out what is written on their papers. Have the audience guess what the actors are doing.

Classroom Supplies
- score four booklets
- pencils

Curriculum Supplies
reproducible pages 243 (Take Action) and 242 (diary sheets)

After the five ways have been guessed, give each student a copy of reproducible page 243. Ask students to match the sentences with the pictures. Discuss how these suggestions can help them be active listeners. Tell them to use this checklist to help them actively listen this week.

Say: **We are going to continue to score four this week. Look at your Score Four Folder. Find the words "listen" and "respond" by numerals two and three in the first column. Every time you actively listen to someone teaching about Jesus and every time you read your Bible and listen to God's quiet voice, write about it in on your diary sheet and then add four to your score this week. Each time you respond to what you heard, write about it on your diary sheet and add four more to your score.** Distribute new numeral four diary sheets to each student.

Say: **You may also score four points every day this week that you say the memory passage. At the end of the week, add your weekly points. Then add those points to last week's points to find your total. Watch your score grow as you grow in devotion to the church by listening and responding to the apostles' teaching about Jesus.**

Growing Up Every Day

Classroom Supplies
none

Curriculum Supplies
none

Say: **The early church grew when people listened and responded to the apostles' teaching. Many people were added to the church. We can grow in our devotion to the church when we listen to teaching about Jesus and respond to what we hear. What opportunities do you have to hear teaching about Jesus?** (Students might listen to sermons, Bible school lessons, lessons in Children's Church or at youth activities, and so on. Students may also count reading God's Word.) **What will you do this week to help you listen more carefully? You will grow in Christ as you respond to what you hear.** Ask a volunteer to pray that God will help everyone to listen and respond in a way that pleases him.

Lesson 3

Growing in Devotion to the Church

Devoted to Prayer

Acts 3, 4

Bible Focus
The church prayed for courage to speak about Jesus.

Life Focus
Participate in prayer for the church and for opportunities to speak about Jesus.

Growing Up in the Word: Acts 2:42, 46, 47
Set up one or both of the following activities to do as students arrive. Greet the students, explain the activities, and invite them to participate.

Memory Activity 1

Classroom Supplies
- snacks that begin with the letters in the word prayer (such as pretzels, raisins, apples, yogurt, candy or hard-boiled eggs, rice cereal squares)
- napkins

Curriculum Supplies
none

Present the snacks and invite students to take a little of each. Say: **These snacks contain clues about today's mystery word. What do you think the clue is that these snacks have?** Allow students to guess. If they have trouble, tell them the clue. **The first letter of the snacks you are eating will spell a word in the memory passage. For example, if you were eating bananas, the letter "B" would be one of the letters in the word from the memory passage. Try to guess the word while you are eating. When you think you know the word, raise your hand, but do not say the word. When all of you think you know the word, I will ask "What's the word?" and you will all say the word together.** If students need help with some of the letters, give clues as needed for the snacks you have selected. When all students have raised their hands, say **"What's the word?"** Allow students to respond. **You are right. The word is prayer. Now let's say the memory passage together.**

Say: **The believers in the early church devoted themselves to prayer. They knew how important it was for them to communicate with God. They knew that the church would grow with God's help. They prayed for God's help; they praised him in prayer; and they thanked him in prayer. In our Scripture lesson today, we will read about the church's prayer for boldness to speak about Jesus.**

Prayer is important for us too. Praying to God will help us grow in devotion to the church. It will help us grow up in Christ.

Classroom Supplies
- papers with memory passage written on them
- crackers

Curriculum Supplies
none

Memory Activity 2

Before class, set up two identical relay stations on opposite ends of the room, one on each end. Each station should include an area marked "temple courts" and an area with a table marked "home." In the temple courts area, place a paper with the memory passage written on it. In the home area, have one cracker for each team member.

In class divide the students into two teams. At your signal, teams will form a circle at the temple courts area. The first team member will read the first verse of the memory passage and pass the paper to the second member who will read the second verse. Teams will continue to pass the paper around the circle, reading one verse until all members have read a verse. Verses must be read in order. After the reading is completed, members will get into a position of prayer by getting on their knees, bowing their heads, and folding their hands. After all members are in position, the team stands and moves to the home area.

At the home area all members must break a cracker and eat it. The team will then form a line. The first person in line will move down the line shaking hands with each team member as he says "praise God." When he gets to the end of the line, he takes his position there and the next person begins to shake team members' hands. Continue until all team members have greeted everyone in line. When finished, the team sits down.

Say: **You just raced through some of the things the early church did everyday. What did you do at the temple courts area that represented what the people of the early church did everyday?** (We read Scripture to represent the apostles' teaching. We got on our knees to represent prayer.) **The church met every day in the temple courts for the apostles' teaching and for prayer.**

What did you do in the home area that represented what the early church did everyday in their homes? (We broke and ate a cracker to represent the breaking of bread. We greeted one another to represent fellowship.) **The early church grew in devotion to the church everyday as they met in the temple courts and in their homes to do the four things of the church.**

Classroom Supplies
- a variety of small items that will fit in a closed hand (coin, button, paper clip, candy, nail, cotton ball, and so on)
- paper
- pencils

Curriculum Supplies
none

Why Grow Up?

Before class, collect enough small items so that each student will have a different item. If you have a small class, collect enough items for two per student. The item must be small enough so that the student can hide it in one hand. Do not let students see the items before the activity.

In class, tell students that they are going to be given an object. They are to hold the object tightly in one hand so that no one else sees it. After giving each student one item, instruct students to stand in different places around the room.

Say: **When I tell you to begin, you are to go to every other student and ask him to show you what is in his hand. When he shows you, thank him and go on to the next person. When someone asks you to show what it is in your hand, open your hand and show the object you are holding. The person will thank**

you and go to someone else. Be sure that you ask every person. Now, begin.

Give students time to see all the objects. When finished, ask them to give the object back to you and be seated. Then hide the objects from view. Distribute paper and pencil and ask students to make a list of all the items they remember seeing. Students should work independently.

After students have had a chance to write what they remember, show the items so students can check their lists.

Say: **During this activity, you asked your classmates to show you what they were holding. You thanked them for showing you the item. Did you remember what they showed you?**

When we pray, we often ask God for something. We ask him to do something for us. God answers our prayers, but do we pray again to thank him? Do we remember what he has done for us? Or do we quickly forget that he answered our prayers? If we devote ourselves to prayer, we will not forget to thank God and we will not forget about his answers to our prayers.

The believers in the early church devoted themselves to prayer. They spent time in prayer. They prayed to praise God. They prayed to ask God for help. They prayed to thank God. They knew that God would answer their prayers.

In our lesson today, the early church prayed for something and God answered their prayer. They used what God gave them to help the church grow.

How to Grow Up

Depending on the size of your class, students may work individually or in small groups. Assign one Scripture reference to each person or group. If your class is very small, assign more than one Scripture reference to each student. Give each student or group one poster board. Tell them to read their Scripture and then draw scenes illustrating what they have read. Students may decide that only one scene will explain their text, while others may need several drawings to fully illustrate the passage. Divide the scripture into these sections: Acts 3:1-7, Acts 3:8-10, Acts 3:11-26, Acts 4:1-4, Acts 4:5-14, Acts 4:15-17, Acts 4:18-20, Acts 4:21-30, Acts 4:31, Acts 4:32-37.

Explain to students that they will be reading only a small part of the story. Tell them to be ready to tell the rest of the class what their Scripture said by using the illustrations they have drawn. When all illustrations are completed, display the posters in chronological order. In turn, have students tell about their part of the Scripture so that the class learns the entire story.

Say: **What a great couple of days this was for the church! A man was healed because he had the faith to be healed. The healing of the man showed that the church was from God. This gave Peter and John an opportunity to teach the people about Jesus.**

What happened to Peter and John, though, because they were teaching about Jesus? (They were put in jail and then brought before the religious leaders.) **This gave Peter and John another opportunity to speak about Jesus. The leaders saw Peter and John's courage as they spoke. How did the religious leaders respond to Peter's teaching?** (They told him not to speak or teach in the name of Jesus ever again.) **The leaders wanted to punish Peter and John, but so**

Classroom Supplies
- white poster board
- pencils
- crayons
- markers

Curriculum Supplies
none

many people had believed in Jesus because of the apostles' teaching, the leaders were afraid to punish them. They only threatened them and then let them go.

When Peter and John went back to their own people, what did the people pray for? (They prayed for boldness to speak about God's Word.)

Peter, John, and the other believers were devoted to the apostles' teaching and to prayer. The fact that they faced the threat of jail and punishment for speaking about Jesus shows us how devoted they were to the apostles' teaching. Because they faced punishment for speaking about Jesus, they prayed for boldness to speak. They knew God would answer their prayers, and he did. They were devoted to prayer.

We are probably not going to be put in jail for speaking about Jesus, but we face other consequences that sometimes make us afraid to speak about Jesus to others. What can you think of that might make us afraid? Encourage students to talk about their own experiences and their fears. Lead them to see that God will give them courage. After they discuss some possible consequences and fears, have a time of prayer asking God for help in specific circumstances and for courage to speak for him.

Classroom Supplies
• score four folders

Curriculum Supplies
copies of reproducible page 242 (numeral four prayer sheets)

Ready to Grow Up!

Say: **How much have you grown this week? Let's look at our Score Four Folders. Did your score grow? Did you find ways to listen and respond to God's Word this week? Were you able to say the memory passage and score four by growing in God's Word? Did you grow in devotion to the church by listening and responding to the church's teaching?**

Ask students to share some of their experiences with active listening and responding to God's Word. Encourage them to read what they have written on their diary sheets. Ask questions that will help them talk about the opportunities they may have had to respond to something they learned. Ask them if following the suggestions for active listening helped them better understand a sermon or lesson this week.

Say: **Today we've talked about how important prayer was to the early church. They devoted themselves to prayer. When we devote ourselves to something, it is very important to us. We want to spend time making it a part of our lives.**

Look at your Score Four Folders. Find items four and five in the first column, which are pray and speak. God wants us to pray. We grow as we pray. The believers in the early church grew in devotion to the church as they prayed. They prayed for each other. They prayed for courage to speak to others about Jesus. And then they spoke about Jesus. God gave them boldness.

God will give us boldness too. Distribute numeral four prayer sheets. **Let's make a list on our prayer sheets of things we can pray for this week. Let's begin by listing two people whom we would like to talk to about Jesus. Fill in the blanks of the first two sentences. Next, let's list some fears we might have about talking to others about Jesus.** Lead students to fill in the rest of the blanks.

Say: **Use these sheets when you pray this week. They will remind you what you need to pray about. Let's devote ourselves to prayer this week. Praying for others and for ourselves will help us grow in devotion to the church.**

This week, score four every time you pray for courage to speak to someone about Jesus. Give yourself four points every time you speak to someone about Jesus or about God's Word. Write about what happens when you pray. Write about your experiences as you speak to someone about God's Word. You may also continue to score four points this week for reciting the memory passage, for active listening, and for responding to what you hear.

We can pray whenever we want and wherever we are. We can pray about everything. Just think about that! We can talk to God about anything whenever we want! He is always listening, and he is always there to help us, just as he was for the early church.

Growing Up Every Day

Give students paper and pencils. Say: **Today we've talked about the importance of prayer. How important is prayer? The number of times prayer is mentioned in the Bible should tell us how important prayer is. How many times do you think the Bible talks about prayer?** Have students write their guess on their paper.

Direct students to find out how many times prayer is discussed in the Bible. Give students concordances and explain how to look for a word, find a reference, and use that reference to locate a verse in the Bible. Assign individuals or groups to find one of the prayer words in the concordance and count the number of times the word is used in the Bible. Include all forms of the word prayer such as pray, prayed, prayer, prayers, praying, and prays. When all counts have been made, have students add the numbers to get a total for all prayer words. They can then compare their guesses to the total.

Say: **Did you know that the Bible has that much to say about prayer? Prayer is important because it is the way we communicate with God. We can't grow up in Christ without prayer.** Close with prayer.

Classroom Supplies
- pencils
- paper
- concordances

Curriculum Supplies
none

Lesson 4

Growing in Devotion to the Church

Devoted to Fellowship

Acts 4:32-37; 6:1-6

Bible Focus
The church cared for believers in need.

Life Focus
Participate in fellowship of the church and share on personal level.

Growing Up in the Word: Acts 2:42, 46, 47
Set up one or both of the following activities to do as students arrive. Greet the students, explain the activities, and invite them to participate.

Classroom Supplies
- construction paper strips
- crayons or markers
- tape or stapler

Curriculum Supplies
none

Memory Activity 1
Before class, cut various colors of one-by-twelve-inch strips of construction paper. In class give seven strips to each student and instruct them to write one day of the week on each strip. Students should then staple or tape their strips together in order from Sunday to Friday to form a chain. Leave the Saturday strip unfastened for now.

Lead the class in reciting the memory passage, Acts 2:42, 46, 47. Say: **How often did the early church meet together in the temple courts and in their homes for the apostles' teaching, fellowship, breaking of bread, and prayer?** (Everyday.) **Doing these four things everyday helped the early church grow.**

Suppose the early church met only one time a week for the apostles' teaching, fellowship, breaking of bread, and prayer; do you think they would have grown very much? Hold up one link of chain. **Suppose they did these things everyday for an entire week.** Have students hold up their chains. **The more days they devoted themselves to the four things, the more they grew. The more links you added to your chain the longer it got. But the early church didn't just grow for one week. They kept doing these important things everyday, every week, every month, every year.** Have students use their Saturday strips to join their chains together. Then hang the chain in the room so that students will see its length.

Say: **Our chain is long. It grew as we added links to it. Each of our links represents a day of the week. We will grow up in Christ if we study the Bible,**

share with others, remember what Jesus did for us, and talk to God everyday. Lead the class in repeating the memory passage again.

Memory Activity 2

Classroom Supplies
- index cards
- four cups of chopped apples
- 1/2 cup pecan pieces
- 1/2 cup mayonnaise
- 3/4 cup raisins
- sixteen containers
- four small mixing bowls
- one large mixing bowl
- four mixing spoons
- paper bowls
- spoons
- napkins

Curriculum Supplies
none

Before class, divide the memory passage into four sections. Write each section on a separate index card. Make four sets. Sort the cards into sets so that all the cards in a set have the same section of the passage.

Divide each of the ingredients for the apple salad into four separate containers. Place the first phrase of the memory passage on each apple container. Place the index card for the second phrase on the pecan pieces. Place phrase three on the mayonnaise and phrase four on the raisins.

Divide the class into four groups. Give each group a different salad ingredient. Group one should have all apples; group two all raisins, and so on. Ask the groups to put the cards in the correct order to complete the memory passage. As they look at their set of cards, they will see that the cards are all alike. Ask one member of each group to read their cards. Ask: **What should we do so that all groups will be able to complete the memory passage?** Give students time to share their cards and put the new set in order. When all groups have finished, ask everyone to read the memory passage together.

Next, instruct groups to mix the four ingredients together in the mixing bowl. They should mix them in the order of the memory passage that is attached to them. Students should recite the memory passage from the card as each ingredient is placed in the bowl. When all groups are finished, have them mix the salads of all four groups into a larger mixing bowl. Eat the snack as you discuss the activity.

Say: **You shared what you had with others so that everyone had what they needed. First you shared the information on the index cards so everyone would have a complete set. Now you are sharing the result of your work—a snack. These are both examples of fellowship. The early church devoted themselves to fellowship. They shared what they had with each other. They shared with glad and sincere hearts, and they enjoyed being together.**

Let's name some things that we can share with others. Give children time to answer and discuss their answers. **We should also be glad to share with others. Enjoying fellowship and sharing together helps us grow in devotion to the church and helps us grow up in Christ.**

Why Grow Up?

Classroom Supplies
- plastic grocery bag with handles
- thread
- scissors
- five pound bag of sugar or flour
- gloves

Curriculum Supplies
none

Before class, place the five pound bag into the plastic bag. Cut eleven 18-inch lengths of thread. Try this activity before class to be sure that your thread is the right strength.

Say: **We are going to try to lift this bag off the table.** Put one thread through the handles of the plastic bag. Using gloves to protect your hands from being cut by the thread, hold one end of the thread in each hand and try to lift the bag with the thread. The thread should break. **One thread by itself cannot lift the bag for us. Let's see what happens when we use several threads together.** Pick up ten threads together, put them through the handles of the bag, and lift the bag using only the threads. This time the bag should easily lift off the table. Some students may like to try this for themselves. Have extra thread available if you have time to allow students to try the activity. Insist that they wear the gloves to protect their hands. **When we put several threads together, those threads working together as one can lift the bag for us.**

The believers in the early church enjoyed a oneness as they shared together. One of the reasons the members of the early church were so strong was due to fellowship—they shared what they had with each other. When one of them was weak, the others helped and together they were strong.

When we lifted the bag, we saw that many threads together could do what one thread alone could not do. When we help each other and work together as one, we accomplish what one of us alone cannot do. We need to care about others spiritually and materially, just as the Scripture says the believers in the early church cared about others. As we share together, we help each other grow in devotion to the church.

Classroom Supplies
- Bibles
- pencils

Curriculum Supplies
reproducible page 244 (No Needy Persons Among Them)

How to Grow Up

Have students locate Acts 4:32-37 and Acts 6:1-6 in their Bibles. Ask students to take turns reading the verses aloud.

Say: **In this Scripture passage, we find that the believers are doing many things that are mentioned in our memory passage. How are the believers devoting themselves to fellowship?** (They were one in heart and mind. No one claimed his own possessions. They shared everything. No one was needy. They sold land and gave the money to be given to others as they had need. They cared about all different kinds of people. They chose seven men to oversee the giving of food.)

How do we know that they were devoted to the apostles' teaching? (The number of believers was increasing. The apostles' continued to testify. The apostles did not want to neglect the ministry of the Word of God.) **How do we know they were devoted to prayer?** (The apostles wanted to give their attention to prayer. The apostles prayed for the seven chosen men.)

The believers were meeting together. We know the Lord was adding to their number because the number of disciples was increasing. Even though there were believers from many different countries and cultures in their number now, the church cared about all people, regardless of differences. They enjoyed the favor of all the people. They cared so much about each other that they thought it was important to choose seven men to make sure everyone was given what he or she needed. Everyone participated in the fellowship of the church. People could see the oneness, the caring, and the sharing and know that this special way of life in the church was from God.

Give each student a copy of reproducible page 244. Instruct students to use their Bibles to fill in the blanks and then find those words in the puzzle. If your class is mostly younger students, fill in the blanks together as a class and allow students to work together to search for the words in the puzzle. When finished, challenge students to find two more words by looking at the unused letters of the puzzle. (The two words are "fellowship" and "sharing.")

Ready to Grow Up!

Before class, cut six strips of paper. On each strip of paper, write one of the following topics: time, money, food, something you know about God or a way God has blessed you, a talent, a favorite possession. If you think you will have more than six groups of three or four in your class, duplicate some of the topics on additional strips of paper.

Say: **Let's enjoy our own fellowship right now. Let's share how we have been growing in devotion to the church as we increased our scores this week.** Pause after each question and allow students to share with each other. Encourage all students to participate. Some students may need extra help in talking about their experiences. Some may prefer to participate only by listening. Comment on their active listening to others as they share. **What have you written in your booklets? Did you use your prayer sheets to help you pray for courage? Did you have an opportunity to use your courage to speak to someone about Jesus? Tell us about those opportunities. What about your other scores? Are you still adding fours for saying the memory passage and for listening and responding to God's Word?**

We can help each other grow in devotion to the church by sharing our experiences. We may help someone else to have courage because of something we say. That is what being devoted to fellowship is all about. We can share material things like food and money the way the early church shared, but they also shared spiritually. They praised God together. They showed they cared about people. They showed love by being one in heart and mind. They shared with glad and sincere hearts. How do you feel when you have fellowship with others? How does it make you feel to share and grow in devotion to the church?

There are many ways to share with others. Divide the class into groups of three or four. Tell students that they will be creating a skit about sharing and then sharing their skits with the class. Lay the strips of paper face down on the table. Have groups select a paper and make up a skit showing a way they might share what is written on their paper. If you have less than six groups, have some groups do more than one skit topic. After the groups present their skits, talk about other ways that they might share that skit topic.

Say: **Now that you have lots of ideas about how to be devoted to fellowship by sharing with others, think of ways that you can personally share with others this week. On your Score Four Folders, find the word "share" in the first column. Remember to score four every time you devote yourself to fellowship this week. Write about it on your diary sheet. Score four for saying the memory passage, for listening and responding to God's Word, and for praying and speaking to someone about Jesus. We will enjoy fellowship again next week when we share our growing scores and our growing devotion to Christ and his church.**

Classroom Supplies
- score four folders
- pencils
- small strips of paper

Curriculum Supplies
reproducible page 242 (diary sheets)

Growing Up Every Day

Classroom Supplies
coin

Curriculum Supplies
none

Say: **We can participate in fellowship now by sharing God's Word. Let's say the memory passage together.** Ask a student to lead in saying the passage. **We can participate in fellowship by sharing our praise to God.** Have students stand in a circle. **Think of some things you can praise God for. When the coin is flipped to you, say one praise to God, and then flip the coin to someone else. Show your love and care for everyone by making sure everyone gets a turn to catch the coin and praise God.** If time permits, allow everyone to have several chances to praise God.

Say: **While we are standing in a circle, let's continue to grow in devotion to the church by being devoted to prayer.** Ask anyone who will to share a sentence prayer. End the prayer by asking God to help all of you find ways to share this week and to grow in devotion to the church.

Say: **The believers in the early church had an attitude of joy about sharing with others. Be joyful this week as you share and as you grow in Christ.**

Lesson 5

Growing in Devotion to the Church

Devoted to Remembering Jesus

Acts 4:1-31; 5:12-14; 5:17-42

Bible Focus

Peter, John, and other apostles stood up for their faith.

Life Focus

Continue to be devoted to four aspects of the church when facing difficult situations.

Growing Up in the Word: Acts 2:42, 46, 47

Set up one or both of the following activities to do as students arrive. Greet the students, explain the activities, and invite them to participate.

Memory Activity 1

Classroom Supplies
- two balls of yarn of different colors
- chalk
- chalkboard

Curriculum Supplies
none

Before class, write the memory passage on the chalkboard.

Divide students into two teams. Have students stand in various parts of the room. Scatter team members so that they are far apart. Position students so that there are chairs, tables, or other objects between team members. Have one team sit and one stand.

Give a ball of yarn to one member of each team. Tell students that their team is to say the memory passage correctly as they toss the ball of yarn from person to person. The first team member will say the first phrase of the memory verse and then, while holding onto the end of the yarn, toss the ball of yarn to another team member. The second team member will say the next phrase of the passage, hold the string of yarn in his hand, and toss the ball of yarn to the next team member. Students should pass the ball of yarn over, under, around, or through any obstacles that are between them and the next team member. Teams will continue until all members are holding the string of yarn. If they finish the passage before all team members have a chance to say a phrase, the team will begin the passage again. If all members have a turn before they finish the verse, the team will continue to toss the ball of yarn to members until they complete the entire passage. The first team to finish the verse with all members holding onto the yarn is the winner of the first round.

Students may not move from their positions during the activity to retrieve the ball of yarn if it rolls out of reach of all team members. If the yarn rolls out of reach of a team, you may return it to the team after one team member tells something that Jesus has done for him or her.

After both teams complete the round, they will race to roll the yarn back into a ball. This time, the team that stood will sit and the sitting team will stand. The first team to reroll the ball of yarn wins the second round.

Say: **Obstacles make it difficult to complete what we are trying to do. As you passed the yarn, there were many objects in your way that made it difficult for you to keep going. Sometimes you lost your ball of yarn. What helped you complete this difficult task?** Students may offer many suggestions. Conclude with the fact that couldn't have completed the task without knowing God's Word—the memory passage—and remembering Jesus—telling something Jesus has done for them.

Say: **Even though early believers devoted themselves to the activities of the church, they faced many difficult situations. It was not always easy for them to stand up for their faith and keep going. However, remembering Jesus always helped them through difficult times.**

We also face difficult situations when we are growing in devotion to the church. It is important for us to continue in the four things of the church that help us grow up in Christ.

Classroom Supplies
- American flag
- wedding ring
- bread and cup of juice used for the Lord's Supper

Curriculum Supplies
none

Memory Activity 2

Give students time to work with a partner to memorize and review the memory passage. After a time of practice, have volunteers recite the passage.

Say: **A symbol is an object that represents another object. It helps us think about or remember something. Our flag is a symbol.** Show the American flag. **What does our flag represent? What does it help us think about or remember?** (The great country we live in, love for our country, freedom, people who have fought for our country, and so on.)

Hold up a wedding ring. Say: **A wedding ring is also a symbol. It is a symbol of the love and devotion a husband and wife have for each other. Can you think of any other symbols?** Give students time to discuss symbols they have encountered.

Say: **Our memory passage tells us that the early church broke bread together. The breaking of bread is also called the Lord's Supper. We share the Lord's Supper to help us remember and to think about what Jesus did for us when he came to earth and died on the cross to save us from our sins.** Show the bread and cup used for the Lord's Supper. **The bread is a symbol of Jesus' body, and the cup of juice is a symbol of Jesus' blood.**

When we take the Lord's Supper, we remember what Jesus did. The Lord's Supper is a special time to give thanks to God for sending his Son and to thank Jesus for dying for our sins. Taking part in the Lord's Supper helps us grow up in Christ. But we don't have to wait to take the Lord's Supper in order to remember what Jesus did for us. Remembering what Jesus did for us helps us face difficult situations.

Why Grow Up?

Place the healthy plant so that everyone can see it. Hide the dead plant to show later. Say: **A few weeks ago, we talked about the four things a plant needs. Do you remember what we decided that a plant needs?** (Soil, water, light, food.) **This plant has been continuing to get soil, water, light, and food. It is healthy and growing. Suppose we put this plant in a closet. We open the door only enough to give the plant water and plant food. We never turn on the light. What do you think would happen to the plant?** Give children time to respond and to discuss the responses. **Suppose we set this healthy plant by a window. The soil has nutrients mixed into it so it is very good soil and supplies the plant with food. However, we do not water the plant for several weeks. What do you think would happen to the plant?** Discuss the responses and then bring out the dead plant. **Of course, the plant would die.**

Think of our memory passage. What are the four things we need in order to grow in Christ and be a part of the church ? (Apostles' teaching, fellowship, breaking of bread, prayer.) **As long as we continue to be devoted to these four aspects of the church, we will continue to grow. Sometimes it is difficult to continue to be devoted to the church. Sometimes it is difficult to stand up for our faith. Our Scripture today tells us that the apostles stood up for their faith when faced with difficult situations, and the church continued to grow.**

Classroom Supplies
- healthy potted house plant
- dead plant

Curriculum Supplies
none

How to Grow Up

Divide the class into five groups. Assign a section of the Scripture passage to each group. If the class is small, divide into fewer groups and assign more than one Scripture section to each group. Have students locate their Scripture in their Bibles and read the passage in their groups.

Instruct students to write a news interview and report about their verses. Select one volunteer from each group to dress as the Bible character to be interviewed and one volunteer to interview the character. The reporter/interviewer will also dress in costume. The interviewed characters and Scripture division will be as follows: Captain of the temple guard in Acts 4:1-4; Annas the high priest in Acts 4:5-22; John in Acts 4:23-31; Peter in Acts 5:12-14, 17-26; and Gamaliel in Acts 5:27-42.

If your class is mostly ten- to twelve-year-olds, they should be able to summarize the Scriptures and write a script that will include questions by the interviewer and answers that tell the main points of the passage.

If your class is mainly eight- and nine-year-olds, they may need help writing interview questions and summarizing the key events in the passage. Help them write appropriate questions such as "Who are you?" "What happened?" "Who was involved?" "Where did it happen?" "When did it happen?" "Why did it happen?" "How did remembering Jesus help this situation?"

Guide students to include some of these key points in their interviews:

Acts 4:1-4. Peter and John were teaching the people about Jesus. The religious leaders were disturbed. They put Peter and John in jail. Many heard their message and believed. The number of believers grew to about 5,000.

Acts 4:5-22. The religious leaders had Peter and John brought before them so

Classroom Supplies
- Bibles
- paper
- pencils
- Bible-times costumes (robes, sheets, large towels, belts or ropes)

Curriculum Supplies
none

they could question them. Peter spoke to them about Jesus. Peter and John had courage. The leaders commanded Peter and John to stop teaching about Jesus. Peter said that they could not help but speak about what they had seen and heard. The leaders let Peter and John go because all the people were praising God because of the man who was healed.

Acts 4:23-31. Peter and John went back to their own people and told them what happened. The people prayed for boldness to speak God's word. The people were filled with the Holy Spirit and spoke God's word boldly.

Acts 5:12-14, 17-26. The apostles performed miraculous signs and wonders. The believers continued to meet together. More people believed in the Lord and were added to their number. The high priest and Sadducees were jealous. They arrested the apostles and put them in jail. During the night, an angel opened the jail doors and brought the apostles out. He told them to tell the people the full message of new life. At daybreak, the apostles began to teach the people. The religious leaders thought the apostles were still in jail. They sent officers to get them. The jail was locked and the guards were at the doors, but the apostles were not inside. The leaders could not understand what happened. The captain and officers found the apostles in the temple courts. They brought the apostles back to the leaders without using force because they were afraid of the people.

Acts 5:27-42. The apostles were taken to be questioned by the high priest. Peter and the apostles told the high priest and leaders that they were going to obey God instead of men. They began to speak about Jesus. The leaders became furious and wanted to kill the apostles. Gamaliel advised the leaders to let the apostles go. He told the leaders that if what the apostles were teaching was from men, it would fail. If it was from God, no one would be able to stop them. The leaders agreed with Gamaliel. They whipped the apostles, told them never to speak in the name of Jesus, and then let them go. The apostles never stopped teaching about Jesus. They remembered all that Jesus had done for them. They wanted others to have what Jesus had given them.

When the research is complete, give students time to practice the interviews. Have groups present the interviews in chronological order. Give them time to dress in costume when it is their turn to present.

Say: **The apostles faced many difficult situations when they tried to stand up for their faith and speak about Jesus. They were questioned and warned, they were put in jail, and they were flogged. They did not let any of these obstacles stop them. They continued to meet together and to teach people about Jesus. People knew the church was from God because of the miraculous signs and because the message could not be silenced. The message did not die out and the church continued to grow.**

The difficult situations we face are not the same as those faced by the apostles, but we still have difficulties that make it hard for us to stand up for our faith and stay devoted to the church. If we remember what Jesus has done for us, then we will be able to face difficult times too.

Ready to Grow Up!

Say: **Your scores show how you have been standing up for your faith and growing in your devotion to the church. Were you able to enjoy fellowship with others last week? Tell us what you did to share with others. Did you have new experiences in any other areas? Did you continue to say the memory passage? Did you continue to listen and respond to God's Word? Did you continue to pray and to speak to others about Jesus?**

Look at the last row on your Score Four Folders. It reads, "Remembering Jesus." This week, score four for every time you remember Jesus. We can remember Jesus at any time during the day. We don't have to wait until Sunday. the disciples remembered Jesus every day; they remembered Jesus in good situations and in difficult situations. Let's name some things we could do to remember Jesus. (Keep Bible nearby, post a note on the mirror, play Christian music, and so on.) **These are some great ideas for remembering Jesus. Every time you use one of these ideas to think about Jesus, give yourself four points.**

We have one column left on our Score Four Folder, but we are not at the end of growing in devotion to the church. Keep doing what the early believers did; keep scoring as you devote yourself to the apostles teaching, to the fellowship, to breaking of bread, and to prayer. If we stop being devoted to even one, we will not grow the way God wants. We will be like a plant that stops growing because it does not have water or because it does not get light.

When difficult times come, remember the apostles and how they stood up for their faith. What kind of score do you think they would have if they had a Score Four Folder? We know that the disciples kept doing what we've been practicing because they were able to face difficult situations. If you continue to study God's Word, fellowship with others, remember Jesus, and pray, then you will be able to face difficult situations too.

What will your final score be this week? Ask for volunteers to pray that everyone will stand up for their faith and continue to be devoted to Jesus and his church. Pray, also, for God's help to keep going even when faced with difficult situations.

Classroom Supplies
Score Four Folders

Curriculum Supplies
none

Growing Up Every Day

Give each student paper and supplies to draw. Tell them to draw a plant to symbolize the way they are growing in devotion to the church. The picture must include a plant, soil, water, and a light source. At the bottom of the picture, have them write the memory passage reference, Acts 2:42, 46, 47. When they finish their drawings, tell them to look at their picture while you lead them in saying the memory passage together. Tell students to take their picture home and display it so that the picture will remind them to continue to be devoted to the church. Every time they look at the picture, they should think about how they are growing up in Christ.

Classroom Supplies
- paper
- pencils
- crayons
- markers

Curriculum Supplies
none

Flip Book

Paste each picture on the right side of separate index cards. Be sure to paste the base of each picture in the same place on each card. Divide Acts 2:42, 46, 47 into 18 phrases. Write one phrase on the left side of each card. Write the reference on the last card. Stack the cards. Hold firmly to the left side and fan through the cards, watching the plant grow.

1. 

2. 

3. 

4. 

5. 

6. 

7. 

8. 

9. 

10. 

11. 

12. 

13. 

14. 

15. 

16. 

17. 

18. 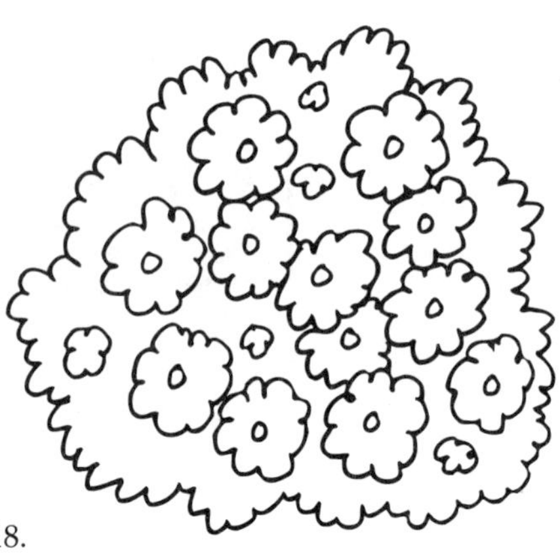

19. 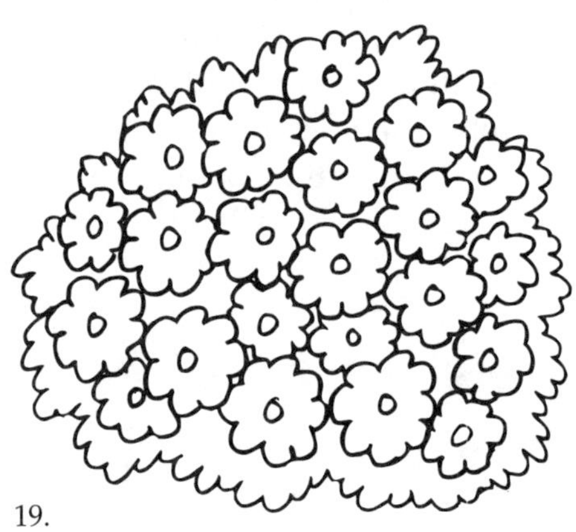

Cut here

Score Four

Fold here

	WEEK 1	WEEK 2	WEEK 3	WEEK 4	WEEK 5
1. Recite Memory Verse					
2. Listen					
3. Respond					
4. Pray					
5. Speak					
6. Share					
7. Remember Jesus					
POINTS WEEK 1					
POINTS WEEK 2					
POINTS WEEK 3					
POINTS WEEK 4					
POINTS WEEK 5					

Cut here

I will pray for a chance to talk to __________ about Jesus.

I will pray for courage to talk to __________ about Jesus.

I will pray so that I will not be afraid of ______________ when I talk about Jesus.

I will pray for ______________ to have courage to talk to someone about Jesus.

I will pray for this person: ________________________.

I will pray for my church: ________________________.

I will pray to thank God for ______________________.

DIARY SHEET

PRAYER CARD

I will pray for a chance to talk to __________ about Jesus.

I will pray for courage to talk to __________ about Jesus.

I will pray so that I will not be afraid of ______________ when I talk about Jesus.

I will pray for ______________ to have courage to talk to someone about Jesus.

I will pray for this person: ________________________.

I will pray for my church: ________________________.

I will pray to thank God for ______________________.

DIARY SHEET

PRAYER CARD

Match the sentences with the pictures. Follow these action steps when you listen to the apostles' teaching.

1. Take notes as you listen.
2. Find Scripture verses in the Bible.
3. Look at the speaker.
4. Write questions about words you don't understand. Ask someone later.
5. Listen for ways you can respond to what you learn.

No Needy Persons Among Them

Use a NIV Bible to find the words to fill in the blanks. Then locate the words in the puzzle.

P	R	A	Y	E	D	P	L	E	A	S	E	D	F
E	L	D	L	O	W	I	S	H	I	P	S	H	A
R	I	I	N	G	F	H	E	L	M	L	O	W	S
R	E	S	P	O	N	S	I	B	I	L	I	T	Y
H	I	T	P	S	H	W	H	A	N	R	I	O	L
N	G	R	F	E	E	O	L	A	D	L	O	G	I
W	S	I	H	N	I	L	P	S	R	H	A	E	A
R	I	B	O	N	G	L	F	E	L	E	L	T	D
O	W	U	S	H	N	E	E	D	Y	I	D	H	O
P	S	T	H	A	R	F	I	N	G	F	E	E	O
L	H	E	A	R	T	L	S	E	V	E	N	R	F
O	W	D	S	H	I	P	S	H	A	R	I	N	G

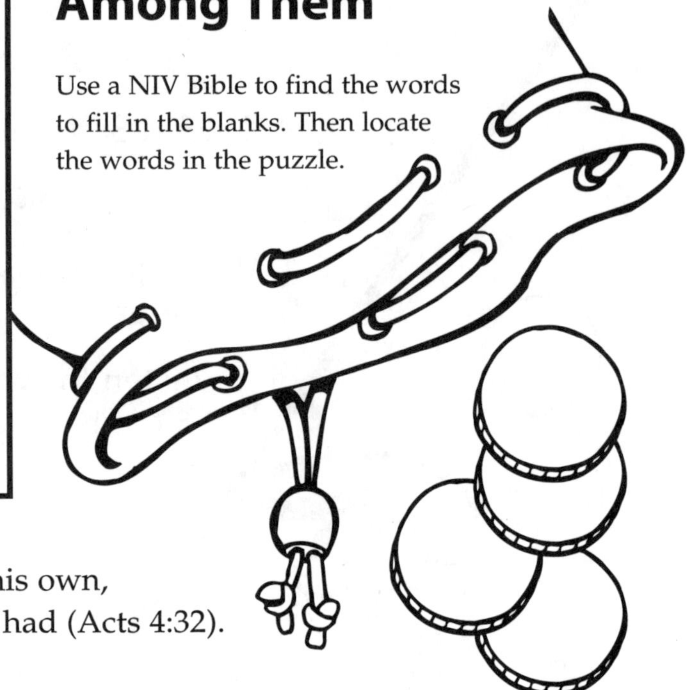

No one claimed that any of his possessions was his own, but they ___ ___ ___ ___ ___ ___ everything they had (Acts 4:32).

There were no ___ ___ ___ ___ ___ persons among them (Acts 4:34).

Money was ___ ___ ___ ___ ___ ___ ___ ___ ___ ___ ___ to anyone as he had need. (Acts 4:35).

Some widows were being overlooked in the ___ ___ ___ ___ ___ distribution of ___ ___ ___ ___ (Acts 6:1).

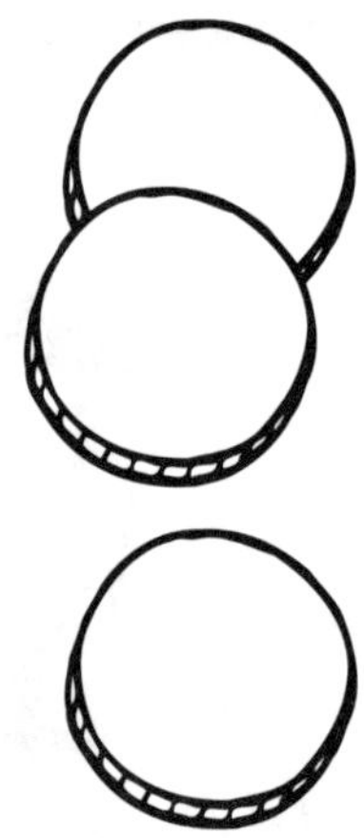

So the twelve gathered all the disciples ___ ___ ___ ___ ___ ___ ___ ___ (Acts 6:2).

"Choose ___ ___ ___ ___ ___ men. We will turn this ___ ___ ___ ___ ___ ___ ___ ___ ___ ___ ___ ___ ___ ___ over to them" (Acts 6:3).

This proposal ___ ___ ___ ___ ___ ___ ___ the whole group (Acts 6:5).

The disciples presented these men to the apostles who ___ ___ ___ ___ ___ ___ for them (Acts 6:6).

The believers continued to devoted themselves to the apostles' teaching and to the ___ ___ ___ ___ ___ ___ ___ ___ ___ ___ (Acts 2:42).

All the believers were ___ ___ ___ in ___ ___ ___ ___ ___ and ___ ___ ___ ___ (Acts 4:32).

Extra: The unused letters in the word search spell out two important words from today's lesson. What are they and why are they important?

UNIT 10

Growing in Grace

Unit Aims

Know:	Identify/describe how individuals in the church showed God's grace to others.
Feel:	Feel compassion for people who don't know Jesus.
Do:	Show God's grace by accepting people in order to help them know Jesus.
Memorize:	1 Peter 4:10, 11

Why Grow in Grace?

Grace is not an often-used word today. Outside of Christian circles it is likely to refer to beauty, movement, dignity in adversity, or a short prayer. But the word grace that is used throughout the New Testament refers to God's grace—his remarkable kindness and forgiving love that we neither earn or deserve. Paul tells us in Ephesians 2:8 that our very salvation is a result of God's grace. As you prepare to help your students grow in grace, study the memory passage 1 Peter 4:10, 11. In this Scripture Peter tells believers to "use whatever gift he has received to serve others, faithfully administering God's grace in its various forms… so that in all things God may be praised through Jesus Christ." The stories of early Christians in this unit will illustrate for your students what it means to exercise God's grace.

The world is always looking for a way to make people get along—civil rights, human rights, multiculturalism, tolerance. Kids today are told from all directions that they need to accept those who are different from them. And yet kids barely in their teens perpetrate some of the most glaring acts of bigotry and hatred. In this unit, your students will learn that Christians don't need to look any further than God's Word for direction on how to treat others. Christians are to show God's grace in the form of kindness and forgiving love even to the undeserving. To treat others in this way is praise to God and is a sure way to help them know Jesus.

Summary

Grow in the grace and knowledge of Jesus by showing God's grace to all people.

- Accept people in order to help them know and accept Jesus.
- Show God's grace by accepting all people as people God loves.
- Showing God's grace helps people know Jesus.

Lesson Aims

Scripture focus	Bible focus	Life focus
Lesson 1 Acts 8:26-40	Philip helped the Ethiopian man know Jesus.	Show God's grace to people from a different ethnic background so you can help them know Jesus.
Lesson 2 Acts 9:1-19	Ananias helped Saul know Jesus.	Show God's grace to people who have been hateful so you can help them know Jesus.
Lesson 3 Acts 10	Peter helped Cornelius know Jesus.	Show God's grace to people from a different cultural background so you can help them know Jesus.
Lesson 4 Acts 11:19-26	Barnabas helped the church at Antioch (first largely Gentile church) to know Jesus.	Show God's grace to all people so you can help them know Jesus.

Memory Passage: 1 Peter 4:10, 11

"Each one should use whatever gift he has received to serve others, faithfully administering God's grace in its various forms. If anyone speaks, he should do it as one speaking the very words of God. If anyone serves, he should do it with the strength God provides, so that in all things God may be praised through Jesus Christ. To him be the glory and the power for ever and ever. Amen."

Classroom Supplies
- scissors
- cellophane tape
- clear packing tape

Curriculum Supplies
reproducible page 264 (cube)

Memory Passage Review Activity

Using the reproducible pattern, construct six Scripture cubes for every pair of students and cover the cubes with clear packing tape for durability. The object of the game is to reconstruct the Scripture passage using the phrases that appear on the tops of the cubes.

Have students play the game in pairs. To play, the first player rolls all six cubes at once. He then picks out the cubes that have different phrases and puts them in order according to the passage. The player then rolls the cubes with duplicate phrases, picking out the missing phrases until all six of the phrases appear on top and the player can put the passage in order.

If the student gets all six phrases in one roll, award ten points. Award eight points for completing the passage in two rolls, six points for completing the passage in three rolls, four points for four rolls, two points for five rolls, and no points for six or more rolls. The first player must construct the entire passage before the second player gets a turn.

Lesson 1

Growing in Grace

Grace Brings People to Jesus

Acts 8:26-40

Bible Focus

Philip helped the Ethiopian man know Jesus.

Life Focus

Show God's grace to people from a different ethnic background so you can help them know Jesus.

Growing Up in the Word: 1 Peter 4:10, 11

Arrive in your classroom a few minutes early to greet students. Set up one or both of the following activities for students to do as they arrive.

Memory Activity 1

Prior to class set the supplies out on tables. Posting the following instructions will make it easier for students to work independently and will allow you to give attention to students as they arrive. Give the instructions verbally to the first students who arrive and ask them to assist those who come later.

1. Find 1 Peter 4:10, 11 in your Bible.
2. Number the phrases in correct order from one to six on your cube pattern.
3. Color the cube.
4. Cut out the cube pattern on the solid lines.
5. Fold the pattern on the dotted lines.
6. Form into a box.
7. Glue or tape the sides together, folding in the flaps.
8. Roll the cube and read the words that come up on top.

When students have constructed their cubes, have them play this game. Divide them into teams of six. All players on one team roll their cubes together and arrange what shows on top in the order of the memory passage. Set aside all the cubes that show duplicate phrases. Roll the duplicate cubes again until each shows a different phrase. Players then arrange the cubes in order and read the passage aloud. Award five points to the team that did not have to roll any cubes again. Give three points to the team that had to roll again only once. Give one point to the team that had to roll again twice. Award zero points to the team that

Classroom Supplies
- colored pencils or markers
- scissors
- glue sticks or cellophane tape
- Bibles

Curriculum Supplies
reproducible page 264 (cube)

had to roll again three or more times. Play as many rounds as time permits.

This is your students' first introduction to the unit memory passage. The concepts of spiritual gifts and grace may be new to eight- to twelve-year olds and are probably not well understood. As students are working, take this opportunity to guide their understanding.

Say: **This Scripture passage has a lot of information for Christians. First it talks about using our gifts. What kind of gifts do you think the Scripture is talking about?** Allow time for student responses and discuss some special abilities they might possess. **What gifts are mentioned in the verses?** (Speaking the words of God and serving.) **Next, it says we are to serve others faithfully. What does it mean to serve others?** Allow time for student responses and discuss them. **The Scripture also says that we are to administer God's grace. Can anyone give an example of God's grace?** (Jesus' death for our sins was the ultimate act of God's grace. He showed us kindness and forgiving love we did not earn or deserve.)

Memory Activity 2

Classroom Supplies
Bibles

Curriculum Supplies
reproducible page 264 (cube)

Before class, cut the cube pattern into six separate squares and discard the tabs.

Ask students to find and read 1 Peter 4:10, 11 in their Bibles. Divide the students into six groups. Assign each group one of the six memory passage phrases. Give the groups their corresponding square from the cube. Each group is to come up with a large gesture that uses their whole body to symbolize the most important words in their assigned phrase. If you have a small class, you may want to have the students act out all of the gestures. Some suggestions follow: Phrase one—students reach up to heaven with both hands, bring their hands into their chest and then reach out horizontally with both hands. Phrase two—students make different shapes with their bodies, such as on hands and knees, knees curled to chest, bent over at waist, stand tall, lie flat. Phrase three—move mouth as if talking while making hand motions. Phrase four—form muscle man positions. Phrase five—lift hands toward heaven and shake joyfully. Phrase six—point to heaven, shake arms, hold up fists.

Read through the passage. As each group hears their phrase, they will act out their motions. Read through the verse at a normal pace. Comment on the good job they did and challenge them to do it again faster. Read through the passage as fast as you can. If time permits, have groups teach other groups their motions.

Say: **How do your motions match the phrases of the memory passage? Why did you choose them?** Allow time for student responses and discuss them. Then ask volunteers to read the passage one phrase at a time from the cube squares. Stop after each phrase and ask the class to think of examples of the following: gifts, grace, the very words of God, serve others, praise and glory.

Why Grow Up?

Pass out the geometric shapes. Give each student two shapes that are identical. If you have a very large class or little time to prepare, give the students a quarter sheet of colored construction paper and have them cut their own shapes.

Divide the class into groups of about six. Each students brings his identical shapes to the group. Give each group a sheet of black construction paper and a glue stick. Tell them they have five minutes to create a design on the black paper using all of their shapes. Bring the groups back together and ask them to display their designs. Comment on the beauty of the designs, the variety of shapes and colors and the contrast with the black paper.)

Ask: **How do you think your designs would look if I had given you all the same shapes such as brown squares?** Allow time for a few responses. **The different shapes that each of you brought to your group helped to make a wonderful design.**

God made people in all different colors, shapes, and sizes. Our differences make the world a lot more interesting. Sometimes, though, it just feels more comfortable to stay around people who are just like us. Sometimes we are even afraid of people who are different from us. Our goal this month is to grow in grace. Grace means showing kindness and loving forgiveness to others. By showing grace to others, even to those who are different from us, we can help them know Jesus.

Classroom Supplies
- two-inch construction paper geometric shapes in a variety of colors
- one sheet of black construction paper for each group of six students
- glue sticks

Curriculum Supplies
none

How to Grow Up

Select two good readers or adult helpers to read the parts of Philip and the Ethiopian. Give them a chance to read their parts silently before they read them orally.

Teacher: I have invited some special guests to come and share with us today. First I would like to introduce you to Philip, a disciple of Jesus and a first century missionary. Let's give Philip a warm welcome! (Encourage applause.)

Philip: Hi, my name is Philip. From the moment Jesus called me as a disciple, I couldn't help telling others about him. After Jesus' ascension into Heaven, I became a full-time missionary. Missionary life is pretty hard. I left my home and all my possessions behind to follow Jesus. I had to rely on friends to provide for my needs. My clothing was very simple—a robe and a pair of good sandals. Those sandals were important because I had to walk everywhere.

I was on a mission trip in Samaria when God's angel told me to get up and go down the road south of Jerusalem. On my way, I met a wealthy African man in a chariot with his servants all around. As I got closer, I heard him reading from the book of Isaiah. It was a prophecy that told of the coming of the Savior. I asked him if he understood what he was reading. He said he didn't, so I did what I always do. I told him about Jesus!

Teacher: Thank you, Philip. Next I'd like you to welcome the keeper of the royal treasury, from the court of Queen Candace of Ethiopia.

Ethiopian: Hi. Yes, I was riding in a royal chariot when Philip came to me. He looked a little scruffy, and I was a bit suspicious of him. I had come from Ethiopia to Jerusalem to worship, and I was reading about the God of the Jews, but the book of Isaiah was a mystery to me. Philip knew the Scriptures and explained to me that Jesus was the Savior. His words made so much sense that I knew God had sent him to me. We were by water, so Philip baptized me right there beside the road. Then he just vanished. For the rest of my life, I told others about Jesus.

Teacher: Thank you sir.

Classroom Supplies
- chalk and chalkboard
- masking tape
- two markers
- Bibles
- slips of paper with prewritten questions

Curriculum Supplies
photocopy of the script printed here

Direct the students to find Acts 8:26-40 in their Bibles. Divide the chalkboard into two columns with the headings "Philip" and "Ethiopian." Depending on the size of your class, give one or more question slips to pairs of students.

Write one of these questions on each slip of paper.

What was Philip's job? What was the Ethiopian's job? Describe Philip's clothing. How do you think the Ethiopian might have dressed? What do you think Philip's home was like? What do you imagine the Ethiopian's home was like? How did Philip travel? How did the Ethiopian travel? Describe how you think Philip might have looked. Describe how you think the Ethiopian might have looked.

Ask the students to read their questions and think of an answer to share based on the Scripture and the messages they just heard from Philip and the Ethiopian. Give the students a few minutes to work. Call the students' attention to the chalkboard and ask them to share their answers as you record them. If you have older students or a helper, you can ask them to record the answers as you go through the questions. Point out the many contrasts between these two men. Rich/poor, walking/riding, well-dressed/simply dressed, one has servants/one is a servant, Jew/African.

Say: **Philip recognized that the even though the Ethiopian man was very different from him, he still needed to hear about Jesus. Our memory passage says that each one should use whatever gifts he has received to serve others. Philip used his gifts as a missionary to show God's grace to the Ethiopian man and to lead him to faith in Jesus.**

Classroom Supplies
- large round sugar cookies
- containers and tubes of frosting in a variety of colors
- plastic knives
- napkins

Curriculum Supplies
none

Ready to Grow Up!

Say: **A very old hymn, a song of praise says, "Tis so sweet to trust in Jesus, just to take him at his word." God's grace that gives us eternal life through Jesus is not something we can earn. We just need to trust in Jesus. And that is very sweet. In our story today, Philip showed God's grace by speaking about Jesus to someone very different from himself.**

Your assignment this week is to speak to someone very different from yourself, someone you have never spoken to before or someone you have spoken to only once or twice. It can be a neighbor or a classmate, maybe even someone here at church. Just say hello or ask them a question about themselves. Maybe you can give them a compliment or find out something about their family. When you show kindness by speaking to someone different from yourself, you pass on some of the sweetness of God's grace.

Today we are going to make a cookie face to help us remember the sweetness of sharing Jesus with others. Hand out the cookies and set out the frosting. Ask the students to decorate their cookie as the face of a person who knows about God's grace. **The sweetness of God's grace brings a smile to everyone's face.** Admire the cookies and set them aside to eat at the end of class.

Growing Up Every Day

Have the students form a large circle. Ask the students to close their eyes and think of the person they plan to speak to this week while you pray. Say: **Dear Lord, Thank you for making a beautiful world with many different kinds of people. Help us to remember that all people need Jesus. Teach us how to show your grace to others. Help us as we share your grace this week. We pray in Jesus' name, Amen.**

Now, let's eat cookies!

Classroom Supplies
decorated cookies

Curriculum Supplies
none

Lesson 2

Growing in Grace

Grace Is Undeserved

Acts 9:1-19

Bible Focus

Ananias helped Saul know Jesus.

Life Focus

Show God's grace to people who have been hateful so you can help them know Jesus.

Growing Up in the Word: 1 Peter 4:10, 11

Prior to class prepare the following activities for students to begin as they arrive. Providing a sample project, posting simple directions, and asking early arrivals to assist those who come later will free you to greet students.

Memory Activity 1

Instruct students to find 1 Peter 4:10, 11 in their Bibles. Read the passage aloud. Write the words "gifts," "grace," "God's Word," "service," "praise," and "glory" on the chalkboard. Tell students they are going to create a torn-paper picture representing the main ideas in the memory passage. Refer to the posted words. Show students how to tear paper into shapes with their hands or by laying a straight edge on the paper and tearing the paper along the edge. The following suggestions for symbols might help students get started: gifts—presents, grace—cross, God's Word—Bible, service—hands, praise—music notes, glory—beams of light.

As the students are working, casually discuss each of the main ideas. Ask the students to think about what the passage means. Help them to understand that the term "gifts" refers to the special abilities or talents that God gives each person. Define grace as kindness and forgiving love that cannot be earned. Explain that speaking God's Word requires knowledge and understanding of the Bible. Ask for examples of service to God and to others. Talk about how God receives our service to others as praise, just like a worship song. Explain that to give God glory is acknowledging that God is the one who gives us the power to do his will.

Classroom Supplies

- construction paper in a variety of colors
- glue sticks
- rulers or other straight edges for tearing paper
- Bibles
- chalkboard
- chalk

Curriculum Supplies

none

Memory Activity 2

This activity needs a large open area. Prior to class write one phrase of the memory passage on each of six sheets of paper: "Each one should use whatever gifts he has received to serve others,/ faithfully administering God's grace in its various forms./ If anyone speaks he should do it as one speaking the very words of God./ If anyone serves, he should do it with the strength God provides,/ so that in all things God may be praised through Jesus Christ./ To him be the glory and the power forever and ever. Amen" (1 Peter 4:10, 11).

Classroom Supplies

- memory passage in six phrases written on separate sheets of paper
- small gift-wrapped box
- cross
- Bible
- serving tray
- cassette or book of praise music
- candle
- stopwatch

Curriculum Supplies

none

Ask students to find 1 Peter 4:10, 11 in their Bibles. Say: **I have some objects with me today. I'd like you to help me match the objects with the words in 1 Peter 4:10, 11.** Hold up one object at a time in random order. Encourage the students to use their Bibles to make the following connections: the gift-wrapped box represents gifts; the cross represents God's grace; the Bible represents the words of God; the serving tray represents serving others, the praise music represents praise, and the candle represents God's glory.

Divide the class into teams of six. Have the students stand at one end of the play area. Place the papers on the floor in random order at the other end. Explain to the students that you will time each team to see how quickly they can match a symbol with the correct phrase from the memory passage, get themselves in order, and read the complete passage.

Hand out the six symbols to the members of one team. Distribute one to each member of the team. Using the stopwatch to time each team, give each team a turn to race across the floor, find the phrase that matches their symbol, arrange themselves in order and say the memory passage. Give each team a rousing cheer and announce the fastest team. Small classes can repeat the activity to achieve faster times. For a large group, set up two or more sets of phrases and symbols and have teams race against each other.

Why Grow Up?

Classroom Supplies

- pencil
- slips of paper

Curriculum Supplies

none

Ask the students to give you some examples of things they find it difficult to forgive. As the students respond, write single word descriptions on slips of paper. Affirm that the situations they describe are difficult to forgive. Make sure you have at least one slip for each student. Repeats are OK. Save the slips to use during the "Ready to Grow Up!" activity.

Say: **Our memory passage tells us that we are to administer God's grace. Can anyone tell me what that means?** Wait for responses. Guide students to the conclusion that God's grace is kindness and unmerited or unearned forgiving love.

Say: **Suppose I offer to give a piece of candy to anyone who helps to clean the room after class today. Does that sound fair? What if some students decide to take off and not help, but I give them candy anyway? How would you feel about that? No, I guess getting candy without helping would not be fair, but it is a pretty good picture of God's grace. Jesus died on the cross for ours sins, not because we deserved to have ours sins paid for by his death, but because God showed kindness and forgiving love that we did not deserve. That is**

grace. Forgiving others, especially when they don't deserve to be forgiven, requires us to administer God's grace.

Classroom Supplies
- colored pencils or markers
- Bibles

Curriculum Supplies
reproducible page 265 (Damascus Weekly)

How to Grow Up

Hand out copies of the *Damascus Weekly*. Ask students to find Acts 9:1-19 in their Bibles. Tell the students that the stories in the *Damascus Weekly* are based on Acts 9. Organize students into small groups to read the stories together. Explain that when they are finished reading they can create a headline, story titles, and "photos" to complete their newspapers. Encourage the students to share ideas and work together. When most of the students are finished, ask for volunteers to share their work.

Say: **Ananias had every reason to feel hatred toward Saul and to stay far away from him. Saul was a murderous hater of Jesus' followers. Ananias may have felt that Saul deserved to be struck blind. But Ananias showed grace to Saul by going to him, healing him, and bringing him to faith in Jesus. How do you think Ananias had the strength to overcome his fear and go to Saul?** Wait for responses. Lead the students to the conclusion that God provided the strength. Refer back to the memory passage. **Our memory passage says, "If any man serves, he should do it with the strength God provides." Ananias called on God's strength to forgive Saul, and we can call on God's strength to show grace to others.**

Classroom Supplies
- slips of paper from "Why Grow Up?"
- small piece of candy for each student
- wastepaper basket

Curriculum Supplies
none

Ready to Grow Up!

Say: **Last week your assignment was to share the sweetness of God's grace by speaking to someone you have never spoken to before. I'd like to hear some of your experiences.** Allow time for students to share. If they are reluctant, share an experience of your own to get them started. After everyone has had a chance to share, distribute the slips of paper you wrote during the "Why Grow Up?" activity. Remind the students of some the things they find difficult to forgive. Ask the students to gather in a circle around the wastepaper basket.

Say: **Your assignment this week is to use the strength God provides to show kindness and forgiving love to someone who has been unkind to you. You may need to control your tongue when someone is rude or smile when your feelings are hurt. It is a very hard thing to do. When you show kindness and forgiving love to someone who is unkind to you, you pass on some of the sweetness of God's grace.**

Let's bow our heads and silently ask God to give us the strength to show grace to people who are unkind to us and who may even hate us. Remember that grace is kindness and forgiving love even towards those who don't deserve it. Allow for a moment of silent prayer.

Say: **Now we are going to go around the circle, and I want each of you in turn to read the word on your slip, tear it in half and drop it in the wastebasket. I'll start first.** After all the students have finished, close in a brief prayer.

Ask: **Do you remember earlier that I said I would give a piece of candy to anyone who helped to clean the room today? Has anyone earned candy yet? No! You haven't even had a chance to earn it. But I'm going to give you a piece**

now, even though you don't deserve it. As you eat your candy, think about the sweetness of God's grace. God shows kindness and loving forgiveness to us even though we don't deserve it. Hand out the candy and enjoy it together.

Growing Up Every Day

Say: **Our memory passage says "If anyone serves, he should do it with the strength God provides." Ananias was able to forgive Saul because God gave him the strength to do it. We have that same power when we call upon the Holy Spirit to help us forgive people who are unkind to us. We can show grace to others because we've got the power of God to help us.**

Tell the students you are going to play a game of freeze tag to help them remember that they've got the power to show grace. Choose "it" and define the boundaries for the game. If you have a very large class, you may want to have more than one who is "it." Explain that when "it" tags a player, that player must remain frozen until another player unfreezes him by tagging and shouting in a loud voice, "You've got God's power." Keep playing until all the players are frozen or until time runs out. Change "it" frequently to give several students a turn.

Close in a brief prayer followed by a shout of "We've got God's power!"

Classroom Supplies
large room or playground area

Curriculum Supplies
none

Lesson 3

Growing in Grace

Grace Is for Everyone

Acts 10

Bible Focus

Peter helped Cornelius know Jesus.

Life Focus

Show God's grace to people from a different cultural background so you can help them know Jesus.

Growing Up in the Word: 1 Peter 4:10,11

Greet students as they arrive and invite them to begin one of the following activities that you prepared in advance.

Classroom Supplies
- scissors
- Bibles
- cellophane tape

Curriculum Supplies
reproducible page 264 (cube and candy pieces)

Memory Activity 1

If memory passage cubes were made for lesson 1, use them for this activity. If not, have students assemble the cubes now and cut out the additional dessert pieces from the reproducible page.

When game pieces are assembled, have students find a partner. At the signal, students will race to roll the cube until they have gathered all the dessert pieces and unscrambled the message. Students gather dessert pieces by rolling the cube and collecting the dessert piece that shows up on top. They must obtain dessert pieces in the order of the memory passage. The first piece the students may collect is the piece that matches phrase one of the memory passage (cupcake). The second piece must be the dessert that matches the second phrase of the passage (bag). Students must roll the cube until the needed phrase comes up on top. When all the dessert pieces are collected, then the player must unscramble them to find a message. (Grace is sweet.)

Say: **What is the message about God's grace?** (Grace is sweet.) **We've been talking this month about the sweetness of God's grace. What makes God's grace sweet?** (Grace is God's loving kindness toward us. It is his favor that we can't earn and don't deserve.) **Who needs God's grace?** (Everyone.) **How does the memory passage say we can show God's grace to others or "faithfully administer God's grace"?** (Through our words, through service to others, through the use of the gifts God has given us.) **God's grace is sweet. Why should we show the sweetness of God's grace to others?** (It helps them to know Jesus.)

Memory Activity 2

Explain to students that one way to use Scripture is to pray it. Hand out a Scripture prayer to each student. Ask them to fill in the blank with a description of how they can administer God's grace. Then they may color their Scripture prayer to make it a prayer for themselves.

Say: **We've learned that grace is God's loving kindness toward us. It is his favor that we can't earn and don't deserve. Everyone needs God's grace. Our memory passage tells us to faithfully administer God's grace. What does that mean?** ("Faithfully" means to keep on doing something. Administer means to give or distribute.) **God asks us to keep on giving or showing his grace to others. How can you keep on giving or showing God's grace?** Allow time for student responses and discuss their responses.

Classroom Supplies
markers or crayons

Curriculum Supplies
reproducible page 266 (prayer)

Why Grow Up?

Write the following headings on the board: "Language," "Food," "Customs," "Music," "Stories and Legends," and "Religion."

Ask the students to help you make a list under each heading. Starting with language, list as many languages as will fit under the heading. Then move on to food and list food items from other countries or cultures that students have tasted or heard about. Under customs encourage students to think about the different ways people celebrate holidays, weddings, and so on. The music list should include types of music, everything from rap to mariachi, rather than titles. Ask the children to think about stories and legends that they have read from other cultures. Finally, list various religions with which the students are familiar.

Say: **Language, food, customs, music, stories, and religion are all parts of what we call culture. There are many different cultures represented in our country and around the world. Do any of you have neighbors or friends whose culture is different from yours?** Encourage responses and discuss some of the differences.

Say: **We may speak different languages, eat different foods, listen to different music and stories, or have different customs. We may even come from different religious backgrounds, but the one thing all people have in common is a need to know Jesus as Savior. By showing grace, kindness and forgiving love to others, even to those from different cultures, we can help them to know Jesus.**

Classroom Supplies
- chalkboard
- chalk
- markers
- masking tape

Curriculum Supplies
none

How to Grow Up

Say: **Today we are going to make a picture scroll about the disciple Peter and a Roman centurion named Cornelius.**

Peter grew up Jewish, and although he was a follower of Jesus, he was most comfortable with his Jewish culture. He spoke Hebrew to his Jewish friends, though he also knew Greek. He ate, dressed, and worshiped according to the Jewish customs, and he had been trained in the Old Testament teachings.

Cornelius was a Roman who was a leader of one hundred Roman soldiers. Cornelius probably spoke Greek. He ate and dressed according to the Roman customs. We know he was a "God fearer," someone who believed that the

Jewish God is the one, true God, but he did not actually become a Jew.

At this time in history, Peter and the other disciples assumed that the salvation offered through Jesus was for those born Jewish and for those who had converted to Judaism. But God had other ideas.

Classroom Supplies
• eighteen feet of banner paper divided into six 3-foot sections and numbered from 1 to 6
• two wrapping paper tubes
• masking tape
• crayons or markers

Curriculum Supplies
none

Divide the class into six groups. Assign each group one of the following passages: Acts 10:1-8, Acts 10:9-16, Acts 10:17-23, Acts 10:24-29, Acts 10:34-43, and Acts 10:44-48. Spread the banner paper on the floor. Instruct each group to read through their portion of Scripture and illustrate its part of the story in the appropriate section of the banner paper. Set a time limit for students to finish. Attach each end of the banner paper to a wrapping paper tube. Roll the banner right to left so that it can be unrolled to reveal one picture at a time.

Have two students unroll the banner beginning with the first section. Ask a representative from each group to tell its portion of the story. Applaud each group in turn. At the end briefly recap the story.

Say: **Peter showed God's grace by looking past cultural differences so that he could share Jesus with Cornelius and his family. Peter was criticized and questioned by others who thought he had done the wrong thing by entering Cornelius' home. Peter didn't worry about what others thought. Our memory passage says, "To him be the glory and the power forever and ever." Peter gave the glory to God by telling others about the vision God sent him. Soon all of Jesus' followers came to understand that they needed to share Jesus with people of other cultures.**

Ready to Grow Up!

Before class, set up a simple six-object obstacle course. Use whatever you have in the classroom such as a table to climb under, a chair to climb over, a ball to throw in a basket, a box to jump over, a tape balance beam. Label the objects with the signs. The students will enjoy helping with the course. If you have a large class, you may want to set up two courses and have team races.

Say: **Let's hear how you shared the sweetness of God's grace this week. How did you show love and forgiveness to someone who was unkind to you?** Allow time for students to share.

Classroom Supplies
• a set of signs that have the following words: Language, Food, Music, Customs, Stories, Religion
• masking tape
• stopwatch
• ethnic treat to share such as Mexican sweet bread, baklava, Danish shortbread, Italian ice, croissants, or bagels

Curriculum Supplies
none

Say: **Sometimes we want to share Jesus with people, but we see their culture as an obstacle like the obstacles on this course. We might even be criticized or questioned for trying to share Jesus with people from different cultures. But if we do it with God's grace, his kindness and loving forgiveness, we will help them to know Jesus.**

Let's get past the differences we have with others so that we can share Jesus. Let's take turns running this obstacle course. Consider timing each student just for fun, but don't over emphasize the competition. When everyone has had a chance to run, gather the students back together in a circle.

Say: **Your assignment this week is to find something to appreciate from a culture that is different from your own. Perhaps you can learn a few words from a friend who speaks**

a different language, or read about another culture in book or encyclopedia.

One thing I know we can appreciate is the good food of other cultures. Let's share a sweet treat from another country to help us remember how sweet God's grace is.

Growing Up Every Day

Say: **God gave us his Word, the Bible, to instruct us, to guide us, and to encourage us. It was written a long time ago, but every word of it is valuable to us today. I know you have heard many Bible stories and verses, but have you ever thought of using God's own words for prayer?** Ask the students to hold the Scripture prayer they decorated from Memory Activity 2. If this activity wasn't done, then pass out the sheets now. Have them fill in the blank with something similar to the following: "Help me to faithfully administer your grace by appreciating the customs of other cultures." While heads are bowed, ask for a few volunteers to read their prayers aloud. Follow this by reading through the prayer together and pausing to allow students to silently fill in the blank.

Classroom Supplies
none

Curriculum Supplies
Scripture prayers from Memory Activity 2

Lesson 4

Growing in Grace

Grace Is Sweet

Acts 11:19-26

Bible Focus

Barnabas helped the church at Antioch (the first largely Gentile church) to know Jesus.

Life Focus

Show God's grace to all people so you can help them know Jesus.

Growing Up in the Word: 1 Peter 4:10, 11

Prepare one or both of the following activities before class. Greet your students at the door and direct them to the activities.

Classroom Supplies

- construction paper in a variety of colors
- pencils
- cellophane tape or glue sticks or staplers
- paper
- masking tape

Curriculum Supplies

none

Memory Activity 1

Prior to class, cut the construction paper into one-inch strips and post the memory passage in the following six phrases on six sheets of paper taped around the room: "Each one should use whatever gift he has received to serve others,/ faithfully administering God's grace in its various forms./ If anyone speaks, he should do it as one speaking the very words of God./ If anyone serves, he should do it with the strength God provides,/ so that in all things God may be praised through Jesus Christ./ To him be the power forever and ever. Amen" (1 Peter 4:10, 11).

Give each student six strips of construction paper. Instruct students to copy each phrase of the passage onto separate strips of paper. When they are finished copying, have them make a chain using the strips and clear tape, a glue stick, or a stapler. As an alternative, draw the lines for the strips on a sheet of white paper, write the phrases ahead of time, and photocopy them onto colored paper. Students then simply cut the strips apart and make a chain. This will be easier for students who have difficulty with writing or copying and will save time, but is not as effective for memorization.

Ask the students to stand in a circle holding their Scripture chains. Say: **Our memory passage says, "If anyone speaks he should do it as one speaking the very words of God." What do you think it means to speak the very words of God?** Allow for some responses. Guide the students to consider whether "speaking the very words of God" might mean that a person who speaks or teaches about God should have a close relationship with God in prayer and Bible study. **One of the ways we can follow this direction is to study Scripture and commit it to memory. Let's use the chains we made to help us learn the words to our memory passage.** Ask students to start with the first link and read through the passage together as a group. Then ask one student to read the first phrase. The next student reads the second phrase. Continue around the circle until the passage has been repeated several times.

Memory Activity 2

Explain to the students that they are going to have a contest to find out who knows the memory passage. Have students locate 1 Peter 4:10, 11 in their Bibles. Divide students into groups of four and instruct them to review the passage for the contest. Give them about five minutes.

Start the contest by placing one bottle for each team on a table in front of the class. The object of the contest is to fill the team's bottle with rice. Each student will be asked to recite the passage. An honest attempt earns 1/4 cup of rice. Reciting it with just a few errors earns 1/2 cup of rice. A perfect recitation is awarded a full cup of rice. The team with the most rice in its bottle after everyone on the team has taken a turn wins.

Read the memory passage aloud. Repeat the phrase "If anyone speaks, he should do it as one speaking the very words of God." Say: **Knowing God's Word is important if we are going to share it with others. That is why we spend time learning Scripture. Can you speak the very words of God? How well did you know the memory passage for our contest? Do you need to study it more?** Allow time for student responses and discuss their responses.

Classroom Supplies

- empty one-liter size soda bottle for every four students
- paper funnel
- large bag of rice
- one set of measuring cups
- small prizes such as gum or pencils or ribbons
- Bibles

Curriculum Supplies

none

Why Grow Up?

Assist the students in linking all of their chains into one circular chain using the extra strips and clear tape. Have everyone sit in a circle around the chain.

Say: **Paper chains are fun and easy to make. Can you think of some uses for a paper chain?** Allow time for responses. **Which link in the chain is most important?** Point out that every link has the same job and is equally important to holding the chain together. **Christians are like this chain. We need to stay connected to each other to do our job of showing God's grace to others. Suppose each of these links represents a Christian. What happens if this one decides it only wants to be with links that are the same color?** Snip the extra link. **What happens if another link decides that the music he likes is the only way to worship?** Snip. **Or that the Bible should only be taught in one language?** Snip. **Or that there is only one proper way to dress for church?** Snip. **What if this link gossips about a link that is struggling with sin?** Snip. **Pretty soon the chain becomes useless. As Christians we become useless if we don't show God's grace to others, even to those who are different from us or who are struggling with their faith.**

Classroom Supplies

- chains from Memory Activity 1 or a paper chain of ten or more links
- one extra chain strip for each student
- clear tape
- one pair of scissors

Curriculum Supplies

none

Classroom Supplies

- masking tape
- large open area
- chalkboard or newsprint
- marker

Curriculum Supplies

list of questions on this page

How to Grow Up

Before class, use masking tape to mark off a large rectangle on the floor that is divided into three equal sections. Each section should be just large enough to hold the whole class. Use this activity to introduce the idea that God calls us to be united with all Christians.

Say: **Today we are going to learn about Barnabas, a first-century missionary who was born in Cyprus, educated in Jerusalem, and called to minister to the Greeks in Antioch. Right now we are going to play a game to help us remember the names of these three places: Cyprus, Jerusalem, and Antioch.**

Show the students the playing area. The middle section is Jerusalem. The left section is Antioch, and the right section is Cyprus. Ask everyone to stand in Jerusalem. When you call the name of a city, everyone has to go to that city as quickly as possible. Anyone who goes to the wrong city, steps out of the lines, or is the last to arrive is out. Practice a few times before you start.

Call out Jerusalem, Antioch or Cyprus in a loud clear voice. Try to trick them by calling the city in which they are standing. Play until there is one player left. Give him a rousing cheer before moving on to the next activity.

Ask the students to get their Bibles and form four teams. Instruct everyone to find Acts 11:19-26 in their Bibles and take turns reading the passage together. Tell them to be sure to read carefully because there will be a little competition when they are finished. Allow the students to silently read the passage.

Post a scoreboard to tally points for each team. Give five points for a correct answer. If a team answers incorrectly, go on to the next question and return to missed questions after you have gone through the list.

- What event caused the disciples to scatter? (Persecution.)
- To what cities did the disciples scatter? (Phoenicia, Cyprus and Antioch.)
- Besides the Jews, who else did the scattered disciples tell the message to? (Greeks.)
- What was the message or Good News? (Jesus died for their sins.)
- Whose hand was with the scattered disciples? (The Lord's.)
- Who was sent to the Greeks at Antioch? (Barnabas.)
- What church sent Barnabas? (Jerusalem.)
- What did Barnabas find in Antioch? (Evidence of the grace of God.)
- What did Barnabas encourage the Greeks at Antioch to do? (Remain true to the Lord with all their hearts.)
- What kind of man was Barnabas? (A good man filled with the Holy Spirit.)
- Who did Barnabas ask to come to Antioch? (Saul.)
- Where was Saul before he went to Antioch? (Tarsus.)
- How long did Barnabas and Saul stay in Antioch? (A year.)
- What nationality or culture did Saul and Barnabas have in common? (Jewish.)
- What was the nationality or culture of the people in Antioch? (Greek.)
- What name was given to the followers of Jesus in Antioch? (Christian.)

Congratulate the winners and compliment the other teams. Say: **Barnabas was Jewish. His customs, language, and religious heritage were different from the Greek believers in Antioch. Yet Barnabas recognized that, in spite of their dif-**

ferences, they shared a common faith in Jesus Christ. Barnabas showed God's grace to the Greek believers by encouraging them, teaching them, and becoming friends with them.

Ready to Grow Up!

Say: **Last week I asked you to find something to appreciate about another culture. Did anyone try a new food or learn a few words in another language? Let's hear about what you found.** Allow time for students to share.

After everyone has had a chance to share, give a world map and a pencil to each student. Encourage students to work together to unscramble the names of the regions. Gather the students in a circle with their maps.

Say: **In the first century after Jesus' resurrection, his followers suffered and often died because they told others about Jesus. Since those times other missionaries have continued the hard work they started. There are Christians all over the world. We may have different languages and customs, but we share a common faith in Jesus Christ.**

Pass around a bowl of chocolate candies and ask the students to take one of each color plus three of brown and place them on the map according to the key.

Say: **We are going to use our maps and these candies to remember the sweetness of God's grace and to pray for Christians around the world. Many Christians are suffering for their faith, others need food and shelter, and some may be struggling with sin.** Ask seven students to pray the following prayer inserting the name of each region.

"Dear Lord, Thank you for your Son Jesus Christ and the grace you show to all Christians especially those in ___________."

Tell the students they may eat the candy for the region at the end of each prayer, remembering how sweet God's grace is. Close with the following prayer: **"Lord, we thank you for the beautiful world you have created and all the different kinds of people in it. Help us to show your grace to all people. Amen."**

Your assignment this week is to pray for Christians around the world using your map and the snack-size bag of candies I will give you to take home. Distribute candy.

Classroom Supplies
- enough candy-coated chocolates (such as M&M's brand) so each student gets one of each color plus three of brown
- pencils
- one snack-size package of candies per student

Curriculum Supplies
reproducible page 267 (world map)

Growing Up Every Day

Say: **When you ate the chocolates, did you taste any difference between the colored candy shells? No! Nobody really eats them for the candy shell. It's the yummy chocolate on the inside that counts. That's how it is with Christians too. A person's language, the clothes she wears, and even the way she worships is just the candy coating. It is the love of Jesus on the inside that counts.**

Classroom Supplies
none

Curriculum Supplies
none

“Each one should use whatever gift he has received to serve others,

faithfully administering God’s grace in its various forms.

To him be the glory and the power for ever and ever. Amen.”
(1 Peter 4:10, 11)

If anyone speaks, he should do it as one speaking the very words of God.

so that in all things God may be praised through Jesus Christ.

If anyone serves, he should do it with the strength God provides,

1. Cut out the cube on solid lines.
2. Fold the cube on dotted lines.
3. Form into a box. Fold in tabs and tape.

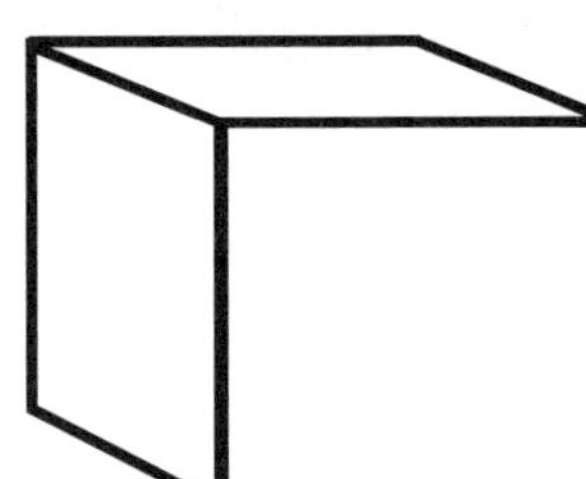

DAMASCUS WEEKLY

Write a headline.

Write a title.

DAMASCUS— A flash of light and a loud voice were reported on the road from Jerusalem to Damascus earlier this week. The light was so bright that it blinded one man, Saul of Tarsus, who was carried by his companions to the home of Judas on Straight Street. He has remained for three days in a state of fasting and prayer. "He thinks he has heard the voice of God himself," stated one of Saul's companions who also said, "As for me, I didn't understand a word."

Draw a picture

Ananias outside the Straight Street house.

Write a title.

JERUSALEM—Saul of Tarsus is known for his hatred and persecution of members of "The Way," a growing group who claim Jesus as the Messiah. Saul has gone from house to house in Jerusalem dragging believers from their homes and putting them into prison. He was present at and approved of the stoning death of Stephen, a sincere follower of Jesus. Having recently obtained permission from the High Priest to search Damascus for members of "The Way," Saul was traveling to Damascus to carry out his plans when he was struck blind.

Draw a picture

Blind Saul and his companions enter Damascus.

Write a title.

DAMASCUS—Ananias, a known follower of "The Way," was seen leaving the home where Saul of Tarsus is staying. Despite Saul's reputation and the real possibility of a death sentence, Ananias is said to have conducted his visit in complete safety. Sources close to both men report that Ananias came to Saul at God's leading and that Saul was expecting him. A witness to the events stated that as Ananias spoke, "something like scales fell from Saul's eyes and he could see again. He got up and was baptized."

Dear Lord,
Help me to use the gifts I have received to serve others. Help me to faithfully administer your grace by ______
____
____
____
________________________________.

When I speak, let it be as one speaking your words. When I serve, let me do it with the strength you provide. So that in all things you may be praised through Jesus Christ. To Him be the glory and the power for ever and ever.

Amen.

God's Grace Covers the World

Unscramble the names of the continents. (Hint: Think about where the animals live.)

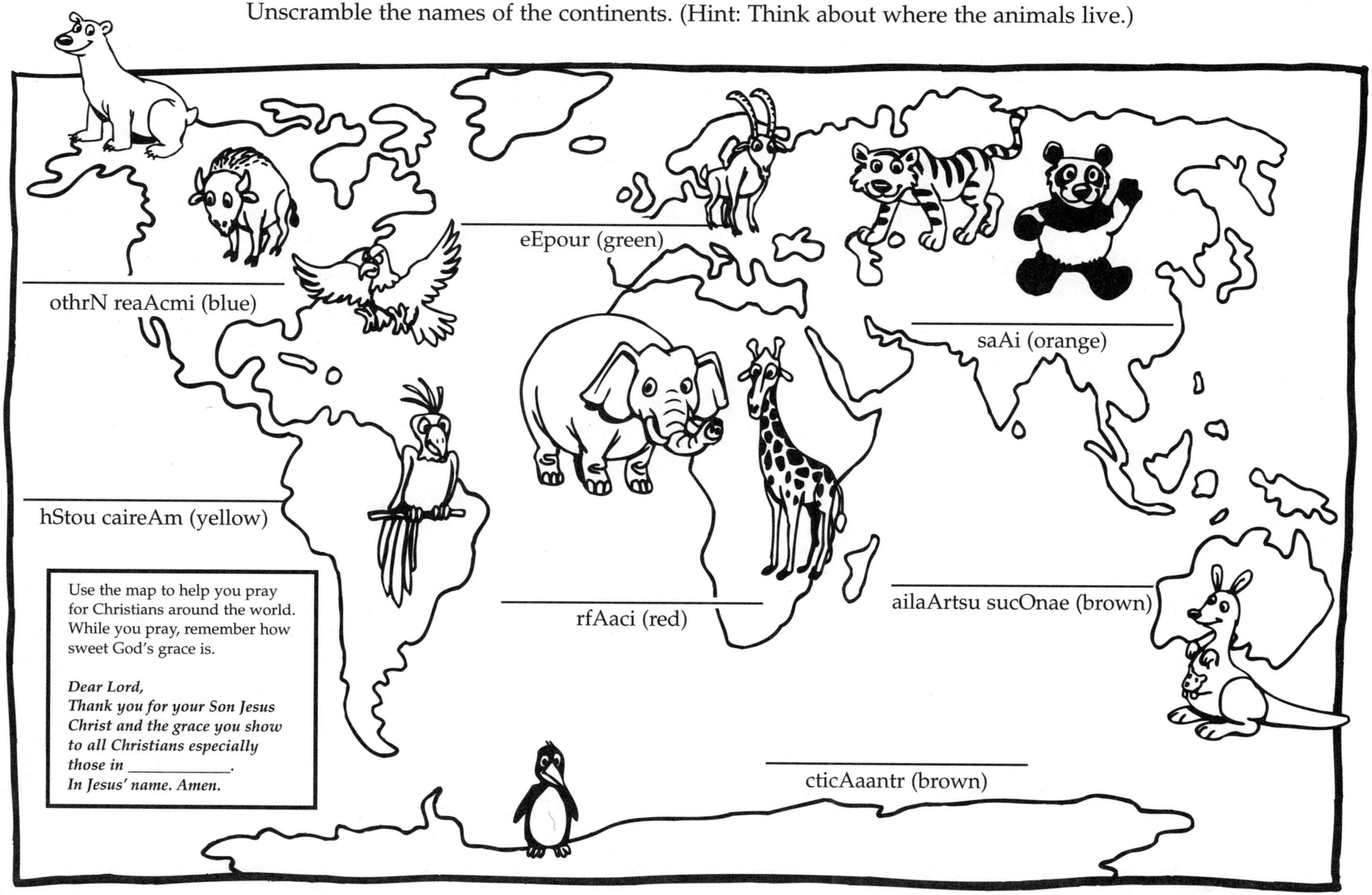

Use the map to help you pray for Christians around the world. While you pray, remember how sweet God's grace is.

Dear Lord,
Thank you for your Son Jesus Christ and the grace you show to all Christians especially those in ____________.
In Jesus' name. Amen.

Growing in Confidence

Unit Aims

Know:	Describe/explain how and under what circumstances Paul told his story.
Feel:	Feel inspired/bold/determined to share the gospel with unbelievers.
Do:	Prepare to share your testimony (your story).
Memorize:	1 Peter 3:15, 16

Why Grow in Confidence?

Today's world desperately needs God's message of salvation, and it is important that we teach our young people to feel confident in sharing that message. This unit is designed to allow students to grow in that confidence through a carefully planned series of lessons and activities. Using the apostle Paul as an example, students will not only learn more about the message that Paul took to the world, but they will also practice ways in which they can make that message their own. The memory passage (1 Peter 3:15, 16) will be used to emphasize that Christians not only need to be prepared to give an answer to the hope that is within them but also must do so with gentleness, respect, and a clear conscience.

The eight- to twelve-year-old is at a critical age. He is developing skills, attitudes, and behaviors that will go with him into adulthood. The world will try to teach him that satisfying self is most important. Parents and Bible school teachers need to help him to see that he was created in God's image and that God has a plan for his life. He needs also to see that God's plan for him isn't meant to start when he becomes and adult; it is meant to start now. In addition, he needs to develop skill in understanding and using God's word. He also needs attitudes and behaviors that are consistent with one whose heart has set apart Christ as Lord.

Summary

Grow in the grace and knowledge of Jesus by telling the story of your salvation.

- Establish a pattern of and build confidence for spreading Jesus' good news.
- Tell about events that led you to become a Christian.
- Tell about a time when you put Jesus first.
- Tell about your hope in Jesus—what you look forward to in Heaven.
- Keep telling your story your whole life—even when it is difficult.

Lesson Aims

Scripture focus	Bible focus	Life focus
Lesson 1 Acts 17:16-32	Paul told the good news about Jesus in a way that interested his listeners.	Prepare testimony (identify what it is).
Lesson 2 Acts 21:27—22:29	Paul told the story of his conversion.	Prepare testimony.
Lesson 3 Acts 24; 25:23—26:32	Paul explained his faith in Jesus.	Share testimony in class (practice).
Lesson 4 Acts 28:17-31	Even under Roman guard, Paul kept telling the good news about Jesus.	Share testimony outside class.

Memory Passage: 1 Peter 3:15, 16

"In your hearts set apart Christ as Lord. Always be prepared to give an answer to everyone who asks you to give the reason for the hope that you have. But do this with gentleness and respect, keeping a clear conscience, so that those who speak maliciously against your good behavior in Christ may be ashamed of their slander."

Classroom Supplies
- two sheets of poster board
- self-adhesive hook-and-loop fasteners (such as Velcro brand)
- markers
- pencil

Curriculum Supplies
none

Memory Passage Review Activity

Use a pencil to divide one poster board in half vertically and into eight horizontal sections. Draw the outline of a heart so that part of it crosses each of the sixteen sections. Divide the memory passage into sixteen sections. Write the words to the memory passage inside the heart shape in each of the sixteen sections. Ink in the heart and the words.

Divide the second sheet of poster board in the same manner as the first—in half vertically and in eight horizontal sections. Ink in the lines. Attach a length of hook-and-loop fastener (keep both sides together) in each section of the second poster board. Carefully place the first sheet of poster board over the first, printed side up, matching the sections. Press down so the fastener is securely attached to both pieces of poster board. Separate the two poster boards. Then cut the first poster board apart, following the penciled lines.

Scramble the poster board pieces and students put the verse in order by attaching pieces to the base poster board. Students may check their work by checking the completeness of the heart outline.

Lesson 1

Growing in Confidence

A Testimony Gives Evidence

Acts 17:16-32

Bible Focus

Paul told the good news about Jesus in a way that interested his listeners.

Life Focus

Prepare a testimony (identify what it is).

Growing Up in the Word: 1 Peter 3:15, 16

Prepare one or both of the following activities for students to do as they arrive. Greet students and invite them to participate.

Memory Activity 1

Before class, enlarge the following copy of the memory passage so that students can easily read it. Assign phrases to students to read. Students may read solo, in pairs, or groups. Instruct students to highlight or underline their parts.

Classroom Supplies
markers or colored pencils

Curriculum Supplies
memory passage printed here

"In your hearts set apart Christ as Lord.
Always be prepared to give an answer
to everyone who asks you to give the reason
for the hope that you have.
But do this with gentleness
and respect,
keeping a clear conscience,
so that those who speak maliciously
against your good behavior in Christ
may be ashamed of their slander"
(1 Peter 3:15, 16).

First, read the passage to the class using expression and emphasis. Then, have the class read the passage together several times and then allow students to practice their parts. Circulate as students are practicing, helping them to pronounce words and use expression effectively. After practicing together, perform the choral reading.

Say: **This memory passage tells each of us to always be prepared to tell others why we are Christians. Certainly we should be ready to do just that. When** we performed our reading and someone was not ready, the performance suffered. If we are not prepared to tell others why we love Jesus, we will miss a chance to help someone know Jesus.**

However, think how wonderful it would be if all of us were working together to tell others about Jesus—just as we worked together in our reading. We could truly make a difference in the world around us.

Memory Activity 2

Classroom Supplies
- poster board or overhead transparency
- masking tape

Curriculum Supplies
none

Before class, write the words of 1 Peter 3:15, 16 on poster board for display or prepare a transparency that can be projected on a screen or on the wall.

Use the masking tape to make a hopscotch diagram on the floor of the classroom. Divide the memory passage into six phrases. Make the hopscotch grid with six sections so that one phrase can be said at each hop.

Allow the students to play a few times while looking at the memory passage. Then have them try to complete the game without help.

Say: **Many people go through life hopping from one thing to another without any purpose. Christians, however, have a purpose because of Jesus. We must be prepared to tell others what that purpose and hope is.**

Why Grow Up?

Classroom Supplies
- items or pictures illustrating ways of communicating such as a telephone, notepad and pencil, radio, television, computer, voice, greeting card, tape recorder, and so on
- slips of paper with the name of people or groups with whom we might want to communicate such as best friend, grandmother, teacher, the world, the president of the United States, parents, and so on
- poster board

Curriculum Supplies
none

Begin the lesson by asking the students to tell what the items or pictures have in common. Lead them to discover that all are ways in which we communicate with other people. Have each student draw out a slip of paper and tell what means of communication he might use if he wanted to give that person a very special and important message. Ask the student to explain the reason for his choice.

Say: **Christians have a very important message that the world needs to hear. Who can tell me what that message is? The message might have several parts. Let's list the things that we think others need to know Christians.** Using the poster board, list what the students tell you. The list might include that Jesus died for us, that God is our creator, that Heaven is for believers, and so on. Reread what is written on the poster board and then ask the following questions, giving students time to reflect and answer. **What would be the result if we kept this message to ourselves and never told anyone else about it? Why do you think people do not share God's message?**

Our goal this month is to grow in confidence so that we will be able to share God's message with those who need to hear it. We are going to study the life of man named Paul as our example and look at ways that he shared God's message with people in his life.

How to Grow Up

Before class, copy the reproducible page and separate the cards for each of the Greek gods and goddesses. Enlarge the cards as you think necessary. Gather a symbol for each.

Begin the lesson by asking the students to listen carefully while you read Acts 17:16-32. When you get to verse 22, you might want to stand on a stool or chair to deliver Paul's sermon.

Say: **We have heard what the Scriptures tell us about Paul's visit to Mars Hill in Athens, Greece. Statues to many of the Greek gods and idols stood at Mars Hill. Let's act out his story. First, we will have to set the stage by creating our own Mars Hill.** Arrange the students around the room as statues, place a card beside each one telling whom they represent and give them a symbol to hold. As you place the card beside each, tell what that god or goddess represented and have the student assume a position that would demonstrate their domain. Hermes could assume a running position. Zeus could sit on a throne. Iris might hold a rainbow between two hands. Place only a card beside the Unknown God. If you have fewer than 11 students, eliminate some of the statues.

Classroom Supplies
- Bibles
- symbols for Greek gods and goddesses such as a heart, sun, moon, crown, fish, flower, rainbow, bow and arrow (these could be cut out of paper)

Curriculum Supplies
reproducible pages 287, 288 (Greek gods and goddesses)

Select a student to represent Paul or portray him yourself. Reenact the scene concluding with the reading again of verses 22-31. When you finish, place the cards with the symbols in a row at the front of the room to be used in the second part of the lesson.

Say: **Paul was an educated man. He not only knew about the Greek gods and goddesses, but he also knew God's Word. These two facts made it possible for him to share the true God with the Athenians. If we are to gain confidence in ourselves so that we can share God with others, we must know God's Word. We must have an answer. What is the answer to the Athenian gods and goddesses? Let's see what God's Word says.**

Assign students one of the Scriptures below to read concerning God. Have them identify the god or goddess that the Greeks thought had that characteristic. When they find the correct match, they can write the Scripture on the back of the card and place it with the card of the Unknown God.

Love: 1 John 4:8
Sun & Moon: Psalm 136:7-9
Wisdom: Proverbs 3:19
King of gods: Revelation 19:16
Messenger: John 1:1
Sea: Matthew 8:24-27
Spring (Seasons): Genesis 1:14
Rainbow: Genesis 9:12, 13
War: Psalm 46:9, 10

Because we know what God's Word says about who he is, we are ready to explain why these idols are false gods.

Classroom Supplies
- pens or pencils
- crayons or a photograph of each student

Curriculum Supplies
reproducible page 289 (passports)

Ready to Grow Up!

Say: **When Paul stood before the Athenians, he was prepared to tell what he knew about Jesus. He was able to tell why the Unknown God is superior to the idols of Athens. As part of his testimony, Paul pointed out the things that only God can do. Let's look at the testimony Paul gave in his sermon about**

God. Point students to Acts 17:24-30. In verses 24-28 students should recognize that Paul testified that God created the world. In verse 31 students should recognize that Paul pointed to evidence that God raised Jesus from the dead.

Say: **Paul was a messenger from God to the Greeks. As a messenger for God, Paul was always ready to give testimony or evidence about God. The Bible tells us that we should all be messengers for him. We should all be ready to give testimony or evidence why we believe in Jesus.**

Another word for messenger is ambassador. Presidents and kings have ambassadors who are their messengers to other countries. The ambassadors are trained to speak for their countries. Sometimes they begin work in small countries, and as they gain experience, may be sent to larger and more important countries. The ambassadors must have visas (or permission) to go to other countries, and they must also have passports that tell what country they represent.

As ambassadors for Jesus, we need a passport to help us accomplish our mission. This passport will tell others who we represent. Pass out passports. To assemble, have students fold on the dashed lines. Then have the students fill in the personal information. If you have access to an instant camera, add a picture or have students draw their picture or bring one from home.

Say: **Now that we have passports, we are ready for our first assignment as ambassadors. Your assignment this week is to share evidence about God with at least one person in your family—a brother or sister, parent, grandparent, and so on. Be sure to tell them the evidence about God that Paul gave when he spoke to the men at Mars Hill. Or tell them how our God is greater than any of the gods or goddesses of Athens.** Review some of those things as you sign the family visa in each passport. Collect the passports so that they can be used each week during this month.

Growing Up Every Day

Say: **An ambassador for the president of the United States needs to know about his country and to be prepared to answer questions about the United States when people ask him. As ambassadors for God, you must also be prepared to answer questions about God. One way we can do that is by knowing about God. We can gather evidence by memorizing Bible passages. A second part of your mission as ambassadors this week is to work on our memory passage, 1 Peter 3:15, 16.** If you used the choral reading activity, pass out the scripts and perform the reading one more time. If not, have the students find the Scripture in their Bibles and read it together.

Close with a prayer, asking God to help each student keep Christ as Lord set apart in their hearts.

Classroom Supplies
none

Curriculum Supplies
none

Lesson 2

Growing in Confidence

Prepare Your Story

Acts 21:27—22:29

Bible Focus
Paul told the story of his conversion.

Life Focus
Prepare testimony.

Growing Up in the Word: 1 Peter 3:15, 16
Set up one or both of the following activities for students to do as they arrive. Greet students and direct them to the activities.

Memory Activity 1
Divide the class into pairs or small groups. Give each pair a bag of sugar cubes and a copy of the memory passage. Allow each student to build his own confidence wall by putting a sugar cube in place as he correctly recites each word in 1 Peter 3:15, 16. One student can act as prompter, using the Bible. Encourage them to recite with confidence and to try to build a wall that is tall and secure.

After students have had at least two turns in building their walls, discuss any problems they might have had. The cubes were not always level. Building too fast made the wall fall. Once the cubes were in place, it would be difficult to remove one.

Say: **Knowing God's Word gives us confidence to share our testimony with others. Just as each sugar wall needed to be built carefully and deliberately, so does our confidence. We need to be sure that we know God's Word. We must also take care to use the right words because words are difficult to take back.**

Classroom Supplies
- at least 60 sugar cubes for each pair or group of students
- Bibles

Curriculum Supplies
none

Memory Activity 2
Before class, copy the questions below on separate index cards.

In class have each student select a hat or tool, read the label, and think about the occupation. Select one student to be the reporter or play this role yourself. The reporter needs a toy microphone. Have the students arrange themselves around the room. The reporter then interviews each citizen, asking for name and

Classroom Supplies

- a hat or a tool for each student in the class labeled with the name of an occupation such as plumber, teacher, salesman, doctor, nurse, fireman, soldier, policeman, secretary
- a toy or real microphone (or a video camera)
- index cards

Curriculum Supplies

questions printed here

occupation. Then the reporter will ask a question or questions that must be answered from the memory passage.

Question: Where should Christ be set apart and how?
Answer: In your hearts set apart Christ as Lord.
Question: To whom should you be prepared to give an answer?
Answer: To everyone who asks you to give a reason for the hope that you have.
Question: How should you give this reason?
Answer: With gentleness and respect.
Question: Why should you keep a clear conscience?
Answer: So that those who speak maliciously against your good behavior may be ashamed of their slander.

If time allows, let different children play the reporter role. If you use a video camera, set aside time for each student to see himself on camera and evaluate his level of confidence.

Say: **Knowing God's Word gives us confidence when we come in contact with individuals who might question our belief in him. However, we do not want to be arrogant or proud in our use of Scripture. First Peter 3:15, 16 tells us to use this confidence with gentleness and respect and with a clear conscience. This means that we must not only know God's Word, but we must also behave in ways that please God.**

Classroom Supplies

- a spray bottle of cologne or a can of fragrant air freshener
- a spray bottle with a small amount of ammonia

Curriculum Supplies

none

Why Grow Up?

Keeping the cologne and the ammonia hidden, have the students go as far away from you as possible and line up with their backs to you. Tell them that you want them to raise their hands when they can smell a different odor. First, spray the cologne or air freshener and wait for a response. Follow with the ammonia and wait for a response. Spray just enough ammonia to cover the cologne smell.

Have the students guess what they have smelled. Ask them how the smell traveled from one part of the room to another. Discuss which smell they preferred. Also generalize as to what the ammonia smell did to the good smell.

Say: **The smells reached your noses as molecules traveled through the air, propelled in this case by a push of air.** Demonstrate the spray bottle. **Words are much like smell molecules. They also travel through the air often propelled by our feelings as we speak. It is important that we learn to send good messages and to remember that bad words and false messages can be overpowering and wipe out our good intentions just as the ammonia covered up the good smell of the cologne. The apostle Paul knew that the world needed to hear good messages, and he was always prepared. Today we want to continue to use him as an example as we grow in our confidence to share the good news of Jesus Christ.**

How to Grow Up

Before class, write one of the following names on separate index cards: Jews, soldiers, commander, centurion.

Say: **Last week we looked at Paul in Athens and saw that he gave testimony or evidence why God is superior to idols. Today, we are going to look at a time in Paul's life when he shared his own story of how he became a Christian. He gave evidence why he believes Jesus is the Christ, the Son of God.**

I am going to let each of you select a card that will give you a role to play in this drama in Paul's life. Read Acts 21:27—22:29 and on the back of your card, jot down what you will say and do when our drama begins. You may also read your parts directly from the Bible.

Give the students time to research their characters. Circulate making sure that they have found the Scripture and located their part in the story. The child who plays Paul cannot be expected to remember all the words, so allow him to use the Bible when it comes time for him to give his testimony.

If time allows, the students could make simple props such as a stick for a spear, paper chains, paper hats for the soldiers, scarves or cloths to cover the heads of the Jews.

Act out the drama. Remember, this is not a public performance so do not worry about perfection. If need be, you can tell the actors when and how to perform as the story moves along. The purpose of this activity is to allow the students feel the circumstances in which Paul gave his personal testimony.

Say: **Paul saw an opportunity to tell others about Jesus, and he was prepared. He was ready to give an answer for the hope he had in Jesus. He gave his testimony—his personal story of how he became a follower of Jesus.**

Classroom Supplies
- Bibles
- index cards

Curriculum Supplies
none

Ready to Grow Up!

Before class, make two copies of the testimony sheet for each student.

Say: **As ambassadors for God, your mission last week was to share evidence about God with your family. Would anyone like to tell us what happened when you carried out the mission?** Allow time for students to share. If they do not share willingly, ask probing questions. **What evidence about God did you share? Why? Were you well-prepared to present the evidence? The story? Did the person you shared with ask questions? If you talked to two or more people, did it get easier? Why or why not?**

It is now time for us to get our passports signed with this week's visa. Pass out passports. **Paul told the people in Jerusalem his testimony—the evidence of how he became a Christian—because he knew that people could grow by hearing it. What evidence did Paul include in his testimony?** Distribute the testimony worksheets. Read over the questions and note that Paul included each item in his testimony.

Say: **This week, your mission has two parts. The first part is to interview one person and ask him to tell you the story of how he became a Christian. Use one testimony worksheet to help you take notes and ask good questions.** Sign the interview visas.

Say: **The second part is to write your own testimony. We're going to work**

Classroom Supplies
pencils

Curriculum Supplies
reproducible page 290 (testimony worksheet)

now on our own stories of how we became Christians or where we are in our process of becoming a Christian. Use one testimony worksheet. Ask yourself the questions on the sheet. Guide students through this activity. If time runs out, send the sheet home with the student to finish at home. Remind them to bring the sheets back with them next week.

Growing Up Every Day

Classroom Supplies
none

Curriculum Supplies
none

Say: **In our Bible lesson today, we learned that Paul was a Roman citizen, an important and valuable position. The commander had paid a large sum of money for his citizenship. To be a Roman citizen meant that you had special privileges and rights such as not being beaten or accused falsely. Roman citizens could also travel wherever they wished without fear.**

In many ways, being an American citizen today is much like being a Roman citizen in Paul's time. We are protected from being accused falsely or being beaten in our country, and we too can travel wherever want. Paul used his Roman citizenship to become a missionary to the Gentiles and to spread the Good News of Jesus Christ throughout the world. Perhaps some of you will use your American citizenship to also become missionaries. But to do so, you will need to set Christ apart in your hearts. And you'll need to be prepared to give an answer for the hope that you have because Jesus has saved you from your sins. Close with a prayer in which you use the words of 1 Peter 3:15, 16.

Lesson 3

Growing in Confidence

Practice Your Story

Acts 24; 25:23–26:32

Bible Focus
Paul explained his faith in Jesus.

Life Focus
Share testimony in class (practice).

Growing Up in the Word: 1 Peter 3:15, 16
Prepare one or both of the following activities for students to do as they arrive. Greet students and direct them to the memory activities.

Memory Activity 1
Before class, write the memory passage on poster board and post in the room. Have the students stand in a circle. Give the Koosh ball to the first student. Tell him to throw the ball to any other child in the circle and to remember to whom he threw it because he will always throw the ball to that person. The second student catches the ball and then throws it to another. He must remember who threw him the ball and to whom he threw the ball. Continue until each student has caught the ball and thrown it to another. (No one can throw the ball back to the person who threw it to him.) Practice again, then add the verse.

The first child begins the verse and then after a word or a phrase, throws it to the next person who catches it, adds the next word or phrase, and then throws it to the next student. The key is not only to remember the verse but also to remember where the ball came from and to whom it should go.

Say: **Did you notice that each time we played, we became more confident and made fewer mistakes? It is the same with being ready to give an answer for the hope we have. The more we think about what God has done for us, the more confident we will be to tell others. In our game, it was also helpful to us when we remembered who threw us the ball and to whom we were supposed to throw it. We were able to look in the right direction. When we remember that our hope comes from God, we will keep our eyes on him.**

Classroom Supplies
- a Koosh brand ball or a beanbag
- poster board

Curriculum Supplies
- none

Memory Activity 2

Classroom Supplies
- small box
- marker
- wrapping paper
- strips of poster board

Curriculum Supplies
reproducible page 264
(cube from unit 10)

Prepare a cube by covering a small square box with paper or use the cube pattern from unit 10. Label the sides as follows: 5, 10, 20, vowel, free turn, lose a turn. Choose phrases and/or words from the memory passage ("reason for the hope that you have," "set apart Christ as Lord," and so on). Put each phrase of word on a strip of poster board, using blanks for each letter.

Students may work alone or if your class is larger, they may form teams. The first student throws the cube. If the top of the cube shows a number, the student can guess a consonant and if that consonant is used in the phrase, he can collect that number of points for each time the letter appears. If the word "vowel" is on top of the cube, the contestant must choose a vowel. If "lose a turn" or "free turn" appears, the contestant either loses the chance to choose a letter or gets a second throw. Fill in the correct letters and keep a list of the letter choices that have been made. When the contestants are confident that they know the phrase, they may choose to solve the puzzle. Award 15 points to a player that solves the phrase.

Say: **What helped you feel confident about solving the phrases? Did it help knowing the passage? How did having the vowels help? How were you prepared to play this game?** (Students had studied the passage; they were familiar with consonants, vowels, and words; they knew what needed to be done.) **The more familiar we are with God's Word, the more confident we will be in sharing the hope we have in Jesus with others.**

Why Grow Up?

Classroom Supplies
- pencils

Curriculum Supplies
- reproducible page 291 (Setting the Record Straight)

Distribute the reproducible to each student. Tell the students that you want to set the record straight. Ask them to think of a time when they were accused of something that they did not do. Have them draw or write the accusation in the situation square. In the accuser square, have them draw or write who accused them of wrong doing. In the plea square, ask them to draw or write about how they answered the charge. Finally, in the judge square, they need to illustrate who decided their guilt or innocence. Complete your own worksheet while the students are completing theirs.

Allow some of the students to share their stories if they choose to do so. Listen but do not make comments. You might want to begin the process by sharing your own story. Comment on how students were ready with an answer to defend themselves.

Say: **We need to be as ready to defend our faith in Jesus as we were ready to defend our innocence in these situations. Last week we found that Paul was again ready to give an answer for the hope he had in Jesus. He told his personal story about how he came to believe in Jesus. As we read further in Acts, we find that the crowd accused Paul of things he did not do. He had to set the record straight, and he was again ready to give an answer.**

How to Grow Up

Before class, write the following roles on separate index cards: Ananias, Tertillus, Paul, Felix, Narrator, Festus, Agrippa. Copy and enlarge Acts 24, 25.

Say: **Today, we are going to use the Scriptures to tell us how Paul was falsely** accused and how he answered the charges. Give each student an enlarged copy of Acts 24-25. Have them draw a role card. Adjust your cards to the number of students by adding a second or third narrator, or a second or third Paul. If your class is large enough, you could have two sets of role cards. **Now that you have a role to play in our court drama, please read the two chapters and underline or highlight what your character will be saying.** Give the students time to mark their passages. Circulate helping those who might need help with vocabulary, pronunciation, and so on.

The court drama can be done in one of the following ways. Choose the one with which you and the students would be most comfortable. Remember the object is to know the story not to present a perfect performance.

Reader's Theater: Students either stand or sit in order to read their parts. No action is necessary other than good verbal expression.

Creative Dramatics: Students may add props, costumes, and action to their parts. The teacher may choose to be the narrator in order to keep the action moving. Each character might provide his own props such as a crown for Agrippa, scroll for the high priest, paper chains for Paul, and so on.

After the drama is completed ask the following questions for discussion. Ask: **What were some of the false accusations against Paul? Why was Paul confident in his testimony? What did it mean to be a Roman citizen? Do you think if Paul had more time with King Agrippa that he might have been persuaded to believe that Jesus is the Savior?**

Close this section of the lesson by reminding the students that Paul had confidence because he knew God's truth. Say: **When we are speaking God's truth, we too can be confident in our message.**

Classroom Supplies
- markers or highlight pens
- Bibles
- index cards

Curriculum Supplies
none

Ready to Grow Up!

Before class, record the following message using a disguised voice or have someone else record it: **Hello, I understand that you have been developing your confidence, and I have a test for you. Your mission is to invite one of your friends to Bible class with you next week. I know this is risky and your friend may refuse, but know that God is with you and will be pleased with your efforts. This message will self-destruct in ten seconds.**

Before you hand out the passports, ask the students to share some of the conversion stories that they heard during last week's mission. You may want to start the conversation by sharing your own story or a story of someone you know.

Say: **Last week our passports and visas took us to meet individuals who told us how they became Christians. We also worked on our own stories of how we became Christians. We're going to use those now and during our mission for this week. I wonder what our mission for this week is. This tape may help us know what needs to be done.** Play the tape that you have recorded before class.

Say: **Perhaps each of you need some practice in order to be ready to receive your visas. Let's role play some situations.** Have the children divide into pairs. Each pair, in turn, should come to the front of the room for their role play. Have them decide who will be student A and who will be student B. Give the pair a situation during which A is to share part of his testimony and to invite B to

Classroom Supplies
- cassette recorder
- blank cassette tape

Curriculum Supplies
- passports
- testimony worksheets (from last week)

come to Bible class with him. Students may use the testimony sheets they prepared last week to help them know what to say. A simple statement of testimony is all students need to share along with the invitation. Give suggestions as needed. For example, "I attend Bible class because I'm thankful that Jesus has forgiven my sins. I'd like you to come with me to Bible class next week."

Situations could include the following: on the school bus, in the school cafeteria, on the playground, in the hall between classes, on the telephone, in gym class, and so on. Student B should respond appropriately. Have pairs play both roles. As each pair completes the role play, sign their invitation visas.

Classroom Supplies
- pencils
- two-inch wide strips of colored construction paper
- stapler

Curriculum Supplies
none

Growing Up Every Day

Give each student one or more strips of construction paper. Tell them that they will be making a prayer chain. Have each one think of a person whom they want to know Jesus. This could be the individual they plan to invite to Bible class. Then have students write a one sentence prayer asking God's help in reaching that person. One by one, let each read his prayer and add it to the chain. Conclude with your own prayer that will link the chain into a circle.

Lesson 4

Growing in Confidence

Tell Your Story

Acts 28:17-31

Bible Focus

Even under Roman guard, Paul kept telling the Good News about Jesus.

Life Focus

Share testimony outside class.

Growing Up in the Word: 1 Peter 3:15, 16

Prepare one or both of the following activities for students to do as they arrive. Greet students and direct them to the activities.

Memory Activity 1

Divide the memory passage into words or phrases so that each child will have at least one. Write the words or phrases on separate index cards. Place the cards in a container and have each child select a card. If there are not enough students for all the cards, make each student's phrase longer by giving them words or phrases that are before or after the ones they have already. Mix the students up and tell them that they are to arrange themselves in the correct order without talking. They may use hand and body motions to communicate. When the class thinks that the passage has been assembled correctly, have them read it. If the order is incorrect, they can make the necessary adjustments.

Ask: **How did you find your correct place? Was it difficult not to speak? How did you feel when you knew that you were in the right place? You were handicapped because you could not speak, but you found other ways to communicate. In today's lesson, Paul finds himself a prisoner in Rome. He cannot preach as freely as before, but he does find ways to communicate God's message.**

Classroom Supplies
- index cards
- marker

Curriculum Supplies
none

Memory Activity 2

Before class, divide the memory passage into words or phrases and write them on separate index cards. Make two identical sets. Divide the class into two teams. Give each team a spoon and an egg. Mark the starting point with a line of masking tape. Place each set of index cards in separate containers and place them at the opposite end of the room. Tell the students that when the relay

Classroom Supplies
- two large serving spoons
- two hard-boiled eggs
- two containers
- masking tape
- index cards

Curriculum Supplies
none

begins, one student is to carry the egg to the opposite side of the room without dropping it. If the egg is dropped, the student who dropped it must return to the starting line and begin again. When the egg arrives safely at the opposite end of the room, the team member may select a phrase or word from the container holding his team's memory passage. He then returns to the starting point, gives the egg to the next student, and places his word or phrase on floor beside his group. When all words are gathered and the team has arranged them in order, the team reads the passage in unison. Tell the teams that they may organize themselves in any way they wish but that all students must carry the egg at some point.

Say: **I noticed that when you carried the egg, you not only did so very carefully, but also you aimed for the finish line. The memory passage tells us to be prepared to give a reason for the hope that we have but to do it with gentleness and respect, much like you did with the egg. In today's lesson, Paul finds himself in a difficult situation, one in which he had to take care as he continued to confidently share his faith with others.**

Why Grow Up?

Classroom Supplies
index cards

Curriculum Supplies
interview questions from this section

To set the mood for this lesson, the students will have the opportunity to interview a Christian who did not grow up in the church. Locate this individual and ask him to be present in class and to answer the students' questions. Give the guest a copy of the questions and a copy of the memory passage so that he may be prepared.

Before class, copy the questions below onto separate index cards. In class before the guest arrives, tell the children that they will be conducting an interview. Distribute the questions, and go over the questions with the class. Ask students for suggestions for other questions to ask. Remind them to be respectful listeners. Interview questions follow:

- Who taught you about Jesus?
- What did you think or feel when this person first talked to you about Jesus?
- What was there about that person that made you want to listen to what he had to say?
- Did the person tell you how and why he became a Christian?
- How did the person act toward you?
- What questions did you ask about Jesus?
- What advice do you have for us about sharing Jesus with others?
- How did it feel to become a Christian?

Introduce the visitor. The visitor may give a brief opening statement as to who, when, and how he became a Christian, or if you prefer, the students may begin to ask their questions.

When the interview is over, thank the visitor and dismiss him. Then briefly discuss the session. Say: **Let's talk about what we learned from this interview. In our lesson today, we will find that Paul continued to share Jesus with others even though he was a prisoner in Rome. Many people were converted because Paul, like the person who taught our visitor, was always prepared to give an answer for the hope that he had.**

How to Grow Up

Begin the lesson by talking about and showing pictures of the city of Rome. Emphasize that Rome was the most important city in the world at the time Paul was taken there as a prisoner. Compare it to a large city today such as New York City or Washington, D.C.

Divide the students into work groups of three to four students and give them the following instructions:

1. Read Acts 28:17-31 carefully.
2. On the work paper, summarize the passage by deciding who, what, where, how, and the results.
3. On the poster board, write a newspaper story about Paul's time in Rome.
4. Give the story a headline.

When the groups have finished, let them read their stories to the rest of the class. Say: **Even as a prisoner, Paul found ways to share his faith. He told everyone who came to see him about Jesus. He spoke boldly and confidently. He was always ready and always prepared to tell about his hope in Jesus.**

Classroom Supplies
- map or atlas
- pictures of Rome (use a library book, textbook, an encyclopedia, or pictures from the Internet)
- poster board for each work group
- work papers
- pencils
- markers

Curriculum Supplies
none

Ready to Grow Up!

Begin by asking students to tell about their experiences in inviting a friend to Bible class. Ask them to share with the class the part of their testimony that they shared with the friend. If there are visitors present, make sure that they are welcome and aware that the class prayed for them.

Say: **Paul was ready wherever he went to share the story of how Jesus saved him. You can begin right now to be ready to share Jesus with others. The best way to share with someone about Jesus is to tell them why you are a Christian. Let's work some more on our testimonies.** Distribute the testimony sheets that students have been working on for the past two weeks. Give time as needed for students to finish any questions on the sheet.

When sheets are complete, have the students take turns telling the story of how they became a Christian to the class. This is important practice. Guide and encourage as needed. Students may use their sheets as needed.

Say: **This week your assignment is share your testimony with someone. We've spent the month thinking about it, writing about it, and practicing it. You are ready to give an answer for the hope that you have in Jesus. With whom do you plan to share your testimony—the story of how you became a Christian?** Have students share names. Then offer a prayer for the students as they share and for the listeners as they listen. Then sign the testimony visas.

Classroom Supplies
pencils

Curriculum Supplies
testimony worksheets (from last two weeks)

Growing Up Every Day

Classroom Supplies
none

Curriculum Supplies
passports

Since this is the last lesson in this series, make a ceremony of presenting the completed passports with all the visas signed.

Say: **This month, we have worked to gain confidence in sharing our faith with others. We have used Paul as our example and have learned that he was always prepared to share his faith whether in Athens, in Jerusalem, in front of kings, or in Rome. Paul was an ambassador for Jesus; he was a citizen of Heaven. Each of us are ambassadors for Jesus too; we are citizens of Heaven. Our passports show that we have worked this month to fulfill our duties as ambassadors. We are ready to give an answer for the hope that we have. Please come forward when I call your name to receive your passport.**

Conclude the ceremony by reciting the memory passage, 1 Peter 3:15, 16, together and then praying together.

Apollo

god of the sun

Artemis

goddess of the moon

Aphrodite

goddess of love

Zeus

king of the gods

Ares

god of war

Athene

goddess of wisdom

Hermes

messenger to the gods

Poseidon

god of the sea

Persephone

goddess of spring (or seasons)

Iris

goddess of the rainbow

Unknown God

Photo

Name ______________________________

Address ____________________________

Signature ___________________________

"In your hearts set apart Christ as Lord. Always be prepared to give an answer to everyone who asks you to give the reason for the hope that you have. But do this with gentleness and respect, keeping a clear conscience, so that those who speak maliciously against your good behavior in Christ may be ashamed of their slander" (1 Peter 3:15, 16).

Testimony Worksheet

What is your name? ____________________

Where were you born? ____________________

Where do you live now? ____________________

How old were you when you became a Christian? ____________________

How did you meet Jesus? ____________________

What was happening in your life at the time you met Jesus?

____

Who helped you to meet Jesus? What did they do to help?

____

How did becoming a Christian feel? ____________________

What is different about you now that you are a Christian?

____

How have you changed? ____________________

____

What do you look forward to in Heaven? ____________________

____

SETTING THE RECORD STRAIGHT

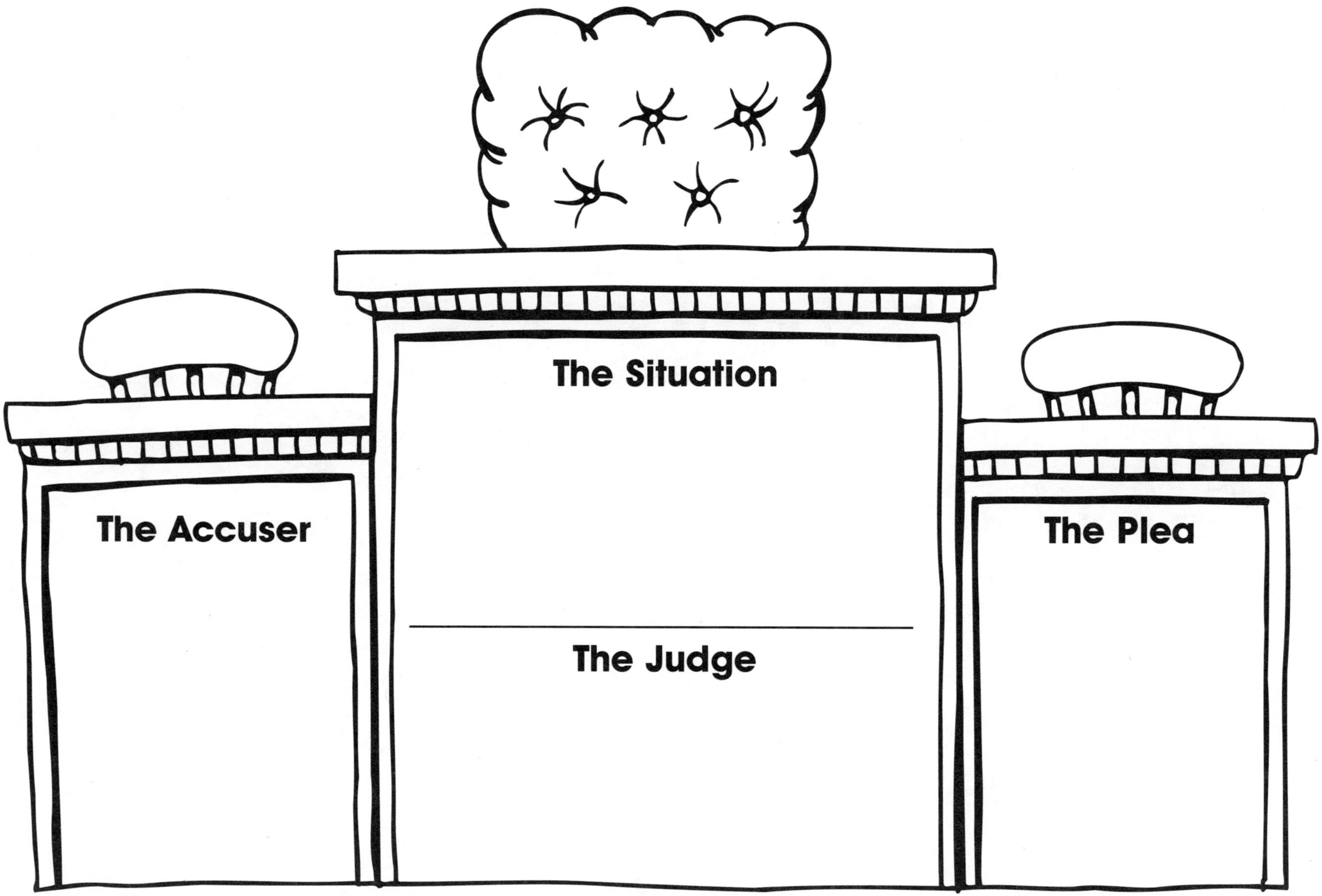

UNIT 12

Growing in Hope

Unit Aims

Know:	Summarize what the Bible says about the end times and life in Heaven.
Feel:	Feel a desire to live in Heaven with Jesus.
Do:	Live so that others see your hope of Heaven.
Memorize:	Matthew 24:36, 42, 44

Why Grow in Hope?

When the apostles saw Jesus ascend into Heaven after his resurrection, many of them believed he would return within a few years. Hundreds of years have passed since then, yet Jesus has not returned. Has he forgotten his promise? Not at all! In fact, in 2 Peter 3:9, we read that the reason Jesus hasn't come back for us yet is that God wants to give more people the opportunity to be saved!

Studying what the Bible says about Jesus' return should motivate Christians to keep watch and be ready. Jesus tells us that he will return like a thief in the night—no one knows when, so it important that we are prepared. Not only does the subject of Heaven and Jesus' return motivate us to be ready, but also it gives us hope. The fact that one day Jesus will return and we will live with him in Heaven transcends earth's sorrows and trials. In today's world eight- to twelve-year-olds need the hope that Jesus' return brings. Your students can live godly lives now, looking forward to the day Jesus does return. And in doing so, they can take others to Heaven with them!

Summary

Grow in the grace and knowledge of Jesus Christ by understanding what the Bible says about Jesus' return and about Heaven.

- Choose to be ready for Heaven and to help others do the same.
- With whom do you want to share Heaven?
- Be ready to go all the time.
- Use gifts to help others get ready.
- Continue to live a godly life.
- Repent and "obey what you know."

Lesson Aims

Scripture focus	Bible focus	Life focus
Lesson 1 Revelation 21:1-8; 22:5, 7, 12, 17-20	Heaven is great! Who do you want to take there?	Live looking forward to Heaven so much that you are always eager to share the reward with others.
Lesson 2 Matthew 24:3-7; 25:1-13	Do what you want Jesus to find you doing when he returns.	Live wisely—be ready for Jesus to return at any time.
Lesson 3 Matthew 25:14-30	Faithful servants use the abilities God has given them.	Use what God has given you to get yourself and others ready for Jesus to come.
Lesson 4 2 Timothy 3:1-5; 4:1-5, 7, 8	Many people will live ungodly lives in the last days.	Continue to live a godly life as an example to others.
Lesson 5 Revelation 1:3-8; 3:1-6	Jesus is coming soon in the clouds—so wake up and be ready.	Repent and "obey what you know" before Jesus comes.

Memory Passage: Matthew 24:36, 42, 44

"No one knows about that day or hour, not even the angels in heaven, nor the Son, but only the Father.... Therefore keep watch, because you do not know on what day your Lord will come.... So you also must be ready, because the Son of Man will come at an hour when you do not expect him."

Classroom Supplies
- 13 large craft sticks
- permanent markers
- masking tape

Curriculum Supplies
none

Memory Passage Review Activity

Divide the memory passage into thirteen phrases. Write each phrase on a separate craft stick. Lay the craft sticks in order and tape the ends so the sticks stay together. Turn the unit of sticks over, and using colorful markers, write the phrase, "Come, Lord Jesus!" on the back. Make sure that one letter of the phrase is printed on each stick. (You could also use the word "Maranatha," which means the same thing; simply write it large enough to cover all the sticks.) Remove the tape and scramble the sticks.

To play, students put the words to the memory passage in order. To check their work, they turn the sticks over to reveal the message. If the message reads correctly, the verse is in the correct order.

Lesson 1

Growing in Hope

Heaven Is Great!

Revelation 21:1-8; 22:5, 7, 12, 17-20

Bible Focus
Heaven is great! Who do you want to take there?

Life Focus
Live looking forward to Heaven so much that you are always eager to share the reward with others.

Growing Up in the Word: Matthew 24:36, 42, 44
Prepare one or both of the following memory passage activities for students to do as they arrive. As each student arrives, say: **"Maranatha! The Lord is coming!"**

Memory Activity 1
Post the memory passage on the chalkboard. Cover the painting area with newspapers. Give the students a paint shirt and a sheet of white paper and have them use a marker to write the memory passage in the center of the page. When they have finished writing, give each student a straw. Drip a few drops of the watered-down tempera paint around the edges of the paper, and have students blow the drops so they look like fireworks exploding around the edges of the page.

Say: **I'm sure all of you have seen a fireworks celebration on the Fourth of July. Fireworks are a great way to celebrate. The bright colors light up the night sky. We marvel at their beauty.**

We have all been invited to a celebration that will have lights so magnificent, they will not compare to the best fireworks show we have ever seen. Heaven will be the biggest celebration ever. The light at our celebration in Heaven will not come from fireworks or the light of a lamp. It won't come from the sun. It will come from the glory of God himself.

Classroom Supplies
- white paper
- markers
- watered-down tempera paint
- straws
- newspaper
- paint shirts

Curriculum Supplies
none

Memory Activity 2
To play the game, set one chair in the front of the room facing the board. Set the rest of the chairs in a row behind the first chair They should also face the board. Write the memory passage on the board. Select one student to sit in the

Classroom Supplies
- a candy bar
- chalkboard
- chalk

Curriculum Supplies
none

front chair and ask the other students to sit in the other chairs. Set the candy bar on the floor behind the front chair. Have the student in the front chair lead the other students in reading the memory passage. While they are reading, have one student quietly walk up to the front chair, take the candy bar, hide the candy, and return to her seat. When the group has finished reading the memory passage, the student sitting in the front chair stands and tries to identify the thief who took the candy bar.

Say: **How did you feel knowing someone was going to steal the candy bar? How did you feel when you had to identify the thief? The Bible tells us that Jesus will return unexpectedly like a thief in the night. No one knows when a thief will come to seal, nor do we know when Jesus will return. We do know God is faithful to keep his promises and that he will send Jesus again. We must be ready. We must keep watch.**

Why Grow Up?

Classroom Supplies
- adding machine tape
- markers

Curriculum Supplies
none

Give each student a different colored marker. Unroll the adding machine tape across the table.

Say: **Imagine you were going to a fantastic party where you knew there would be nothing but fun. There would be plenty of good food to eat and lots of interesting people to be with. You just knew you were going to have a great time. Wouldn't you be excited about being invited?**

Now imagine that the person who invited you to this great party said you could invite anyone else you wanted to come along with you. In fact, you could invite as many people as you wanted. There would be no limit to the number of people you could bring. Who would you invite?

Right now all of you are going to line up along the edge of the table. You are going to list the names of the people you would invite to this fantastic party. We are going to make this list as long as we can. Keep unrolling the adding machine tape to add more names. Allow time for students to come up with a long list.

Say: **Look at this list! Who are some of the people you included on the list?** Have students read the names on the list. They might mention friends from school, family members, other kids from their neighborhoods, and so on.

Say: **Perhaps you've never thought of it like this before, but you really have been invited to a fantastic party. It's called Heaven! God has invited all of us to come to Heaven to be with him, and he wants us to bring as many of our friends and family members as we possibly can. He hasn't set any limit on the number of people who can come. He would be thrilled if all the people on this list came to Heaven with us!**

How to Grow Up

Before class, write the following verses on separate index cards: Revelation 21:1-4; Revelation 21:10-14, 21; Revelation 21:22-27; 22:5; Revelation 22:1-3.

Say: **In just a few minutes, I am going to divide the class into four groups. Each group is gong to be given an index card with a passage of Scripture on it. Your group is to find those verses and read them. Then you are going to work**

together to design a mural that illustrates what the verses say what Heaven will be like.

After each group has finished, have one member of the group read the Scripture verses the group illustrated, and then another member serve as the spokesperson and explain what the group has drawn.

Highlights of the verses include the following:

Revelation 21:1-5: a city coming out of heaven; no more death, no more crying; no more pain, everything new; Revelation 21:11-14, 21: high, shining wall; twelve gates made of giant pearls; three gates on each wall; streets of gold. Revelation 21:22-27: no sun or moon; glory of God lights Heaven; no night; nothing impure will enter. Revelation 22:1-3: clear water from the river of life coming from God's throne; tree of life on each side of the river.

Say: **Heaven is an exciting place. Everyone is invited, but not everyone will choose to go. We must realize that only those who are ready when Jesus returns will enter Heaven.** Have students read Revelation 21:6-8; 22:7, 12, 17-20. **There is no doubt that Jesus will return. Are you ready?**

A person who is ready for Heaven looks forward to the return of Jesus, and he wants everyone he knows to be with him in Heaven.

Classroom Supplies
- Bibles
- index cards
- butcher paper
- markers

Curriculum Supplies
none

Ready to Grow Up!

Before class, make two copies of the maranatha strips for each student. If possible, make copies on several different colors of paper.

Say: **During the past few years, several survey companies and churches have asked church members why they started going to their churches. Some of the reasons included:**

- **The church is close to my home.**
- **I visited because I was curious and just kept coming.**
- **I came for a special program and liked it so I stayed.**
- **The most common reason people gave for attending a particular church was because a friend or family member had invited them to come!**

A few minutes ago we came up with a long list of people we would invite to attend a party with us. I'm sure if you had more time, you could have included more people on the list. Right now, I'm going to ask that you take your scissors and carefully cut apart the list so each one of you can gather the names that you wrote on the list. Allow time for students to separate the names and gather the ones they wrote on the list.

Say: **Now look through the names you have in your hands. Which of these people do not know Jesus? Have you ever talked to these people about Jesus or invited them to come to church with you? When we remember that Jesus is coming soon, we remember how important it is that we invite people to Jesus.**

Let's be ready for Jesus' return this week by reminding one person on our list that Jesus is coming soon. Let's also be ready for Jesus' return by reminding each other that Jesus is coming soon. When the early Christians wanted to remind each other about Jesus' return, they greeted each other by saying "Maranatha." Maranatha is a Greek word, which means "the Lord is coming." When you see each other at school this week, greet each other by saying "Maranatha!"

Classroom Supplies
- adding machine tape list of names
- scissors
- small plastic bags
- bag ties

Curriculum Supplies
reproducible page 315 (Maranatha Pharmacy)

Distribute the reproducible sheets, plastic bags, bag ties, and scissors. Read through the messages on the sheet. Have students cut the strips apart and roll each to form a pill. Put each of the pills in the plastic bag and close with the tie. After completing the labels, students should attach them to the bags with the tie. Students should make two sets or maranatha prescriptions, one for themselves and one for the person they have chosen from their list.

Say: **Your job this week is to give one maranatha prescription bag to someone on your list. The other bag is for you. Once a day, take a pill out of the bag and read the Scripture about Jesus' return.**

Growing Up Every Day

Classroom Supplies
none

Curriculum Supplies
none

Say: **God has promised us that Heaven is going to be the most wonderful place we can ever imagine. There will be no pain, no crying, and no death. Our heavenly home will be beautiful with streets of gold, gates of pearl, and walls that shine.**

Because we know that God keeps his promises, we know that someday he will send Jesus back to earth to take his followers to be in that fabulous place with him. God is waiting to send Jesus back because he wants as many people to join him in Heaven as possible! Lead students in prayer for the people they've chosen to remind about Jesus' return.

Who is going to be at Heaven's party? If your friends are going to be there, it may depend on your inviting them to the party.

Lesson 2

Growing in Hope

Keep Watch!

Matthew 24:3-7; 25:1-13

Bible Focus

Do what you want Jesus to find you doing when he returns.

Life Focus

Live wisely—be ready for Jesus to return at any time.

Growing Up in the Word: Matthew 24:36, 42, 44

As each student arrives, have him address a postcard to himself. Postcards will be used at the end of today's lesson. Prepare one or both of the following activities for students to do after they finish addressing the postcard. As each student arrives, greet him by saying "Maranatha!"

Memory Activity 1

Classroom Supplies
- 10 shoe boxes with lids
- marker

Curriculum Supplies
none

Before class, write the words to the memory passage in six shoe boxes and put the lids on them. In the classroom, set one of the shoe boxes in which you have written on a shelf or in a cabinet. Mix the other five boxes with the four with no writing and place them against one wall in the room.

When all the students have arrived, they are to open the boxes and work together to build a pyramid and reconstruct the memory passage using the boxes with the memory passage words. This will be impossible because one of the necessary boxes is hidden.

Say: **What is the difficulty you are having? Is it possible for you to complete the task? What is missing?** At this point you can provide the missing box so the students can complete the memory passage.

Say: **It is impossible to complete a task if you don't have the tools you need to do it. Have you ever started something without having what you needed? For instance, have you ever tried to complete a homework assignment when you have left your book at school? Have you ever tried to study for a spelling test when you have left the list at school? You can't prepare for something unless you have the right stuff!**

In order to be ready for Heaven, you need the right stuff too. What do we need to be ready for Heaven? As we learned earlier this year, the only way to

Heaven is through Jesus, our Savior.

It is also important for us to memorize God's Word. The truths in the Bible are tools God has given us to help us live our lives each day. He has given us verses to help us in any situation we can imagine, and if we hide these words in our hearts, they will be valuable tools in helping us to be ready when Jesus returns.

Classroom Supplies
- potato
- stop watch or a wrist-watch with a timer

Curriculum Supplies
none

Memory Activity 2

To play, have the students sit in a circle on the floor. Give one student the potato. The students are to pass the potato around the circle. Set the watch or timer to go off after 15 seconds. The student holding the potato at the buzzer must recite the memory passage.

Say: **Hot potato has always created feelings of anticipation. How did you feel when you knew the potato was coming your way? Did you take your time passing it to the person sitting next to you, or did you hurry and shove it in his hands? It's hard to stay calm when you know the timer is about to go off!**

This month we are talking about the second coming of Jesus. We don't know exactly when this is going to happen, but we do know that the time is getting closer every day. And although we don't have anything to be nervous about, we do need to be alert and anticipate his coming. We need to be ready!

Classroom Supplies
- paper lunch bags
- small household items

Curriculum Supplies
none

Why Grow Up?

Before class, gather a few small items that follow a theme and place them in a lunch bag. For example, a small measuring cup, a spoon and a potholder would all be put together in a bag. A nail, a hammer and a screwdriver could be in another bag. Other suggestions would be craft items, dinnerware, game pieces, and so on. Fill as many bags as you think would be necessary for this activity.

In class, have a student come to the front of the room and select a bag. Have him remove the items from the bag, identify each, and state what he would be able to do with the items. Continue this way until all of the bags have been opened.

Say: **It wasn't too difficult to figure out just what you could do if you had those particular tools. If you want to eat, you need silverware. If you want to cook, you need potholders and measuring cups. Just about any activity you do requires some kind of tool.**

But what about being ready for Jesus to come back? We can't pack a suitcase or a bag of fun things to take on the trip with us! Just how are we supposed to be ready? Today, we are going to learn how we can be ready.

How to Grow Up

Before class, gather six to eight flashlights, but only put batteries in half of the flashlights.

Ask the students to open their Bibles to Matthew 24:3-7 and 25:1-13 and read the passage silently. Then summarize the parable.

Say: **There were ten ladies who were all going to be in a wedding. Perhaps one was the bride and the other nine were her bridesmaids. They were all**

waiting for the groom, and he was running late. Night came and when the girls all tried to light their lamps, five of them didn't have enough oil to keep their lamps going. They asked the other five to share, but if those girls did, then they wouldn't have enough oil, and they wanted the groom to find them ready for the wedding when he arrived. The five girls without oil had to leave the wedding party to get oil. While they were gone, the groom finally arrived and the wedding party got started. When the five girls returned with their oil, they found the door locked. They knocked, but the groom wouldn't let them in because he didn't recognize them.

Sometimes these stories can be can seem a little strange to us because the way people lived in Bible times is so different from the way we live today. So we're going to retell the story in a little different way.

Classroom Supplies
- Bibles
- a large flat bed sheet or a tent that will set up inside
- flashlights

Curriculum Supplies
none

Set the stage for the skit by creating a tent from a table and a sheet or with an actual tent. Ask one student to be the guest of honor at a backyard sleepover. The remaining students are the guests at the party. Each guest gets a flashlight or two guests can share a flashlight. Have the host ask the guests to wait by the tent for the host to return from getting snacks in the house. While they are waiting, night begins to fall, and the guests need to turn on their flashlights. Those without batteries ask the others to share, but they are told to go home or to call their parents to get some. While they are gone, the host returns, locks the gate in the backyard, and the people in the backyard go into the tent for fun! When the others return, they can't get in the gate. The host won't let them in because he can't see who they really are.

Say: **It sounds like the host of the party was mean to those who had to go get batteries, doesn't it? But all the guests knew what they were supposed to bring. Those who had batteries were ready. Those who didn't have batteries should have checked their flashlights to be sure they worked before they got to the party. It wasn't the host's fault that some of the guests were not prepared.**

The same is true for us as we live our lives. We know Jesus is coming again, and we know it is going to be soon. We need to be prepared for his coming as the party guests who were prepared!

A person who is ready for Heaven looks forward to the return of Jesus, and he does what he wants Jesus to find him doing when Jesus returns.

Ready to Grow Up!

Classroom Supplies
- paper lunch bags
- scissors
- pencils
- Bible concordance

Curriculum Supplies
reproducible page 316 (tools)

Say: **Maranatha! Last week you made a pill bag of verses to give to someone who needed a reminder that Jesus is coming again. Who did you give the bags to? How did you feel? Did the person say anything to you about what they read? Did you remember yourself to watch for Jesus' return?** Discuss.

Since Jesus could return at any time, what could he find us doing when he returns? Discuss. **Jesus could find us doing many different things. Jesus could find us doing the things he has asked us to do, or he could find us sinning. What do you want Jesus to find you doing?** Discuss.

God has given us tools to help us be ready when Jesus returns. If we use these tools, then we will being doing something Jesus will be proud of when

he returns. God's tools will help us be ready no matter what the time or hour of Jesus' return. What are some of those tools?

Brainstorm with the students about what some of those tools are. List them on the chalkboard. Items on the list might include: reading the Bible, praying, hanging around with Christian friends, listening to Christian music, attending church, obeying parents and those in authority, helping and serving others, using gifts and talents.

After the students have finished their list, give each student a lunch bag and a copy of the tool sheet. Have students cut apart the tools and place them in a pile in front of them.

Have students choose five activities from the list on the board and write a Bible verse that goes with each of these activities on each tool. Have a Bible concordance handy if you need help finding a passage for one of the tools. Be sure they write only the Bible verse, not anything else. Some examples follow:

- Reading the Bible—Psalm 119:9
- Praying—Colossians 4:2
- Christian friends—Proverbs 12:26
- Christian music—Ephesians 5:19
- Obey parents—Ephesians 6:1
- Working— Colossians 3:23, 24
- Using gifts and talents—1 Peter 4:10

Say: **When we use the tools that God has given us, we are living wisely. We are living like we are ready for Jesus to return. We are doing what we want Jesus to find us doing when he returns.**

Now that you have the tools you need for this week, put them in your bags. Every morning this week, take one of these tools out of the bag, look up the Scripture passage and read it. All through the day think about what the verse said and how you can use it that day. These tools will help you do the things that you would want Jesus to find you doing when he returns. What tools will Jesus find you working with when he returns?

Growing Up Every Day

Classroom Supplies
- postcards
- crayons or markers
- half a sheet of poster board

Curriculum Supplies
none

Before class, write the word "Maranatha" in large letters on the poster board.

Say: **The early Christians helped each other remember that Jesus said, "I am coming soon." Instead of saying hello when they greeted each other, they said "Maranatha."** Point to the word and help students pronounce it. Distribute the postcards and have students use markers to write a colorful version of the word "Maranatha" on their card.

Say: **When you receive your postcard this week, remember that Jesus is coming soon and remember to do what you want to be found doing when Jesus returns.** Collect the postcards and close with prayer. Early in the week, mail the postcards.

Lesson 3

Growing in Hope

Be Faithful!

Matthew 25:14-30

Bible Focus
Faithful servants use the abilities God has given them.

Life Focus
Use what God has given you to get yourself and others ready for Jesus to come.

Growing Up in the Word: Matthew 24:36, 42, 44
Greet each student by saying "Maranatha" and direct them to the Memory Activity that you prepared before class.

Memory Activity 1
Before class, write phrases of two or three words from the memory passage on individual index cards. Make two sets. Fill the grocery bags with tissues and bury the index cards in the bags. Use the masking tape to mark a starting line at one end of the room, and set the bags on the floor eight to ten feet away from the line.

To play, divide the students into two teams. Have each team line up behind the starting line. At the signal, the first member of both teams races to the grocery bag and digs for a card. When he has a card, he races back to the team, touches the hand of the next person in line, and that person races to the bag. As each member returns to the team, they must arrange the words of the memory passage in order on the floor behind the team. The first team to complete the memory passage wins.

Say: **Digging for the words to the memory passage was a lot of fun! What other reasons do people have for digging?** Answers might include an archaeologist digging for artifacts, kids digging in the sand at the beach, construction workers digging a foundation for a building, and so on. **In our lesson today, we'll talk about a man who did some digging.**

Classroom Supplies
- index cards
- paper grocery bags
- tissues
- masking tape

Curriculum Supplies
none

Memory Activity 2
Before class, write one or two words of the memory passage on each coin. Place them in a basket.

Classroom Supplies
- candy coins wrapped in foil
- a thin-tipped black marker
- a small basket

Curriculum Supplies
none

In class, place the basket of coins in the center of the table. Instruct the students that they are to work together to put the words of the memory passage in order. Give them four or five minutes to accomplish this. Give them no more instructions, allowing them to figure out who will contribute in what way. The teacher need only encourage those who are not actively involved to participate.

Say: **Great job! Let's read the memory passage together. Now, these coins are worthless if we were interested in purchasing something, but they are good for a treat! Give each student a candy coin for a treat.**

Our lesson today is about money—not candy money, but real money called "talents." Talents were a measure of money used in Bible times. And just like in today's world, some Bible times people used their money wisely and others did not.

Classroom Supplies
- 10 pennies for each student
- plastic sandwich bags

Curriculum Supplies
none

Why Grow Up?

To play, place ten pennies in each bag, and give a bag to each student in the class. When the teacher gives the word, each student approaches another student and both pull a penny out of their bags. Each student reads the date imprinted on the face of his penny. The student holding the oldest penny takes both and each player moves on to challenge another student. If the years imprinted on the pennies are the same, the students return their pennies to their bags and move on to another student. Give students five minutes to play and then call them back to their seats. Have them count the number of pennies they have in their bags to see who has the most.

Ask: **How did you feel when you had to give someone else a penny? Maybe you didn't feel too bad about it; after all, you weren't giving away your pennies. And you were just losing a penny, not a whole lot of money. But if the penny really was yours or if it was something bigger, maybe a quarter or a dollar bill, would it have been harder to give away?**

Satan tries to teach us that the most important thing we can do is to take care of ourselves. He wants us to put ourselves first, ahead of everyone else, so we get what we want. Satan wants us to believe that it isn't important to share what we have with others, whether it is money, possessions, or even talents and abilities we might have. He's happy when we selfishly want things for ourselves.

The Bible tells us, however, that this way of thinking does not prepare us for Heaven and for Jesus' return. God has given each of us different talents so we can serve each other and help each other grow closer to Jesus.

Classroom Supplies
- Bibles
- chalkboard or marker board
- chalk or markers
- pennies from the opening activity

Curriculum Supplies
none

How to Grow Up

Begin by having the students find Matthew 25:14-30 and read the passage aloud. Then select four students to do a brief, modern-day version of the story, one to be the master and the other three to be the servants. Give the master ten pennies. Then give one servant five pennies and another servant two pennies. The third servant does not receive any. It might help students better understand if each penny represented $100 or about a day's wage.

Ask the students to list as many jobs they can think of that are done in the church, then say: **Many jobs need to be done in the church. Some of these jobs seem to be more important than others. Some take specialized training to be able to do them well. Let's think about some of these jobs and the talents and abilities a person must have in order to do these jobs well.**

The list might include some of the following: The pastor needs training in communication and Bible study. The organist or pianist needs to know how to play the instrument. The choir director needs training in music and singing. Teachers needs to know what activities will help students learn.

Say: **Many times people think they cannot serve others because they can't get up in front of the church and preach or they can't sing well. Some people think those are the only ways to serve God. But there are many other jobs in the church that need to be done. Some of them require special abilities; others just require a willing spirit.**

The person who is ready for Jesus' return faithfully uses what God has given him whether it is money, a possession, a talent, or other special gift.

Classroom Supplies
paper lunch bag or a small basket

Curriculum Supplies
reproducible page 317 (talent cards)

Ready to Grow Up!

Before class, cut the cards apart and place them in the basket or the bag. Also make enough copies of the blank talents so each student will have two.

Say: **Maranatha! Last week we kept watch for Jesus' return by using some of the tools God has given us. How did your week go? Did you keep watch? Did the postcard help remind you to watch for Jesus?** Discuss. **This week we will continue to look at ways to be ready for Jesus' return.**

Call a student to the front of the room to draw out a card and read it to the rest of the students. Brainstorm with the students what jobs each of these people could do with the special gifts God has given them.

Say: **God has created each person with special gifts and talents to help others grow. Maybe you have been blessed with a wonderful singing voice. Maybe you can organize and file. Perhaps you can play an instrument or you can memorize Scripture easily. Whatever it is God has blessed you with, he can help you use it so you and others can grow closer to Jesus.**

Take some time right now to think of two things you can do well. How can you use those abilities to help others be ready for Jesus' return ? Distribute blank talents and have students list their talents on them. Gather them to use during the closing.

Say: **Use the talents God has given you, so when the master comes back, he'll find you using your gifts, and you'll be able to hear him say, "Well done!"**

Growing Up Every Day

Classroom Supplies
none

Curriculum Supplies
none

Say: **What happened to the talents in today's story when the servant used them?** (They increased.) **What happened to the talent that was buried in the ground?** (The servant lost it.)

You've listed the talents that God has given you on these papers. As I pass them out to you, remind yourself that these talents are from God. How will you use them this week? The more faithful you are in using what God has given you, the more he will give you to use. Distribute all the talents back to the students.

Say: **A person who is ready for Heaven looks forward to the return of Jesus, and he faithfully uses his abilities to serve the master, Jesus.**

Lesson 4

Growing in Hope

Be Prepared!

2 Timothy 3:1-5; 4:1-5, 7, 8

Bible Focus
Many people will live ungodly lives in the last days.

Life Focus
Continue to live a godly life as an example to others.

Growing Up in the Word: Matthew 24:36, 42, 44
Prepare one or both of the memory passage activities for students to do as they arrive. Greet each student by saying "Maranatha!"

Memory Activity 1
Before class, write two-word phrases of the memory passage on separate index cards. Make three or four sets so the students can be divided into teams for the activity. Mix up the cards in each set.

In the classroom, divide the students into teams and give each team a set of the cards. Give the students time to arrange the words of the memory passage in order. Then shuffle the cards and tell the students that they will race this time. Set them up to begin the race, then stop the count by giving an excuse why you or one of the students isn't ready. For example, say: "Get ready, get set, oh, wait, I need to tie my shoe." Continue in this fashion to the point of student frustration. Suggested reasons follow: light needs to be off/on, card is missing, student is holding cards in the wrong hand, teams are even/uneven, the room is too cold/hot, someone is thirsty. Finally, let the students race.

Classroom Supplies
- index cards
- marker

Curriculum Supplies
none

Ask: **This was a difficult race, why? What were the factors that made this difficult?** (It took forever to get started; some students may not have known the verse; too many people working at the same time caused confusion.) **Our memory passage tells us to be ready because we don't know the day or the hour that Jesus will come. You all were ready to start this race, but you began to wonder if it would ever get started! I noticed that some of you remained ready until the minute the race actually began. Some others of you lost interest because it took so long to get the game going. While we are waiting for Jesus to return, we can let other things take our focus off of the fact that he is com-**

ing back. That is why we are warned to be ready. Our lesson today warns us not to let the sins of the world cause us to lose interest in Jesus' return.

Classroom Supplies
- masking tape
- adding machine tape
- markers
- cellophane tape
- cotton balls
- straws

Curriculum Supplies
none

Memory Activity 2

Before class, use the masking tape to mark a starting line for this activity.

Give each student a four-foot piece of adding machine tape and a marker. Have each student write the memory passage on the strip of paper. When everyone has finished, have all of the students line up, shoulder-to-shoulder, along the masking tape starting line. Kneeling down, each person tapes one end of his paper strip to the starting line, stretches out the strip of paper, and tapes down the other end of the paper strip.

Give each student a cotton ball and a straw. The object of the game is for students to use the straw to blow the cotton ball to the end of the paper strip without having the cotton leave the paper strip. If the cotton ball is blown off the paper, the student must return to the starting line and begin again.

After the game, say: **Great job! Now, this was probably more difficult than you thought it would be. How easy was it to keep the cotton ball on the paper strip? Did anyone else's wind affect your cotton ball? Was it hard to keep blowing? Did you ever get to the point where you wanted to quit?**

In our lives, there will always be situations that are challenging. Sometimes other people will affect what we are doing. Other times we might get tired of doing what we know is right, and we will want to quit. But we must remain faithful to God and to his way of doing things because in doing what we know is right, we might influence another person and introduce him to Jesus. And in doing things God's way, we make sure we are ready for Jesus to return.

Classroom Supplies
- white paper
- a paper clip
- scotch tape
- dental floss

Curriculum Supplies
none

Why Grow Up?

Give the students a piece of white paper and have them each make a paper airplane. Make one yourself as well. When everyone has finished, have each student fly her airplane. Make note of the flight path each plane takes. Though some might veer one direction or another, all of the planes will probably fall quite quickly. Most will not reach the other side of the room.

Say: **Some of your airplanes went quite a distance, but eventually the same thing happened to all of them—they fell to the ground. There are certain forces that act on the planes—gravity and friction—that caused these airplanes to fall. We can't stop gravity or friction. They are part of our world. So how could we get the planes to stay up in the air?** Discuss.

When the students have finished coming up with ideas, take out the paper airplane you made and tape the paper clip in the middle of the center section so a little loop shows on the top of the plane. Break off a long piece of dental floss and thread one end of the floss through the loop on the top of your airplane. Select two students to come to the front of the room. Ask them to hold on to one end, pulling the floss firmly. Select a third student to come up and fly the airplane by pushing it along the string.

Say: **Like this paper airplane, we need something in our lives to hold us up** and to help us keep moving in a straight path. That something is God. He can help us when things in our lives get difficult and confusing and when we don't think we can stay up any longer.**

How to Grow Up

Before class, write each of the following words on separate index cards: devout, impious, transgressing, perspicacious, iniquitous, vaunting, forbearing, acquiescent, vainglorious, magnanimous.

Direct students to locate 2 Timothy 3:1-5; 4:1-5, 7, 8 and read it silently. Give each student one card and a pencil. Have each student read the word on his card. Then ask students to draw a smiling face on the front of the card if they think this is a positive word or a frowning face if they think the word is a negative word.

Once everyone has completed this, pass out dictionaries and have the students look up the words to see if they were correct in their guesses. Students should write the definition on the back of the card. Have the students read their words to the class and discuss their meanings. Divide the students so those with positive words are on one side of the room and those with negative words are on the other side.

Say: **The Bible tells us that in the last days we will see people acting in negative ways, like the negative words we looked up. We need to be careful that we do not act like this! These are the behaviors that will cause us to fall as the paper airplanes we flew earlier. The Bible says that we should have nothing to do with behavior like this.**

Rather, we must choose to live godly lives and do good things, like the positive words we looked up. When we make a choice to live for God, he promises that he will help us. He will be like the dental floss that held up my airplane. He'll support us and help us stay up and keep us moving in the right direction.

A person who is ready for Heaven looks forward to the return of Jesus, and he lives God's way, having nothing to do with behavior that displeases God.

Classroom Supplies
- dictionaries
- pencils
- paper lunch bag
- index cards

Curriculum Supplies
none

Ready to Grow Up

Say: **Maranatha! Are you ready for the Lord to return? Last week you were be ready for Jesus' return by using one of your talents. What did you do?** Discuss. **A person who is ready for Heaven looks forward to Jesus' return. And while he is waiting, he faithfully uses the talents he has to serve others. Let's look at another way that we can be ready for Jesus' return.**

Give each student a copy of the reproducible page. Help students as need to form the page into a booklet.

Say: **This journal will be a special tool to help you this week. Each morning when you get up, take a few minutes to look up and read the verses on one page. Think about these verses all day long, and when you use that verse during the day, write it down on that page. For example, let's say one morning you read the verses that go with the word "magnanimous." Later that afternoon, your little sister is playing on your computer and deletes a report you were working on for school. If you generously forgive her instead of getting angry and yelling at her, record that in your journal. That verse has helped you stay on the right track and do what is pleasing to God!**

Classroom Supplies
- scissors
- markers

Curriculum Supplies
reproducible page 318 (booklet)

When we are ready for Jesus to return, we avoid evildoers and instead live our lives God's way so we can receive the crown.

Growing Up Every Day

Classroom Supplies
none

Curriculum Supplies
none

Ask: **Have you ever heard an athlete talk about how easy it is to train? Probably not. Most people who are serious about training for a sport will tell you about how tired they get, how sore they get, and how they are sometimes tempted to give up.**

Our Christian lives are a lot like that. Many times we seem to do wrong things. We can get frustrated and be tempted to give up. But if we use God's Word, the tool he has given us to help us when we need it, we stay in training and can win the victory he promises us! And the prize for the victory is an eternity with Jesus! With God's help, we can do it! Everyone put your right hands into the center like a team huddle before a game. I'm going to count to three and we're going to yell, "Maranatha! Come quickly, Lord Jesus!" Ready? 1-2-3.

Lesson 5

Growing in Hope

Wake Up!

Revelation 1:3-8; 3:1-6

Bible Focus
Jesus is coming soon in the clouds—so wake up and be ready.

Life Focus
Repent and "obey what you know" before Jesus comes.

Growing Up in the Word: Matthew 24:36, 42, 44
Say "maranatha" to welcome each student as they come in the room, and direct each one to the activity that you have prepared.

Memory Activity 1

Classroom Supplies
- construction paper
- masking tape

Curriculum Supplies
none

Before class, write the following memory passage phrases on separate sheets of construction paper. Tape them in order to the floor in a circular pattern.

"No one knows/ about that day/ or hour,/ not even the angels in heaven,/ nor the Son,/ but only the Father./ Therefore keep watch,/ because you do not know/ on what day/ your Lord will come./ So you also must be ready,/ because the Son of Man/ will come at an hour/ when you do not expect him"/ (Matthew 24:36, 42, 44).

To play, have students walk the circle in the opposite direction of the passage. Instruct them to read the words as they walk. This may be fun at first but should become frustrating. At a signal, students should stop and turn around and start walking in the correct direction to read the passage sensibly. Repeat as time permits.

Say: **Sometimes doing things our way is fun for a while. But the fun soon turns into frustration. This happens when we want to live our way and not God's way. In order for us to be ready for Jesus' return, as our memory passage warns us, we must be willing to repent of what we are doing that displeases God. Repentance means to stop doing wrong and to start doing right. When we repent, we change directions.**

We walked the memory passage backwards and didn't gain much practice in memorizing it. But soon we stopped, changed directions, and walked the passage so that it made sense to us. Then we were able to make progress in mem-

orizing it. Turning around was an important action in helping us memorize the passage. Turning around—repentance—is also an important action in being ready for Jesus to return.

Classroom Supplies
- poster board
- black marker

Curriculum Supplies
none

Memory Activity 2

Write the words to the memory passage on the poster board. Have students sit on the floor in a circle. Select one student to be "it." This student walks around the outside of the circle, tapping the other students gently on the head as he passes them saying "dead" until he gets to a student he would like to choose. When he taps that student on the head, he says "alive."

The student who was tapped stands and recites the memory passage before "it" walks all the way around the circle and taps the reciting student on the shoulder. Use the poster board as a prompt if the student doesn't remember all the words to the memory passage.

Say: **The words "dead" and "alive" refer to how a Christian can live his Christian life. And though this is a fun game to play, we can't tell by looking at a person if she is really living for Jesus. Take a look at the people sitting around the circle. Can you tell who visited a sick friend this week? Can you tell who read their Bibles or said their prayers every day? Can you tell who thought bad things about a brother or sister?**

Just by looking at the outside of the people here, we can't tell if a person is dead or alive in his Christian life. This information can only be found in a person's heart, and no one can see the heart but God. We need to be sure what is in our hearts is God's stuff! Having God's stuff in our hearts is a sure way to be ready when Jesus returns.

Classroom Supplies
- three-by-twelve-inch strips of construction paper
- markers
- cellophane tape or Plastic-Tak

Curriculum Supplies
none

Why Grow Up?

Give each student one strip of construction paper and a marker. Have the students work together to brainstorm the activities they do each morning to get ready for school, and have each student write a different activity on a strip of paper. Some suggestions might include the following: eating breakfast, brushing teeth, flossing, combing hair, showering, getting dressed, packing lunch, and so on.

Say: **This is quite a list of things you do every morning! Now, I'm going to take a minute and put these in order.** Put the strips in some logical order on the board. **Is this the order all of you use to get ready in the morning? If not, what do you do first?** Allow time for responses. There should be quite a bit of conversation about the order of these activities since no two of the students will have the same morning routine. **What would happen if we switched the order of some of these activities? What if you ate breakfast before you got dressed? What if you brushed your teeth before you combed your hair? Would it make any difference?**

Switching the order of your morning might seem strange, but just changing when you do something won't have much of an impact on your day. But what would happen if you left something out? What if you didn't eat breakfast? Could that change how your day went? Sure it could! If you are a person who

eats breakfast every morning, your body would have a hard time adjusting to missing that meal, and you would probably not have a great morning.

What if you forgot to brush your teeth? You might get some comments from those close to you about your breath! If you make a habit of not brushing your teeth, you will end up with a mouth full of cavities!

Leaving something out of our morning preparations can contribute to us having a bad day. That's one reason why we are careful to do the things we know are important such as eating breakfast or packing our lunches. We do what we know is important to do.

While we are waiting for Jesus to return, life can get pretty routine. And if we are not careful, we can leave some important elements out of our Christian lives. And that can certainly contribute to us having a bad day! When that happens, we need to wake up and get back to doing what we need to do. That's what happened to the Christians at Sardis. They were living the routine of being Christians, but something was missing. So Jesus told them to wake up. Let's find out what happened.

How to Grow Up

Classroom Supplies
Bibles

Curriculum Supplies
none

Begin by having the students find and read Revelation 1:3-8 and 3:1-6.

Ask: **How would you feel if you were listening to the letter being read to your church? How would you feel if someone told you that you are dead? If you were reading the letter and hearing the words, how could you be dead? Wouldn't you have to be alive to read and hear? Let's look at another passage of Scripture that might help clear up some of this for us.**

Turn in your Bibles to 1 Corinthians 13. Ask a volunteer to read verses 1-3. **All three of these verses tell us the same thing. We might be able to do some pretty fantastic things, like having great faith or understanding parts of the Bible that are difficult for others to understand easily, but if we are leaving out one thing—love—than we really have nothing. Our love for God should motivate us to obey what he has told us to do.**

Being alive in Jesus is more than going through the motions. It is looking at your life through God's eyes. It is adjusting what you are doing so that you do what God wants you to do. We call this adjustment of ourselves repentance. The church at Sardis needed to wake up to the fact that they were not loving God. They needed to repent—to stop doing wrong and start doing right. They needed to change directions. We need to do this as well.

The person who isn't doing what he has been taught to do will have a terrible surprise. Because that person is asleep, he will be surprised by Jesus' return, as we would be surprised by a thief in the night.

Jesus warns us to be awake and not asleep. We can't be ready for his return if we are asleep. But the person who is ready for Jesus to return is awake. He looks at what he does to see if he needs to repent and to start doing what is right. He watches the sky for Jesus to return. He won't be surprised when Jesus returns.

Classroom Supplies
- pencils
- Bibles
- markers

Curriculum Supplies
reproducible page 319 (Wake Up!)

Ready to Grow Up

Say: **Maranatha! We spent last week being ready for Jesus to return by doing things God's way. We prepared a book with suggestions for doing things God's way. What happened? What did you write in your book about doing things God's way?** Have students share.

We're going to continue this week being ready for Jesus to return. A person who is ready for Jesus to return looks at his life through God's eyes. He looks to see what he is doing right and wrong. If he finds something wrong, he repents and starts to obey.

Let's continue to look at 1 Corinthians 13:4-8 where we will find some of the right things to do. And if we discover that we are not doing what it says, then we need to repent.

Love is patient. Are you willing to wait to get what you want? Are you patient with those who are slower than you? If not, you need to wake up, repent, and start doing what is right.

Love is kind. Are you kind to the kids at school nobody wants to talk to? If not, you need to wake up, repent, and start doing what is right.

Love doesn't envy. Are you happy for another student who beats you in a contest? If not, you need to wake up, repent, and start doing what is right.

Love doesn't boast. Can you win a contest without making other people feel bad about themselves? If not, you need to wake up, repent, and start doing what is right.

Love keeps no record of wrong. Do you keep reminding your friend about the time she spread a secret you told her? If so, you need to wake up, repent, and start doing what is right.

We've talked about several ways that we've been taught to treat others. In which area do you need to wake up? Which area is keeping you from being ready? Distribute the reproducible sheet and pencils. Have students spread apart so they have some privacy. Instruct students to choose one thing they will stop doing and write it on the sheet. Then have students fill in how they will start doing right. Encourage them to be specific. Students may color the sheet if time permits.

Classroom Supplies
none

Curriculum Supplies
none

Growing Up Every Day

Have students remain where they are, some distance away from the other students in the class.

Say: **No one knows the exact day Jesus will be coming back. All we've been told is that someday he will return. And every day that passes brings us one day closer to his return.**

In his Word, God has given us important things to do. When we do these things, we are not only obeying God, but we are showing others the right way to live. We are setting an example in our words and actions, and we just might help someone else come to know Jesus through our example.

We are going to close our class today with a time of silent prayer. Take a few minutes to ask God's forgiveness in the area where you have been asleep. Talk to him about what you have written on your worksheet. Tell him that you will start doing what he has asked you to do. Allow several minutes to pray, then close in prayer.

Maranatha! Pharmacy

RX # Coming Soon

For: ______________________________

Read one every night before bed. Remember that Jesus is coming soon.

Maranatha! Pharmacy

RX # Coming Soon

For: ______________________________

Read one every night before bed. Remember that Jesus is coming soon.

Maranatha! The Lord is coming! Revelation 22:12, 13.

Maranatha! Be ready! Matthew 24:36-41

Maranatha! No one knows the hour! Luke 12:39, 40

Maranatha! Heaven is great! Revelation 22:5.

Maranatha! Keep watch! Matthew 24:42-44.

Maranatha! Be faithful! Matthew 25:23.

Maranatha! Be prepared! 2 Timothy 4:8.

Maranatha! Wake up! Revelation 3:1-3.

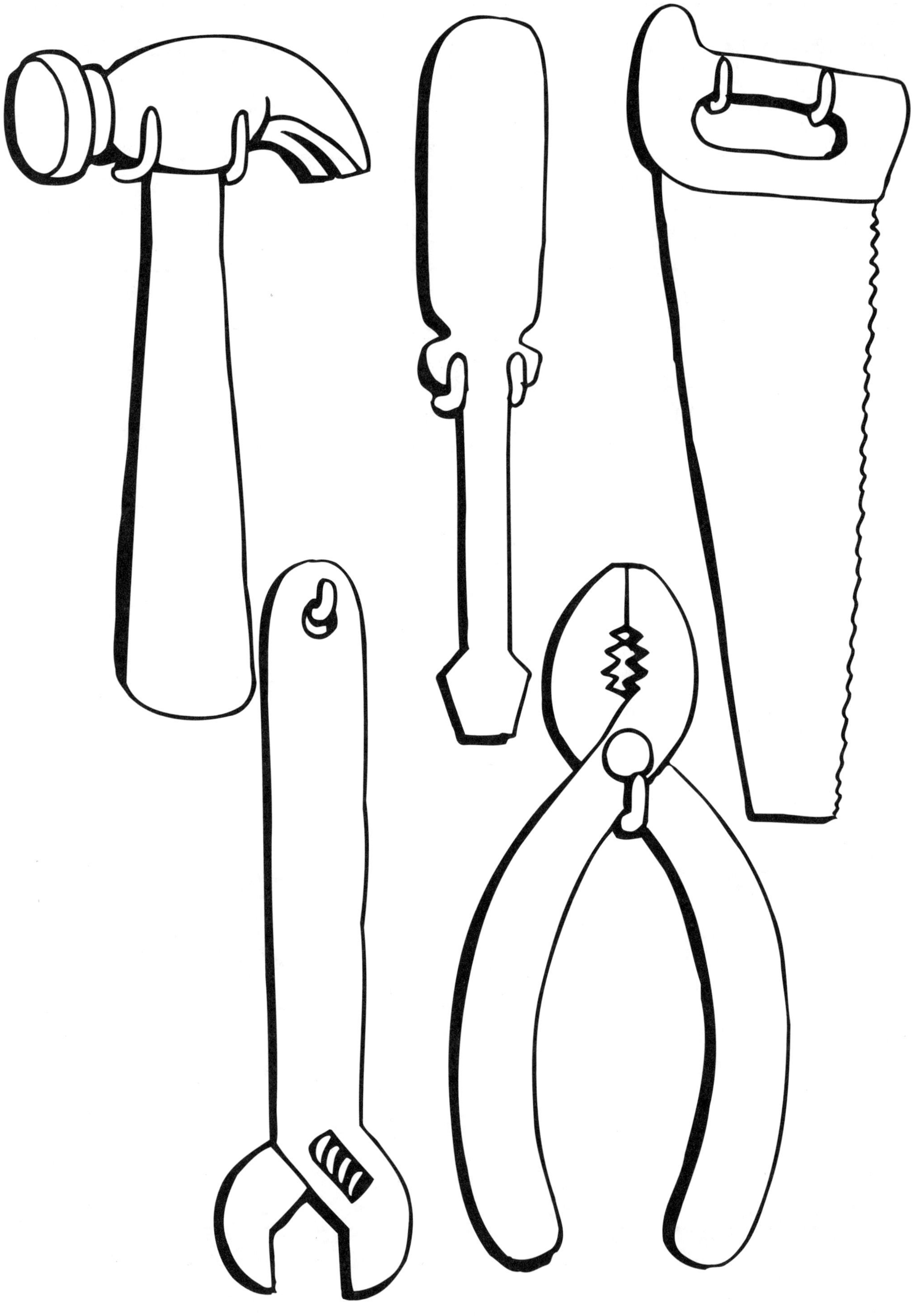

I can't play the piano at all, but I can type and use the computer.

I get a great feeling when I can encourage someone.

I love to cook. I make fantastic cookies!

I like young children.

I like to ride my scooter.

I can draw.

I love to clean!

I have a gift for talking!

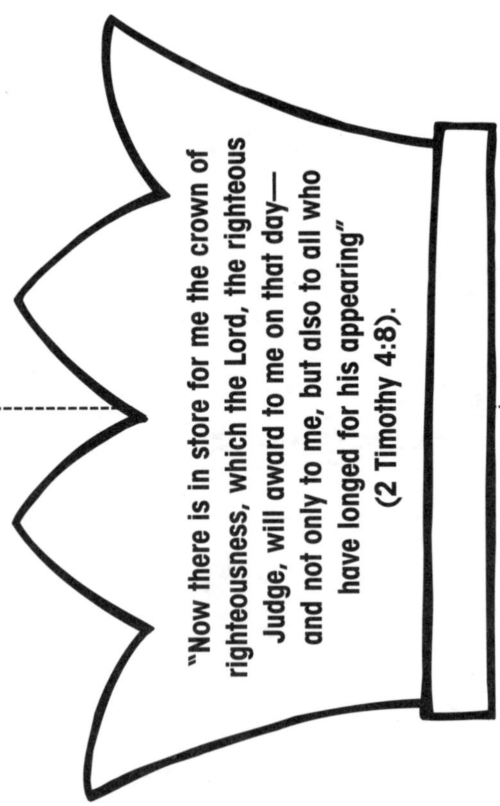

"Now there is in store for me the crown of righteousness, which the Lord, the righteous Judge, will award to me on that day—and not only to me, but also to all who have longed for his appearing" (2 Timothy 4:8).

1

Devout

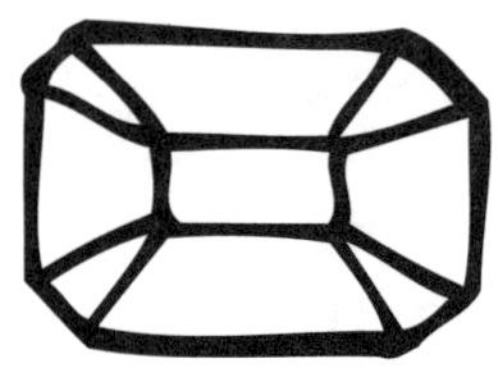

means devoted to worship
Psalm 100

2

Forbearing

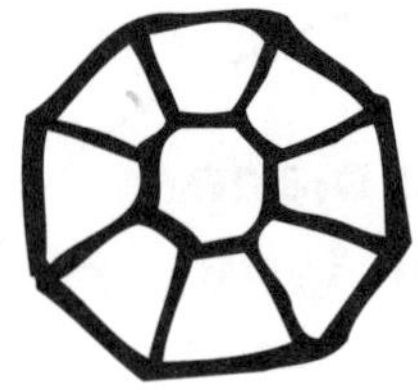

means patient endurance
2 Timothy 2:10-12

3

Acquiescent

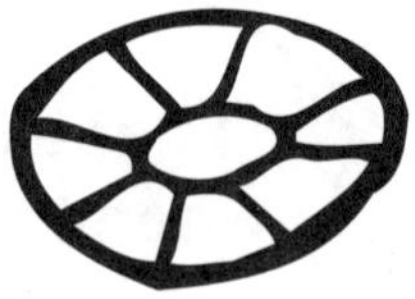

means to obey without protest
Proverbs 1:8, 9

4

Perspicacious

means having keen mental discernment
Proverbs 14:6; 15:14; 18:15

5

Magnanimous

means generous in forgiving
Matthew 6:12-14

6

"No one knows about that day or hour, not even the angels in heaven, nor the Son, but only the Father. . . Therefore keep watch, because you do not know on what day your Lord will come. . . So you also must be ready, because the Son of Man will come at an hour when you do not expect him" (Matthew 24:36, 42, 44).

7

8

fold — cut — fold

Follow these instructions to turn this page into a book.

Step 1—Cut out the book following the solid lines. **Step 2**—Cut along the solid line in the center of the book between pages 1 and 6 and also pages 2 and 5. **Step 3**—Crease along all the dashed lines. **Step 4**—Open the page and then fold in half lengthwise. **Step 5**—Push the two sets of outside pages to the center, causing the two sets of inside pages to push out. The pages should form a plus shape. **Step 6**—Fold the book so the pages are in order from 1 to 8.